D0948731

The Practitioner Inquiry Series

Marilyn Cochran-Smith and Susan L. Lytle, *SERIES EDITORS*

FROM ANOTHER ANGLE: CHILDREN'S STRENGTHS AND SCHOOL STANDARDS

The Prospect Center's Descriptive Review of the Child

EDITED BY MARGARET HIMLEY
WITH PATRICIA F. CARINI

TEACHERS COLLEGE PRESS

Teachers College, Columbia University
New York and London

Published by Teachers College Press, 1234 Amsterdam Avenue, New York, NY 10027

Library of Congress Cataloging-in-Publication Data

From another angle : children's strengths and school standards : the Prospect Center's descriptive review of the child / edited by Margaret Himley with Patricia F. Carini.
    p. cm.—(Practitioner inquiry)
  Includes bibliographical references and index.
  ISBN 0-8077-3931-6 (paper)—ISBN 0-8077-3932-4 (cloth)
    1. Child development—Vermont—Bennington. 2. School children—Vermont—Bennington. 3. Schools—Standards—Vermont—Bennington. 4. Prospect School (North Bennington, Vt.) I. Himley, Margaret. II. Carini, Patricia F. III. Prospect Archives and Center for Education and Research. IV. Series.
                                                                99-055549

ISBN 0-8077-3931-6 (paper)
ISBN 0-8077-3932-4 (cloth)

Printed on acid-free paper
Manufactured in the United States of America

07 06 05 04 03 02 01 00   8 7 6 5 4 3 2 1

We learn to see a thing
by learning to describe it.
—Raymond Williams, *The Long Revolution*

CONTENTS

ACKNOWLEDGMENTS

First and foremost we express our gratitude to Gabriel, Victoria, and Nile, whose stories are the heart of this book. We are honored to be allowed to join in this telling of their school lives and wish for them future educational opportunities to match their individual and considerable talents and strengths—as thinkers, as learners, and as persons. We also thank their families for permission to share these stories with a wider audience of readers—all of whom we know will benefit from them as we have.

We extend our heartfelt admiration to Karen Khan, Tara Shaw, and Kiran Chaudhuri, each of whom as busy classroom teachers so ably prepared and presented the descriptive reviews of Gabriel, Victoria, and Nile. Our thanks, too, to the many teachers in both New York and Philadelphia who participated in the reviews and, by their active questioning, helped a full and complex picture of each child to emerge.

A multiauthored book is a complex undertaking. We are grateful to the many authors, all of whom lead active professional lives, for their generosity as the book made its way through several revisions, and for the grace and good humor with which they stayed the course.

The Prospect Board of Trustees sponsored this book project as part of its long-range plan to make Prospect and the Prospect descriptive processes more accessible to a wider spectrum of parents and teachers. Every member of the Prospect Board contributed to this project—some as convenors of one of the descriptive reviews, many as authors, and all as readers and responders to the manuscript at every stage in its development.

In addition, the board sponsored a "Writing Week" which brought authors together, all in one location, for concentrated work with the support of onsite readers and editors. In addition to the board members, we want to recognize the contributions to the writing week of Elaine Avidon, Andy Doan, Anne Martin, and Karen Woolf. We also thank Lou Carini for his steadfast and careful reading of various drafts of the manuscript. To the Prospect Board, and Cecelia Traugh, in her capacity as president, our thanks for unwavering support of our efforts from start to finish.

We thank Marilyn Cochran-Smith and Susan Lytle for including this book in the Practitioner Inquiry series. We are delighted to be in the series. We appreciate too the support given to us all along the way by Carol Collins, Acquisitions Editor for Teachers College Press; Cathy McClure, freelance development editor; and the copyeditor and production staff.

Patricia F. Carini
Margaret Himley

INTRODUCTION

A PAGE FROM
THE PROSPECT ALBUM

Patricia F. Carini

Walking or driving up West Street from the center of the village of North
Bennington, Vermont, you arrive at Prospect School, located in two build-
ings on the edge of the village. The Main Building, once a guest lodge for the
Park-McCullough House across the street, is home for the younger children,
ages 4½ to 11 (see Figure I.1). The middle school–age children (11–14) are
located in the nearby Bleau House. There is a teacher for each group, with
parent volunteers, and sometimes a teacher intern working alongside. The
setting is distinctly rural, yet the school serves children from all across the
community, including the downtown Bennington industrial areas. The total
population is small in number, never more than 100 children, and more typically around 65 or 70. In the lower school, these groups usually include 23
to 26 children; in the middle school, the number is mostly under 20. It's the
early 1980s, when Prospect is about 18 years in the making.

Walking into the school, you may feel as many visitors have as if you
are entering a home. The rooms are small and adjoining; there are no hallways, but since each room opens off another, and short flights of stairs accommodate additions made to the original dwelling (circa 1840's), there are
nooks and crannies aplenty. You discover, on a meandering walk through
the building, a child-sized kitchen, many block areas, and the "big room,"
once a game trophy room and the only space large enough to conduct movement classes or to accommodate all the staff and children at one time.

The building is old and scuffed, in need of paint and other repairs. This
isn't a rich school. Yet everywhere you see children in small multiage groups
or alone, engaged with paint, blocks, cardboard and paper, sewing materi-

FIGURE I.1. Photograph of Prospect School

als, cooking supplies, woodworking materials, books of all sorts, maps, globes, timelines, a wide variety of mathematical equipment, and natural science supplies and tools.

Later in the morning, you listen in on one of the whole-class discussions or lessons, joining the children seated in a circle on the floor. The point of departure for one of these discussions may be a child's or group of children's project. In another, it may be a theme that emerged from interests current in the group, such as animals or mechanics or pioneer life or nature study. In yet another, it may be the teacher's choice of a topic or idea, such as geometric forms or a history timeline. Perhaps you spend some time after the class meeting, and before lunch, watching a group of children researching and designing plans for a large-scale construction or you decide to observe a teacher working individually with a child on reading or writing or math.

After watching the children so deeply and actively involved with making things, you would certainly want to spend a considerable amount of time looking at the collections of children's works housed in the Prospect Archives. By the 1980s, there are upwards of 250,000 works arranged by child, often spanning as much as nine years of a child's school life, and including artworks across a spectrum of media, writings of all kinds, and constructions (e.g., see Figure I.2).

FIGURE I.2. Photograph of Block Construction

In terms of the archives, it happens you have arrived at a propitious moment. Through funding from the Bush and Jessie Smith Noyes Foundations, Prospect in concert with the Center for Teaching and Learning at the University of North Dakota is embarked on publishing a *Reference Edition of the Prospect Archives* (Prospect Center, 1985). Thirteen scholars, some from education, others from art, anthropology, history, and literature, are at this moment cataloguing collections and selecting works for the slide selections that will compose part of the publication.

You might decide to join one of the scholars' seminar sessions, listening in on an overview of one of the collections presented by the scholar responsible for cataloguing it. Perhaps you decide to stay and participate in a descriptive review of a child's story or painting selected by the scholar as a focus for this session.

Later, you go upstairs to the adult library to meet the students enrolled in Prospect's Teacher Education Program and to sit in on a class. This day it is a session on observing in which students and teacher are recollecting their own favored play as children and what they learned from that play. Starting from their own experience, the students and teacher are launching a series of observations of children at play. Staying on in the library after class, you have the opportunity to meet with the teacher and the student teachers to talk about your observations in the school earlier in the day and to ask questions.

On the second day of your visit, after another extended period of observation in the school, you return to the adult library to read some of the Prospect publications and to talk with me or some other staff member about the program for longitudinal, school-based inquiry. From among the publications, I might hand you three monographs: *Observation and Description: An Alternative Methodology for the Investigation of Human Phenomena* (Carini, 1975); *The Art of Seeing and the Visibility of the Person* (Carini, 1979); and *The School Lives of Seven Children* (Carini, 1982)—all published under the sponsorship of the North Dakota Study Group on Evaluation.

As you and I sit down to talk about these monographs, I call your attention to ideas key at Prospect and for me when I wrote them. The importance of the child's or any person's uniqueness, complexity, and integrity. The role of description in representing these. The attentiveness to the manner in which, for any person, dynamic polarities, seemingly contradictory, enact that person's expressiveness and complexity. The assumption of human capacity, widely distributed, as the taproot value nurturing all these ideas.

To illustrate what I mean, I might read you a paragraph from an early unpublished descriptive study of a child from age 5 to age 13, one which predates the first of the monographs by several years:

> The person who emerges from these descriptive statements is unique and complex—and in his uniqueness and complexity, he reflects the uniqueness and complexity of all persons. If he [can be] explosive and angry, he is also persistent and concentrated. If he is physical and energetic, he is also expressive. If material goods compel him, he is also drawn to music and the arts. If he plays to win and must win, he can also be generous and helpful. *And he is all of these things at one time, an integrity that escapes any attempt to "type" him or to classify his particular behaviors.* . . . [What we] are seeking [in this kind of inquiry are] the patterns of continuity and the patterns of transformation in . . . the multiple expressions of an individual life that are the statement of that [person's] unique expressiveness.

From those early beginnings, I would call your attention to the most recent of the monographs, *The School Lives of Seven Children* (Carini, 1982), since it reports on a full-scale application of this longitudinal, descriptive methodology. I would explain that it is based on a five-year inquiry Prospect designed and conducted as a component of an evaluation of New York State's Experimental Prekindergarten Program, in which we followed the school lives of children from seven different districts across the state from ages 4 to 9.

With your visit drawing to a close, I would also call your attention to documentations published in-house of Prospect School and of Prospect's adult education programs, including the summer institutes. Along with these, I would certainly also supply you with flyers for Prospect's upcoming conferences, workshops, and institutes. With your interest piqued by your visit, it is possible you would decide later on to enroll for the coming summer's institute.

Assuming you did make that choice, you would arrive on a late July day in any of the summers from 1980 to 1984 to find yourself in the company of teachers from Philadelphia, New York City, Ithaca (New York), Grand Forks (North Dakota), and the Greater Boston area. Just as they have, you have brought with you your own works-in-progress. Among these you might include observations of children and descriptive records, collections of children's works, a teaching journal, class newsletters and other writings, and materials for a Descriptive Review of Teaching Practice.

During the next two weeks, you are going to be part of collaborative inquiry groups focused on description of these kinds of materials and on learning and reworking processes for that description. At other times you may choose to join in on a teacher's Descriptive Review of her Practice or one of several Descriptive Reviews of Children or their Works or Issues. Topics in the early 1980s included, among others, children's responses to the threat of nuclear war, the value of diversity in the classroom, tests and the history of testing, increasing class size, and bilingual education.

Each morning of the institute, you participate along with everyone else in a seminar on the institute theme, which, depending on the summer, is The Growth of Language or Values/Valuing or Science. Perusing documentations of summer institutes for those years, I discover that readings for the seminars included, among others, Alfred North Whitehead's (1938) *Modes of Thought*, Raymond Williams's (1976) *Keywords*, Howard Nemerov's (1978) *Figures of Thought*, Clara Park's (1972) *The Siege*, and Evelyn Fox Keller's (1983) biography of the renowned geneticist Barbara McClintock, *A Feeling for the Organism*.

This is Prospect at a moment in time: A school for children. An archive of children's works. A center for descriptive inquiry. Adult education programs, including conferences, workshops, and summer institutes for experienced professionals.

The other story of Prospect is of an institution without an adequate financial base. Operating without public funds except for the federal monies that subsidized the early years, and continuing to serve many families for whom an independent school tuition was not affordable after that funding ended, Prospect eked out its existence from year to year. The sources were several: gifts from local benefactors, most consistently and generously, Jane and Lucien Hanks and Babs and Bill Scott; contributions from the membership; what was earned through workshops, institutes, and other adult education programs; and consulting fees and grants. In particular, Prospect was the grateful recipient of grants spanning a number of years from the Jessie Smith Noyes Foundation, the Rockefeller Brothers Fund, and the Bush Foundation for the publication of the *Reference Edition of the Prospect Archives* (Prospect Center, 1985).

In June, 1991, the always weak financial base gave way. With deep regret and sorrow, the school was forced to close—26 years after it was founded. It has remained closed since that time.

In November 1991, Prospect reorganized under a newly formed working board with a national membership. The board retained Prospect's name, "Prospect Archives and Center for Education and Research," with the aim of continuing many of its functions and adding others. Much has been accomplished, and many resources and activities now define Prospect in 1999.

There are the collections of children's works and *The Reference Edition of the Prospect Archives* (Prospect Center, 1985). This edition—which documents 36 children, each over at least five years, in slides, microfiche, and text—is available from the Prospect Center and in use for teaching and research purposes.

Teachers, parents, administrators, teacher educators, and researchers participate each year in Prospect's annual institutes and conference. One- and two-week summer institutes, which are focused on observation and descriptive processes and inquiry, are offered every year in Bennington (Vermont), Philadelphia, and New York City. Since 1991, the Fall Conference is held annually near New York City and serves as a weekend introduction to Prospect ideas and processes.

Members of Prospect's working board, and others in the membership, have also brought these ideas and processes to a variety of schools, teacher centers, and universities. Often these consultations set in motion a descriptive inquiry group within a teacher center or school, or initiate descriptive studies of children's or adult students' works, or help teachers and parents learn a particular process such as the Descriptive Review of the Child. A major research effort in the 1990s involved the teachers' participating in Summer

Institute II serving as consultants for a National Science Foundation Science Project, directed by Edward Chittenden for the Educational Testing Service, Princeton, New Jersey.

Another aspect of Prospect's work is its publications (see Appendix). *The Prospect Review*, started in 1993 and published twice yearly, presents Prospect-related writing from across the membership. *Prospect Papers* are issued occasionally, typically featuring talks presented in one or another of Prospect's annual events. With this book on the Descriptive Review of the Child and its companion volume, *Schools in the Making, A Collection of Talks, 1988–1998* (Carini, in press), we are publishing some portion of the accrued work of the past thirty years. This book engages the reader in the actual doing of descriptive reviews, while *Schools in the Making* invites the reader to consider the wider context of the values and ideas foundational to these processes and relates both to current educational, social, and political issues. At a time when education is threatened by pushes on all sides for conformism and standardization, we believe this is the *right* time to get the Prospect ideas and descriptive processes out to classroom teachers, parents, administrators, teacher educators, and the research community.

CHAPTER 1

PROSPECT'S DESCRIPTIVE PROCESSES

Patricia F. Carini

> *Every experience is a moving force. Its value can be judged only on the ground of what it moves toward and into. . . . It is then the business of the educator to see in what direction an experience is heading. . . . Failure to take the moving force into account so as to judge and direct it on the ground of what it is moving into means disloyalty to the principle of experience itself.*
>
> (Dewey, 1938, p. 38)

When Prospect's doors opened in mid-September of 1965, there was a multiage class of 23 5- through 7-year-olds from all walks of life and from all across the Bennington community. There was one teacher, Marion Stroud, who brought with her substantial experience in the British Infant Schools, including her understanding of ungraded, mixed-age classrooms. The other founders were Joan Blake and Patricia and Louis Carini. All four of us actively participated in the school and in shaping its philosophy and commitments.

We brought with us substantial knowledge of John Dewey's philosophy, and progressive educational and social aims more generally. I was (and am) especially fond of the phrase "moving force" in the passage I have quoted. It says quite well, I think, what we at Prospect were striving for: learning experiences that lead on, and which, as Dewey (1938) also says, "arouse curiosity, strengthen initiative, and set up desires and purposes sufficiently intense to carry a person over dead places in the future" (p. 38).

From its very beginnings, the classrooms at Prospect featured plentiful choices for children, opportunities to make things from a rich array of open-ended and natural materials, ample use of the out-of-doors, and reading, writing, and math taught with individual attention to each child. As an observer on a daily basis, what I saw in Prospect's classrooms matched Dewey's vision: children engaged with media, ideas, experiences and in motion with these, both following their lead and making choices of where to go next.

The passage matches just as well with another Prospect aim. From the start, we were committed to an examination of the school's practice through observing, recording, and describing what happened in the classrooms and for children on a daily and continuing basis. The idea was that a school and a staff could create a comprehensive plan for doing this kind of observational inquiry and that such an investigation could be school-based—that a school could itself generate knowledge of children, of curriculum, of learning and teaching.

The aim was straightforward: to have those observations fold directly into practice. By documenting the children's growth and learning, the curriculum and the classrooms, and the school more generally, we expected to do what Dewey says: to sustain the school as a "moving force," leading on from the edges of its own experience and thinking.

Speaking personally, although so much of what I now think and know about this kind of descriptive inquiry unfolded from these original commitments, some things were fairly clear to me from the start. For example, I knew that the design of the multifaceted inquiry plan we envisioned had to focus on *process*. In practice, this meant to me paying close attention to how a child goes about learning or making something, and not only to assessment of what the child learned, made, or did. I reasoned that it is when a teacher can see this process, *the child in motion*, the child engaged in activities meaningful to her, that it is possible for the teacher to gain the insights needed to adjust her or his own approaches to the child accordingly.

At Prospect, I felt that to an unusual degree we had a setting optimal in its opportunities to see children in action and in motion. I was well aware, and so was everyone else at Prospect, that this was a context offering opportunities for teachers as well as learners that were different from those available in a school that relied mainly on verbal responses to assignments with built-in answers. In that other and more familiar circumstance, what counted and also what was observable were mostly end-products—responses that could be assessed on the spot as "right" or "wrong." The child either got the correct answer or didn't. In this kind of conventional educational arrangement, it was the child who was being inspected and assessed, and it was up to him or her to conform and measure up to the demands set by school in whatever terms the school set them.

What we at Prospect were aiming to do argued with that construction. Our aim was to tailor learning to the learner. For that aim to be credible, it was essential to be able to see and to reflect on how a child was going about making sense of the world. Otherwise how could we go about reexamining and reworking the educative surround to support better the child's efforts? The ever-strengthening commitment to a setting with natural and malleable materials and opportunities for both choice and sustained involvement provided an extraordinary opportunity for teachers to do this kind of observing. We had other advantages. None of us at Prospect was working solo. Committed to a collaborative inquiry, we could count on the perspectives of all of us in making sense of the educative process we observed. Ours was a collective effort from beginning to end.

TAKING A DESCRIPTIVE STANCE IN THE CLASSROOM

It was also clear to me that the classroom teachers at Prospect were the only staff in a position to make these regular observations of process, since it was they who were with the children all day, every day. My observations, and those of other staff, could supplement, but the backbone for the plan had to be the teachers' observations and records. The second teacher hired at Prospect—Jessica Howard—and I were the ones who tackled how this might happen. How could a teacher both teach and observe? How would she or he keep track of all that happened in a day? Were there formats that could support the teacher's efforts?

Process again proved the key word in working through these questions. The plan depended not merely on devising ingenious formats to guide teachers as observers and to systematize how they recorded their observations. Between us, we did devise and try out formats, changed them as circumstances changed—and then more often than not, once underway, discarded them as more hindrance than help. *The most important yield from our efforts was getting clear that observing is something a teacher is always doing all the time he or she is teaching.*

Rather than a paucity of observations, mostly teachers are surfeited by the end of the day with all that has happened. The question then became how to tap and give some order to these. What evolved from our experiments was indeed a layered enterprise, but one that, with hitches and lapses and periodic corrections of course, worked surprisingly well over many years.

According to this plan, each teacher worked out for her- or himself a way to keep daily track of children's choices of media, play and work partners, and so forth. At the end of the week, or on some other regular schedule, the teacher wrote four or five sentences for each child describing what the child did that week, with whom, and any other observations the teacher may have made. The standard for this writing was to be descriptive, which meant, in practice, to stay clear of judgmental, evaluative language and as much as possible to include an illustrative example or two.

Although each weekly entry was brief, their cumulative weight and depth proved extraordinary. About 15 years after we initiated them, I had occasion to compile these records for 36 former Prospect students. On average, the teacher records, including the narrative report parents received twice yearly, and any Descriptive Reviews of the Child or other collateral pieces, *were 100 typed pages, single spaced.*

Alongside the daily choice lists and the weekly descriptive records, each teacher also devised other records: a way to keep track of a child's reading, mathematics, and other assignments; a way to maintain collections of children's works in the classroom; and ways to document the curriculum on a semester and yearly basis. These records took a variety of forms, but, as Jessica Howard and I discovered almost at the beginning, rather than formats and schedules, it was the ideas that mattered. As I saw it then (and now), the rationale for any longitudinal inquiry is the assumption that something continues and that paying attention to the continuation is going to yield knowledge that is not findable in isolation and in the short term.

For recording observations, *describe* played a companion role to attentiveness to process. The point of the Prospect plan for observing and recording was to build a layering narrative account, developed over time, of a child's learning or of the school's curriculum or of the school itself. It was by reflecting together on these narratives as the story unfolded over time and in relation to context that our understandings of where the child or the group was tending, and the meaning of what was happening, became visible.

Alongside the observing and the recordkeeping, the Descriptive Review of the Child and the entire family of descriptive processes were evolving: the Descriptive Review of Children's Works (visual art and writings of all kinds, constructions, etc.) as well as the Descriptive Reviews of Curriculum, of Teacher Practice, and of Issues. Connected to these were the Reflective Conversation and Recollections. Later, and in connection with public school teachers in a variety of locations, we developed the Descriptive Review of the Work and Art of Teaching, the Descriptive Review of Classroom Activities, and the Descriptive Review of a School.

These collaborative reviews conducted on a weekly, monthly, quarterly, or yearly basis were our way of making sense of all that we were gathering and recording. From these we collected the fruits of our inquiry and discovered the questions and leading edges—the moving force—that pointed the way ahead. I am surprised, looking back, at how quickly all this happened.

It was in this climate, and specifically as a way to learn from the children and to get to know them, that we began the practice of meeting each week for about an hour and a half to do a Descriptive Review of a Child.

This was a firmly held-to resolve. Other business didn't get done at these meetings. This was the time when we as a staff gave undivided attention to a particular child and to pooling our knowledge about that child.

THE DESCRIPTIVE REVIEW OF THE CHILD

It's a Tuesday after school. We are meeting in the staff room, which doubles as an adult library and study room for post–B.A. adult students enrolled in Prospect's Teacher Education Program (see Figure 1.1). While the staff and teacher education students are gathering, the chair for the review and the teacher who is primarily responsible for describing the child who is at the center of this particular descriptive review session are attending to last-minute details: laying out some of the child's drawings, writings, and constructions, and perhaps making an adjustment or addition to the focusing question for the review. Each of these roles, chair and presenting teacher, rotate from week to week among the staff, as does the role of note-taker, the staff member who keeps a record of main themes from the description of the child and the recommendations that are made as the descriptive review draws to a close.

As these last-minute arrangements between chair and presenting teacher suggest, the descriptive review that is about to happen already has a history.

FIGURE 1.1. Photograph of Staff Room.Library

Sometime in the preceding week, the chair and presenting teacher met to plan the review. With the chair acting as a listening ear, this was the opportunity for the presenting teacher to work through how she might focus the descriptive review for her colleagues and how she would organize her own portrayal of the child. For the portrayal, she would rely heavily on her daily and weekly records.

If you were to sit in on that meeting, one of the things you would learn is that the focus for the review doesn't have to reflect some major problem or crisis. The presenting teacher might, for example, mostly want the help of other staff in getting to know better a child who often seems not to be visible in the class. "How is it," she might ask, "that this child seems always to slip by me? How can I get a clearer picture of where she is making her presence felt in the group?" Or the teacher might be wondering if some concern she feels is actually well founded. For example: "This is a child who is altogether competent academically, but it isn't at all clear to me what ideas, questions, or materials fire her imagination or arouse any strong enthusiasm. I want to think that through. Am I missing something? Am I making too much of what I perceive to be a lack of any strong personal interest? Is it enough educationally that the child complies with whatever I suggest and participates in whole-class activities?"

Now, on the day of the descriptive review, the chair makes sure the chairs are arranged in a circle so everyone participating will be visible to one another and visually invited to take an active role. Today, including the teacher education students, there will be 10 of us. Figuratively, the child who is the occasion for all of us to gather is situated at the center of that circle and at the center of our collective attention.

The chair convenes the session. The presenting teacher is ready with her portrayal of the child in the form of notes she made in advance of the session. On a low table, she has positioned close to hand the child's artworks, writings, and projects she means to call attention to as she talks. Everyone in this review group, not only the note-taker, is equipped with paper and writing implements. We will use these to keep track of questions and observations that occur to us while the presenting teacher is describing the child—a portrayal which will take upward of 30 minutes and is uninterrupted.

Since the presenting teacher and chair have decided on a reflection on a word to preface the review, the chair announces what that will be. Setting aside *visible/invisible* and *presence*, the presenting teacher has settled on *slip/slips* because it seems closer to how she experiences the child she is going to describe. The chair invites everyone in the review circle to write down words, images, and phrases that these words—*slip* or *slips*—call to mind. After we have had time to reflect on the word individually, each of us reads aloud what we have written. The word surprises us, as words tend to do, with its variety and richness of meanings. Among these: slide, silk; silent or quiet; a whisper on the wind; slippage; slippery slope; an undergarment; sideways; to slip between, by, around, or into; a clay slip; to pass unnoticed; a space between; slight or small as in "slip of a girl." The chair pulls together clusters of these meanings, reminding us that we will *not apply* the reflection to the child; rather it will serve as surround and context for the picture of her that the presenting teacher will paint.

With the reflection completed, the chair talks about the values that guide the Descriptive Review of the Child process. The chair gives this especially careful attention since the teacher education students attending this review are relatively new to the process. What she emphasizes in her remarks are confidentiality and respect: that everything said during a review is kept strictly within the circle of participants; that each of us is to strive to speak descriptively and provisionally, to honor the child's strengths and capacities, and to avoid speculations about the family and its circumstances. The chair suggests that a good rule of thumb is not to speak of the family or the child in language we would not use if they were present.

What does it mean to speak descriptively and provisionally? It means to set aside heavily judgmental language and diagnostic or other categorizing labels such as "hyperactive" or "learning disabled" or "developmentally delayed." The chair explains that no child is *always* moving or invisible or pestering or whatever—no matter how much it seems that way to the harried or concerned parent or teacher. She suggests that phrases like "it seems to me" or "from my perspective" leave room for the child to be other than what any of us might think. The chair stresses that what is most important is to ground language used to describe a child in examples and illustrations so that the language is well rooted in observation.

As the chair comes to the end of these framing comments, she calls attention to the procedure of the descriptive review, which has been circulated in advance to those who are unfamiliar with the process. The Descriptive Review of the Child is comprised of the following elements:

Reflection on a key word (this is optional)
The chair's framing remarks and the focus for the review
The presenting teacher's map of the classroom and description of the schedule
The presenting teacher's portrayal of the child, according to:

1. physical presence and gesture
2. disposition and temperament
3. connections with others (both children and adults)

    4. strong interests and preferences
    5. modes of thinking and learning.

The chair gathers main threads from the portrayal (also called "integrative restatment")
Additions to the presenting teacher's portrayal: observations by other staff
History of any significant illness, unusual absences, and so forth (very brief)
Chair restates the focus question(s) and invites questions and comments from the participants in the review
Questions, comments, dialogue
Chair gathers main themes from the discussion and restates the focus question
Responses and recommendations from the review group
Evaluation of process, with particular attention to respect for the child, the family, and the teacher
Plans and calendar for any upcoming descriptive reviews

She introduces the child we are going to review, giving the child's name and age, the names of family members and/or other caregivers, the length of time she has attended Prospect, and the multiage group in which she is currently enrolled. The chair reads the focusing question the presenting teacher and she have put together to frame the review.

With that preamble, the descriptive review is under way, and the presenting teacher takes over. She speaks briefly about the classroom setting, perhaps showing a map of the room and highlighting important features of the daily schedule. With this context established, she moves on to her description of the child, organized under the five headings that, though they have been revised and renamed over time, are the consistent framework for every Descriptive Review of the Child presentation:

    1. Physical presence and gesture
    2. Disposition and temperament
    3. Connections with other people
    4. Strong interests and preferences
    5. Modes of thinking and learning

This portrayal of the child is the heart of the descriptive review. After a restatement of main themes by the chair, and any observations by other staff, the next large chunk of time is devoted to the review group's questions and other responses to what they have heard. All working together—chair, presenting teacher, staff members, and teacher education students—we inquire and, inquiring, add dimension and depth to the picture of the child. As new insights emerge from this collaboration, the question the presenting teacher used to focus the review is illuminated by the perceptions and angles of viewing brought by the members of the descriptive review group. As the review comes to a close, the chair invites recommendations.

When these are completed, what remains on this Tuesday afternoon at Prospect is to evaluate the process: Did we respect the family, the child, and the teacher? How did we enact that respect? As we prepare to leave, we are already anticipating next Tuesday: Who has a child he or she wants to present? Who will be chair? Who will be note-taker?

For us at Prospect, these weekly descriptive reviews served us well in at least two ways. The first benefit was always to the child, since the child's particular teacher(s) left the meeting with fresh insights and expanded ideas for building on that child's capacities and strengths. The equal benefit was to us as a staff committed to children. By immersing ourselves weekly in one child's school life, that child became a lens to other children and to the school itself.

I don't mean that the child described became the caller of a tune for other children to dance to. Rather, the opposite. Looking closely at the one child exercised and sharpened our powers of observation, making us more keenly attuned to each child who came our way. The habit of observing and describing and pooling our knowledge and perspectives on a child made us disciplined students of childhood. The same habit gave substance and meaning to the claim of being centered on children as the context for educating.

This was perhaps our great advantage at Prospect. Starting from the commitment to examine our own practice, we were oriented from the first toward noticing, with a responsibility to record, reflect on, and describe these noticings. Starting from the idea of human capacity and possibility, widely distributed, we were oriented to look for and to particularize the capacities and strengths of each child. Starting from classroom settings rich in media and materials, we were in a position to see and make visible each child's strong interests and characteristic modes of engaging and learning. Committed to the long view and the child's growth over time, we were able to document these interests and modes of learning for as many as nine years of a child's school life.

PICTURE THIS . . .

On any day in the 1990s, a group of teachers, support staff, and administrators are meeting in a school to hold a Descriptive Review of the Child. Or, changing the venue and players, it is a group of parents and teachers meeting in an after-school collaborative inquiry group. Or it is a teacher cooperative group meeting at a teacher center or at one of the teacher's homes. Or it is a professional development class or a college seminar for women and men preparing to be teachers. Or it is a descriptive inquiry group convened at a local college to do a long-term study of adolescence or reading or mathematics. Or it is a Prospect conference or Summer Institute convened to teach descriptive inquiry and practice.

Listing these venues, I am mapping the spread of the Prospect descriptive processes across 30 years and a spectrum of actual locations, from New York City, Mamaroneck (New York), and Philadelphia to Boston, Ithaca (New York), Chicago, Grand Forks (North Dakota), and Phoenix. When Prospect's board, with a membership reflecting this spectrum, decided that after three decades of use and study the time was particularly *right* for wider publication of these processes, it was in relation to that spread. Looking across the span of locations where Prospect is a presence, the variety gave us confidence that the descriptive processes have achieved a sufficient thickness and toughness from years of dialogue and reworking to justify the decision to publish them more widely.

The time also seemed *right* because the ideas and values that center them are articulatable and accessible, as I think they were not even 10 years earlier. *Right* because for all the setbacks, the larger visions of human possibility that the descriptive processes promote and sustain are on the horizon even as, at the same time, there is mounting pressure for a national curriculum, for standardization, for sameness. *Right* because these processes can enact and translate into practice that vision of human possibility: a vision of children as complicated, interesting, and active in making some sense and meaning of the world and their own lives (for a full explication of these ideas, see Carini, in press).

This avenue of enactment and application that the descriptive processes provide is needed more than ever by the teachers, administrators, parents, and teacher educators who are struggling against the pressures for standardization.

To accomplish this, Prospect members across the country were alerted to tape any reviews of children for which they had permission, but especially those given by or for teachers and parents with little or no experience with descriptive processes. From this rich but unvarnished material, we selected three descriptive review stories. Making that selection, we were not looking for perfect reviews, flawlessly enacted. We wanted the children to be diverse in age. We wanted the locations of the reviews to be varied. We hoped for variety in terms of the focus for each review. We wanted these reviews to be what we call "starting-up stories," which by being that might inspire readers of this book to do and practice the kinds of observing and describing on which these stories hinge.

The first review is the story of Gabriel, age 7, from a public alternative elementary school in the Bronx. This review was held as part of a seminar offered by the Elementary Teachers Network in New York City for classroom teachers, all of whom, except for Gabriel's teacher, were new to the descriptive review process.

The second review is the story of Victoria, age 9, from a Philadelphia public school. This review was held during one of the Philadelphia Teachers Learning Cooperative's weekly Thursday meetings. Presenting such a review was a new experience for Victoria's teacher; the teachers participating in the review included many with extensive experience with the Descriptive Review of the Child.

The third story is the review of Nile, age 13, a ninth-grader at a public alternative high school in New York City. This concluding review happened as part of an Adolescent Study Group convened at Lehman College in which all participants, including the presenting teacher, had experience with the descriptive review processes.

The teachers who served as chairs for these three descriptive reviews were all experienced in that role.

The aim is to invite readers behind the scenes to join with the teachers who are the presenters or main storytellers for these reviews and with others participating in them. Through this behind-the-scenes look, through participating in what is a kind of guided tour through the process, readers are invited to learn how to think about and prepare to do this kind of review.

I have deliberately inserted here the language of *story*, and for several reasons. First of all, it was story as metaphor that freed us, the authors of this book, to think of ways to present the Descriptive Review of the Child process without reducing it to an outline or protocol. Then, developing story as we use it here, we tied it to rigorous observation and description, and in the telling of the story, to the use of ordinary language held to a standard of particularity and aptness.

It is story understood in this context of language that is vivid and particular to the child and securely grounded in observations which distinguishes the descriptive review from more clinical or psychological approaches; for example, the case study or developmental history or personality profile, as well as school evaluations in which the main purpose is to categorize or diagnose the child for referral to special services. This is an important distinction, and one that is explored in several essays in this book, but particularly in Chapters 3 and 7.

Each Descriptive Review of a Child that appears here is also understandable as a story from another slant: Each is a story of adults joining together in a spirit of collaborative inquiry in which the aim isn't to scrutinize or "solve" the child like a puzzle but to build from the child's capacities and strengths.

This story of circles of adults enacting descriptive reviews illustrates, by portraying it, how each person's perspectives and knowledge contribute to enlarge and complicate the story of each of these three children. This story also portrays how pooled knowledge assists teachers to make the changes in program and practice that are needed in order to support the child. Additionally, it is a story that tells by example how a constructed, disciplined conversation that keeps children at the center of thought and practice can be started by a group of teachers in any location who want to make that commitment.

The three descriptive reviews of Gabriel, Victoria, and Nile, enacted through edited transcribed tapes, are the heart of the book. Through this use of many voices and stories told in the voices of the persons closest to the child, we strive to show the underside of the tapestry, the working side, the side where all the knots and threads are visible. This choice means that rather than a seamless or transparent dramatization of the finished event, readers are in on the making of it.

To create other kinds of thinking space and to elaborate points touched on but not fully disclosed in the texts of the reviews, we have interspersed essays between the reviews. These are grouped in twos, each set offering the reader another angle for understanding how the descriptive review process works or the ideas and values at its root. There is also a progression across these pairs of essays.

Part I is comprised of the Gabriel review and a pair of essays that stay close to points of process. Chapter 3 tells how either a parent or teacher gathers and organizes her or his observations and knowledge for a descriptive review presentation. Chapter 4 is the story of two teachers choosing a child for a descriptive review and putting the review together.

Part II is comprised of the Victoria review and a pair of essays that explore description as method. Chapter 6 deepens the discussion of what it is to describe and to inquire through describing by referring to the phenomenological roots of the project processes and by taking a close look at how language works in them. Chapter 7 introduces the reader to an extensive literature in which teachers from the Prospect membership draw on their observations to write textured and layered stories of life in the classroom.

Part III is comprised of the Nile review and a pair of essays that illustrate descriptive processes at work in school and program settings. Chapter 9 tells how a year-long, schoolwide descriptive inquiry moved along a staff's understanding of what it means to commit to heterogeneity as a value and describes the politics of enacting that commitment. Chapter 10 tells by example and story how disciplined description and oral inquiry serves democratic aims.

The Appendix at the end of the book contains a list of resources available from The Prospect Center, including locations nationwide where Prospect work is happening and information about board members, conferences, institutes, and the Archives. A reader eager to do further reading of works published by Prospect-connected teachers will find an extensive bibliography, too, collated by Karen Woolf.

We, the authors (and there are a lot of us!), invite you to join actively in these descriptive processes, the philosophy that frames them, and the discipline of taking a descriptive stance.

PART I

LEARNING THE DISCIPLINE OF DESCRIPTION

We invite you to the first descriptive review, which took place in a course taught by the Elementary Teachers Network (ETN) in New York City in the spring of 1996. The presenting teacher is Karen Khan, a K–1 teacher at the Bronx New School who had some prior experience with Prospect processes. The other teachers in the review group were brand-new to the processes. Typical of newcomers, they were at first awed by Karen's knowledge of Gabriel and her ability to describe him so fully to them. Then, slowly, they came to recognize how the processes draw on knowledge and ability that all teachers always already have. With that dawning recognition, they progressed from finding the review "incredible" to understanding its value in the "real" day-to-day demands of teaching. This shift in perspective is discussed in an essay we asked Elaine Avidon and Mary Hebron, who taught the ETN course, to write in lieu of presenting edited transcripts from the questions and recommendations section of this review.

After the review, in Chapter 3, you will find a letter Patricia F. Carini wrote several years ago as a guide for assisting teachers and parents interested in learning how to describe children by using the five headings of the descriptive review. She offers concrete and specific suggestions for remembering the child, for gathering impressions and images together, for drawing together story and observation. This letter is often used by experienced teachers who are helping teachers new to the process learn how to prepare for a review.

Chapter 4, by Betsy Wice, documents how an experienced teacher "joins with" a teacher new to the processes in preparing for a review. A longtime member of the Prospect network, Betsy had volunteered to chair for her friend and colleague, Cheryl. Using transcripts from those planning sessions, Betsy revisits the work she and Cheryl did together. Her chapter illustrates how preparing for a review—that is, how learning the discipline of description—makes the child more visible as a full and complex person through the language the teachers develop in their efforts to do justice to that complexity.

In this planning session, the word *interesting* marks the shift in this enlarged, engaged way of thinking and describing children. The chapter also illustrates how preparing a review opens up for teachers issues that are critical to their daily practice, such as labeling children, mandated testing, and official assessment.

We have permission to use the real names for all three children reviewed in this book. To protect the privacy of other children, we have used pseudonyms.

CHAPTER 2

GABRIEL

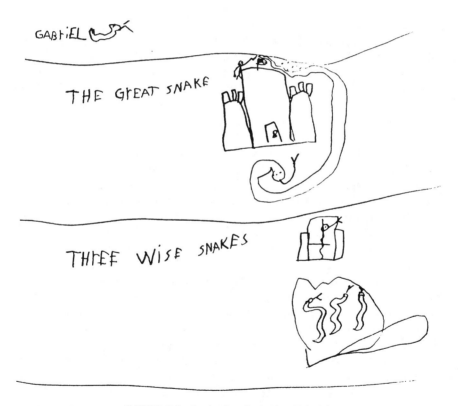

FIGURE 2.1. Snake Symbols, by Gabriel

CONTEXT

Elaine Avidon

Karen Khan, the early childhood teacher who prepared the review that follows, has worked in nursery school settings and large neighborhood public schools in New York City as both an art teacher and a classroom teacher. Karen is one of the founding members of the Bronx New School (BNS), a small, public alternative elementary school begun in the mid-1980s by a group of Bronx parents and teachers interested in open education. For many years Karen was the school's art teacher. She began her work as a classroom teacher for a mixed-age K–1 class in the fall of 1993.

The 200 children attending the BNS live in Community School District 10. This is the district of Jonathan Kozol's (1991) *Savage Inequalities*, serving one of New York City's poorest and one of the city's wealthiest neighborhoods. Families who send their children to the BNS are selected by a lottery process that is structured to ensure that the school's population will reflect the ethnic and racial diversity of the district—African American, African Caribbean, Asian, Latino, and White. The Prospect descriptive processes were introduced to the BNS community in its early years when the founding director, Beverly Falk, brought to the school as a consultant Mary Hebron, associate director of the Art of Teaching graduate program at Sarah Lawrence College and a member of the Prospect board. As a member of that staff, Karen used the processes extensively both to inform and enhance her teaching.

The BNS maintains its child-centered focus. But over the years the school has more and more been subject to external pressures—to district and citywide curricular initiatives, frameworks, and standards. Today teachers at the BNS occasionally participate in Descriptive Reviews of Children and of Work, but the Prospect processes are no longer part of the regularly scheduled practice of the school. So when Karen learned about a course that mentioned the Prospect documentary processes and had Mary Hebron as the instructor, she jumped at the opportunity. On our end, Mary was thrilled when she saw that Karen would be one of the teachers in the group.

The Elementary Teachers Network (ETN), a professional development program of the Institute for Literacy Studies at Lehman College, works with teachers and schools to promote a child-based practice. At the center of this work are the visibility of the child and the visibility of the teacher and his or her practice. The course Karen registered for, "Observation and Documentation: Building from Children's Interests," was one of several reflective practitioner study groups offered by ETN in the spring of 1996. The flyer for the course, offered specifically for teachers in Community School District 10, indicated that teachers would use the Prospect processes to document children's learning and look closely at collections of children's work; use recollection and storytelling, oral and written, to reflect on their own learning and their practice as teachers; use talking, reading, and writing-to-learn strategies to respond to readings in the field; and consider the implications of all this for teaching and learning. The study group/course would meet for seven three-hour sessions over a four-month period.

The structure of the ETN's District 10 study group/course where Karen presented her review of Gabriel was pretty straightforward. Each week Mary and I, as instructors for the course, provided frameworks for seeing the particularity of the child and for responding to that particularity. Participants spent their class time building their descriptions of a child, using guided writings that we developed from the descriptive review headings and the amplification of these in Pat's Letter to Parents and Teacher (see Chapter 3). We also provided lots of time for talk about what it was like to describe a child, to recall a child, and to share these descriptions with colleagues in small groups. And to frame this work we read from Patricia F. Carini's (1986) "Building from Children's Strengths," Mary Jane Drummond's (1994) *Learning to See: Assessment Through Observation*, and Eleanor Duckworth's (1987) *The Having of Wonderful Ideas*.

Why this content and structure? Mary and I were concerned with what teachers might take with them that they could draw on in their home settings, with what ideas they could articulate for themselves that would support their work with children in classrooms. Our decision to focus the course on each teacher's study of one child, to use each session for teachers to document what they already knew about the child, and to use the headings of the descriptive review to shape these documentations was greatly supported by Karen's presence in the course. We knew that we could ask her to present to the group a full descriptive review. We believed that the review, in addition to allowing Karen to think about Gabriel from such a full vantage point, would make visible the power of looking at the child, at any child, more fully, more wholly. We also hoped that Karen's review would make of the course a piece.

Sixteen teachers participated in the course. Each time a teacher described a child and then talked about the child, that sent the teacher back to look again, to see if what was recalled was so, how it was so, when it was not the case, and to ask what else might be done to enable the child to be seen, to be visible. During the fourth meeting of the group, one of the teachers brought a collection of a student's work, and we described one piece. The full descriptive review of Gabriel occurred during the sixth meeting. We met that day in Karen's classroom rather than at the college so that we might imagine more broadly the whole of this child in his classroom context. We hoped the group would make use of the setting as well as of the review to support Karen and her work with Gabriel and to support their own work with children.

On the day of Karen's review, and throughout the course, the Prospect processes supported structured discussions focused on children and their work. The processes helped us to see a child—in this instance, Gabriel—and together to build knowledge about that child and begin the work of finding questions that might further our understanding.

PLANNING THE REVIEW

Mary Hebron and Karen Khan

Karen Khan and Mary Hebron meet in Karen's K–1 classroom at the BNS to prepare for the descriptive review that she will present for the ETN class. Karen has come to this planning session having already chosen a boy in her class to describe. Because she is an experienced teacher and has had some experience with the Prospect descriptive processes, she also comes with many observations of this child and stories from the classroom.

As trains speed by on the elevated track just outside her classroom window, Karen begins to tell Mary about Gabriel, the 7-year-old she has chosen. As chair, Mary's role during this planning session is to listen carefully for fullness in the description of the child, aiming toward learning about the child across all five headings of the descriptive review. She listens, too, for language that is particular and apt, not judgmental or mere jargon.

During the planning session, Mary takes notes to keep track of questions, themes, and connections that will help them find the focusing question for the review as well as to select a word for reflection. The following is an edited transcript from this meeting in May 1996:

Karen: I have started thinking a little bit about focusing questions. When Gabriel first came into my room, my question was, "Will he get enough here?" He is very interested in scientific things, clearly a deep thinker, a great strong reader, and a quick learner. I just wondered if this would be the right environment. I thought perhaps it might have been better if we had had a 1–2 class for him.

After several weeks of getting to know him, I realized that this was, in fact, a good environment because emotionally he really needed to learn more about relating to children. I felt that he behaved in a way that very young children behave. He did well with children who weren't like him in certain ways, like with children who took longer to learn, or for whom he could be the one who showed them what to do. But he needed to learn how to make friends and how to sustain relationships with children who were like him, where there was more of a give-and-take, where they were thinking in the same depth that he was thinking. He could relate more in that way to adults, but he's not a seeker-out of adults. It took me a long time to get to a place where I saw that he was comfortable with me. He's just quiet. *Quiet* is the word for Gabriel.

Mary: Is that a possible word to reflect on in the review?

Karen: Maybe. He's just so quiet. Sometimes he pantomimes things rather than speaking about them. That has become an issue at times when it confuses people. It's like when you don't use words to explain your actions, when you think your actions are self-explanatory—and in fact they're not. That's something that I've been pointing out to him, and we have a relationship now where he can hear what I have to say and sort of nod, like, "Oh, you know." It seems like it's nothing that's ever occurred to him.

Mary: So when you are saying "quiet," you mean nonverbal, too?

Karen: Well . . . the thing is, he can speak . . . long paragraphs in such a soft voice. But he is so quiet that even when he's speaking, it's very hard to hear him. I think sometimes he's just moving his mouth. I'm not even sure if he's actually producing sound. Again, he doesn't do that as much as he used to, but in the beginning he really was very quiet. But he *would* talk about snakes because that was his thing. He always communicated around snakes right from the beginning.

At this point in the conversation, Karen gives Mary some of Gabriel's school history and explains how he came to be at the BNS after completing kindergarten somewhere else. Karen describes how she made Gabriel comfortable during his first visit to the school and in the process began to get to know him.

Gabriel spent a week coming here, and he was very happy. I knew of his interest in snakes, so I put out books for him, and I borrowed Ronnie's snake for a period of time. He and his father went out and bought food—live goldfish—for the snake to eat, and he really enjoyed being here. I could see that his skills were really strong. He read right away. He could decode everything, and he understood it, even though the way he read was choppy. He was using a phonetic approach to the decoding, but he pulled it together and understood what was being said. He always understood what he read, and it was always nonfiction, and it was always about snakes in the beginning.

Karen goes on to describe what she noticed during that first week when Gabriel was visiting at the BNS.

I remember teaching him how to use the index. He wasn't aware of an index. We were trying to find out about snakes in books that weren't apparently snake books. He was just an exuberant learner; when he found out something new, he was thrilled. I could see that he went off and looked into all kinds of books to see if they had an index and if he could find snakes. When he noticed that the index was alphabetical and that it could go over more than one page, he was deeply excited. That's just his style of learning.

I felt like he talked more regularly at those times, but always about snakes. I only heard his voice when it was about snakes; otherwise he didn't always answer. When we did our self-portraits, he did a portrait of a snake, and he signed his name "Gabriel Agent Python." He never writes just "Gabriel"—it's "Gabriel Agent Python."

By thinking back to Gabriel's entry into her classroom, Karen is laying out for herself and for Mary the complexity of getting to know this child and the layers of questions about teaching him.

Karen: So once he was in my class, I really worried about him. I really worried that he was going to be a challenge, because he absorbed things so quickly. I felt, "How am I going to feed that hunger to learn?" I had a wonderful group of kids that pulled together right away this year, but they were very young. Even some of my first-graders were very "young" first-graders. I was a little concerned about that and about the friendship thing because his mother had made me aware that that was something that might be a problem for him.

The next thing I noticed he liked to do, during free time in the morning, were the multilink cubes. He would construct snakes, and the kids—you know how kids are—watched and saw and were interested. Who's this new person? They knew immediately that he's an information holder—a child who has a lot of information, accurate information—and someone who thinks things through. They knew they could count on him for certain things. I felt like the children knew that immediately.

Mary: Talk more about his connections with other children.

Karen: At first I think that they were confused about his interest in snakes, because sometimes Gabriel would hiss instead of talk in a group and because he signed his name "Agent Python." When he first did his self-portrait as a snake, the kids were a little wary about that. It seemed odd to them. Now his love of snakes is totally accepted.

He's totally accepted. But I wasn't sure at the beginning how it was going to go, if he was going to turn out to be this oddball that kids were going to continue to think this way about.

One child, Alex [pseudonym], who is a first-grader, was so wonderful with Gabriel. He just took Gabriel under his wing and helped him out. I mean, he really took on the role of introducing Gabriel to the class and to whatever we do, and Gabriel really seemed to feel like he had a friend.

Mary: Were there other children he related to?

Karen: Gabriel became Scott's [pseudonym] partner during reading center time, which we do down in Ronnie's room with the other class. Scott is a very strong reader. He probably taught himself how to read when he was 3, and I mean he can read anything. He can read out loud beautifully from chapter books with expression. Gabriel is a strong reader but not as expressive. He's gotten smoother over time; I don't know if it's been helped by just his growth or Scott's style, as they've given each other a lot and they read together a lot.

Scott didn't have a really close friend, and I thought, "Those guys should get along well." But Scott didn't like working with other people very much and always kept away from that one-to-one closeness. He'd rather be close to an adult than with a child. So when they first started partnering up, it was a little difficult.

Karen has a great deal of knowledge of Gabe's relationship with Scott, and she shares stories of their on-again, off-again friendship, many of which she includes later in the review. In describing their work together, aspects of Gabriel's standards for himself and his work emerge.

Gabriel would try writing stories during writing time about snakes. He would write sometimes about soccer, but you had to be motivating him all the time and it wasn't really coming from him. When he did work on his own, it was drawings of snakes. There would be a lot of overworking of them, but not out of boredom, like some kids do when they can't think of anything else to do. He would do these elaborate snake drawings, and there would be some words, but it wasn't clear what he was doing with them or what he was thinking. He could be coerced into writing a story, but nothing was helping him grow as a writer.

Then a couple of months ago he was writing lists of snakes—just sitting and writing these long lists of names of snakes. He and Scott were sort of working together, but it wasn't clear what they were doing, and after seeing this for a couple of weeks—this list of snakes just growing and growing—I said, "What are you going to do with this?" He responded, "I just want to write it."

Karen goes on to tell Mary how she then worked with Gabriel and Scott to develop their snake lists into a computer project about snakes and what she learned in the process about Gabriel's standards for his writing.

Karen: When I first talked to them about writing a book about snakes, Gabriel said to me, "I can't write about the facts I learned about snakes, because I read it in other people's books and I can't do that." I said, "I have to tell you something. Do you know where those people learned those facts? They probably learned a lot of them from other people's books and from observing." I explained to him what you can't take from a book and what you can take, like you can't write the words exactly the way they're written in the book because that is stealing. I told him about plagiarism, too, but also how you can gather information and repeat it back in your own words. You can observe and add that, too. I told him there were many sources that writers use.

Mary: Is what he says about the different snakes his own?

Karen: Yes, that's what he and Scott are researching. They are reading during the reading time, and I'm inputting it. They say it to me, and then I type it in. At first Scott had no qualms about plagiarizing at all, so some of it really sounded like somebody else's words. I said, "Where did this come from?" They showed me, and I said, "This is not okay. This you cannot do. You read this or reread it now and then tell me what you got from it. Tell me what the important part is and what you want me to put in the project." That's how they are doing it now: They're telling me what they know. And Gabriel does know a lot. He tells me snakes, and I don't know how to spell some of them, because I really don't know snakes. So that's how we're doing it now, like a long-term project that they're very content to stretch out.

Mary: Okay. Let me look over my notes and say some things that I've been thinking about for the review. You said a lot about Interests and a lot about Connections with Other Children, especially Scott. You gave a physical description. And his Disposition and Temperament obviously come through all of this.

But because we will be doing this review with teachers who are really beginners in descriptive processes, I want to make sure that they hear the headings of the review. We might in this instance say, or have you say, specifically that you're moving from one heading to another.

Karen: Okay.

Mary: I will say in my introduction to the whole process that these headings always overlap, and when you're thinking about where you want to place a particular observation or description, you may have any one of three places to say some of the things you just said about Gabriel.

Karen: So I should sort of put them under the headings?

Mary: Yes, to help people follow your thinking. What we're saying is that with the help of these headings, we get as full and balanced a picture of the child as we can. That's why we use the headings. Include things about Scott. I also think it's important that you give them Alex's story. It's an interesting story, with the whole notion of his choosing in the beginning kids with whom he was able to sort of be the teacher.

Karen: Sort of like the big brother. I should also say Gabriel has two older brothers.

Mary: In the beginning, as chair, I'll state his age, the ages of his siblings, and his previous schooling.

Karen: He's 7. His brothers, I would have to find out how old they are.

Mary: Okay, and he went to kindergarten at a different school? And so this is his first year here?

Karen: Yes, that's right.

Mary: And that's really all I'll say by way of background. Family data are kept minimal in a descriptive review, sharing only what the family agrees to have shared or what we would be comfortable saying in their presence. Are you going to use his name?

Karen: I feel like I will, whether I want to or not. Probably it's going to pop out. Is that okay or should I change things?

Mary: Generally, the rule of thumb is that when you do a review outside of the school, you use a pseudonym or the initial unless you've checked it out with the parents.

Karen: Well, I could ask his mom. That's no problem. I have a relationship with her. And I suspect it will be okay.

Mary: Good. One of the things I'm going to press hard on is the issue of privacy and how important that is for people to think about—to be respectful of the teacher, the child, and the family. I will tell people in the review circle that what is shared in the review is to remain within the circle, that what is shared about the child or the family is not spoken of in other contexts. When the review is completed, we will go around the circle and critique our process by commenting to our respect for the child and the family.

At this point in the conversation, Karen and Mary discuss how recognizing the child's Strong Interests and Preferences leads to knowing the child's Modes of Thinking and Learning. Mary wants to be sure that the description of Gabriel will be broad as well as deep, so she asks Karen to share with her other interests Gabriel has pursued, in addition to snakes, emphasizing the value and importance of knowing places where the child diverges from his or her strong preferences to try out new ideas and interests.

Mary: The other thing is the way that knowing what Gabriel is interested in will so clearly lead into knowing how he thinks and learns. Think about how to lay that all out—the incredible focus on one interest, the deep investment in that, and the different ways that he's pursued that interest. Has it been through observing? Is he reading as well as observing these snakes? Is observing part of it?

Karen: It's more reading, thinking, drawing. He does a lot of artwork around it. At home he does other artwork. He even brought in an aluminum-foil snake this morning, a cobra, and I said, "Did you make that?" He said, no, his mother had. I try to steer him toward some stuff, but he doesn't go for it. He and Scott were thinking they could make a big snake, like a papier-mâché snake, but they decided to stick with the computer project, and they haven't pursued the snake—which I thought would be really a neat project.

Mary: Are there other interests that show another side of Gabriel? Something else he has connected to? You started to say earlier that he got interested in something . . . I forgot what it was.

Karen: Oh, in science! We've been doing a balance and motion study. He has such theories. I definitely have to talk about that—his theories. He experiments with everything, and he comes up with these great theories, which in fact become often the class's next starting point. He is definitely a leader in that way in his thinking.

Mary: Say that in the Interests section, and in the Modes of Thinking and Learning section, note that he has scientific bent, a theorizing mind.

Karen: He also does other stuff. He wrote a rhyming game. He loves rhyming, and we had some rhyming work we were doing, and he brought this in for people to work on. He had this game, where you can only rhyme with the Bronx New School. What is the school where the cows go? It's the Bronx Moo School. Which school do all the animals go to? It's the Bronx Zoo School. His mind is really a riot.

Mary: That *is* interesting because you were saying before how, in addition to all this heavy-duty nonfiction, he likes things like *Bony Legs* [Cole, 1983] and things that have a little irony or a little twist to give another angle.

Karen: He's so into all these intellectual pursuits or scientific pursuits that I might have thought that rhyming words would not really turn him on, but he just loves it. And he loves to be read fiction, like chapter books. We're reading the *My Father's Dragon* [Gannett, 1988] series. He just loves those. Then he also was doing *The Magic Tree House* series by Mary Pope Osborne [1992].

Mary: That's so interesting because that's very kind of innocent and . . .

Karen: It also may be that he has gotten pulled into the culture of the class with that one, because the kids couldn't get enough of it. They just all sprawled all over the place, just listening to these stories.

Mary: But the Bronx moo stuff, has he shared that with the kids?

Karen: I think he does.

Mary: You need to describe that part of him.

Karen: Yes, he has a totally silly part. He is like this little preschooler in some ways. He pushes people, he tumbles. He doesn't do it so much anymore, but he still will suddenly be tumbling on the rug with somebody.

Mary: So under the heading of Physical Presence, you may want to say something about that or under the heading of Disposition and Temperament.

Karen: Okay. If he's sitting next to someone, he'll start one of these foot-pushing things—no words, but he'll do that kind of stuff. He's a fascinating kid. I would like to just watch him all the time. He eludes me when I'm not sticking near him. He totally eludes me: I'm looking at him and then he's gone.

After Karen describes some observations she made of Gabriel using meditation and yoga to regain control in situations that were loud or confusing, Mary suggests that Karen include these stories in her description. They then try out some additional words for reflection. *Resourceful* and *communication* come to mind.

Mary: Now let's start thinking about the focusing question. One of the questions raised here is bigger than just Gabriel. It is the question of when kids are not visible in a certain way, usually because they're not very verbal: First of all, how do you refrain from making quick judgments and then how do you get to know these children in other ways? There is a question, too, of how to allow the child to make himself visible at his own pace.

Karen: Yes, Gabriel really slowed me down. He really told me, "You're moving ahead of me."

Mary: This descriptive review should be useful for you, Karen, so the
   focusing question has to help the group think about something that
   they can work through with you. Do you have a sense of where you
   would want to have help at this point?

Karen: I guess the question has two parts. One part is for Gabriel to be
   comfortable—to move at this own pace—and then for me to have
   trust and faith that he is clearly going somewhere with everything that
   he's got.

Mary: For you to trust, then?

Karen: Well, for me and the teacher who comes next. I would also like to
   see where this is all going. I want to see more actualizing, all the
   thinking and all the theorizing, and he's a baby, just a little kid. It's
   really hard because there is such a disparity between the depth of his
   thinking and who he is in the world. I'm feeling now like I'm in a good,
   settled place with him. I feel like he's got a great combination here. He
   can go off thinking and he can be the little kid that he is. I'd like to see
   him continue to do that until he doesn't need to do that anymore.

Mary: That struck me right from when you started talking—how you
   worried that your classroom wasn't going to be challenging enough
   for him and that idea of allowing him to be 7.

Karen: I know, and he's *so* 7. He's just *so* 7. And he's also all the years
   that came before still. He's just such a rich kid to look at. You can see
   so much when you actually get to see him. I don't know what the
   question is, but you know he's been such a gift to me. He's so visible
   that I don't know how I couldn't have seen him. He is so visible.

Mary: Well, we probably need to have a brief phone conversation either
   Monday or Tuesday night to firm this up. I will try to form the
   focusing question around what you just said. The two parts of the
   question, as I heard it, are how to have the classroom provide enough
   to support Gabriel's modes of thinking and learning, and how to
   allow him to be who he is, to be 7, and to trust that he is going somewhere even if he does not conform to all classroom expectations. I
   think there is a lot in this that will generate thought and conversation.
       As far as selecting the word for reflection, we have discussed *quiet,
   resourceful*, and *communication*.

Karen: I know that most presenters do not write their review out, but I
   prefer to, and as I write, the word may just leap out at me.

Mary: Absolutely. You can call me over the weekend, too. This is going
   to be great, Karen. There is so much here.

In the phone conversation that follows this planning session, Karen
rethinks the importance of having all children participate in all classroom

activities and wonders if a child has to be engaged in everything that they do in a classroom. Gabriel opens this issue up for her because of his strong inclination to pursue his own ideas and approaches to learning. Karen acknowledges, too, that she hopes to think about the role of the teacher and of the classroom in providing for Gabriel. The question that emerges is, "What is enough?" She thinks that might be an interesting word to reflect on.

Class Schedule

We did Science Workshop two or three times per week. On other days, we had Reading Centers, Book Buddies, Music Buddies—all of which we did with other classes. Writing was often in the morning, math in the afternoon.

Karen's Class 209 1995–1996

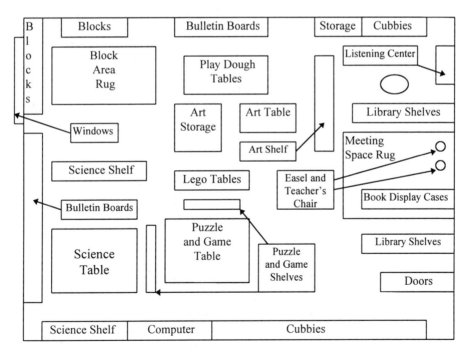

FIGURE 2.2. Map of Karen's Classroom

7:50	Jobs, routines, writing, reading
8:10	Morning meeting
8:20	Work time
9:05	Science workshop—balance and motion study
9:50	Read together (shared reading)
10:00	Music
10:50	Math workshop
11:35	Lunch
12:00	Clubs
12:30	Story time (read-aloud)
12:45	Quiet book time (independent reading)
1:15	Writing workshop
2:10	Dismissal

REFLECTIVE CONVERSATION ON A WORD: *ENOUGH*

Elaine Avidon

Often, before a descriptive review begins, the group assembled participates in a structured conversation focused on a particular word (as described in Chapter 1). The word chosen intersects in some way with the child who will be described; the word may also relate to the adult's/teacher's relationship with the particular child.

What follows is my integrative restatement of the group's reflection on the word *enough*, which took place right before Karen Khan's descriptive review of Gabriel.

> We spoke of *enough* as a word of measure having to do with both persons and things, quantity and quality. We placed our depictions of *enough* on a continuum with notions of adequate and appropriate at its center, of too much and too little at the edges. On this continuum, *enough* was a boundary line, a standard either achieved, not yet realized, or exceeded. At issue was whose measure, whose standard, whose evaluation.
>
> When we characterized *enough* as just right, as the right amount, we used words and phrases like *sufficient, satisfactory, ample, okay, complete, closure, perfect.* But also, *bare minimum.* And this difference between *just enough* as perfection or as bare minimum was as visible in our tone of voice and expression as in our choice of words. *Enough* also implied no more needed, and *just right* was to feel full, satisfied, though not satiated.

Not enough had to do with physical and societal deprivations. But the matters we most associated with *not enough* had to do with our role as both parent and teacher, as provider. Two key phrases used here were *just not enough* and *never enough*, and on our list were *time, room,* and *space* as well as *money, materials,* and *supplies.* We also spoke of *performance*—of adults and children we believed could do more or better, of machines that could perform more consistently or more reliably, and of our own efforts and output, which never seemed quite enough. Implied was both a belief and an expectation that one could or should do more, that the child or teacher or parent, for instance, with some effort, could perform better or had the capacity to do more. We hear ourselves saying to children and to ourselves: too little; that's not enough; you didn't do enough; you can do more. And one of us wondered, "Can I ever do enough?"

Too much was about going overboard—the pushing of someone or something beyond the limit. And this we noted could be both positive and negative. When positive, it is about exceeding our own or someone else's expectation, about accomplishing the impossible. When negative, we talked about going beyond what one could tolerate, take, manage, deal with, hold onto. In such instances, in an attempt to set limits, to gain control, we hear children and ourselves calling a halt, putting a stop to whatever is taking place: Stop! That's it! That's all! I've had it! Enough is enough! I've had enough! Enough already!

When we spoke of persons, objects, things, or events—whether our emphasis was on output, relationships, or capacity—*enough* had to do with measurement in a tangible/literal sense (enough space, enough food, enough oxygen) and measurement of a more qualitative, individual, and particular sort. We asked: When is enough enough? When is enough too much, too little? Because notions of *enough* differ from person to person, because what seems enough to the child may seem too little or too much to the teacher, we noted that this required of us a vigilance having to do with timing, with pacing, with watching. We might very well have to step outside our own frames of reference to understand what is enough for another person. And this, we noted, is hard to do.

Embedded in our sense of *enough* are matters of fairness and equity. Is there enough to go around, enough for everyone? Did you get your share? Sharing will yield less for each individual but some for everyone. So the individual may believe he or she does not have or get enough, yet the compromise yields some for all. Here for us was the dilemma of individual/group need.

We implied that in schools, in our daily living, our judgments of *enough* are almost always a matter of purpose, stance or position, perspective, and preference. Enough sugar is relative to what it is needed for. Vacation time is never enough. From the tester's stance, there is sufficient time provided for the test; from the child's perspective, the time is hardly enough. So the standard of what is enough for one person or situation might well be too much or too little for the other person or in another circumstance; what is emotionally too much for one might be just fine for another. On our continuum, the word is full of borders and boundaries; the definition, both elusive and malleable.

And finally, one of us remembered the song "Once Is Not Enough," and another of us found the word a strange one to reflect on, and even stranger to spell.

DESCRIPTIVE REVIEW OF THE CHILD

Karen Khan

Focusing Question

Part One:

"How can Gabriel be supported in being all of himself—the deep thinker and theoretician, the little boy who needs to play footsies and tumble and shove; the snake specialist, an expert at something meaningful to him; the shy person who speaks when he is ready. Is Gabriel getting enough in my classroom?"

Part Two:

"Does a child have to be engaged in everything that we do in the classroom?"

History

Mary Hebron: Gabriel is a 7-old-boy, who is in Karen's K–1 classroom at the Bronx New School. He lives with his mother and father and is the youngest of three boys in the family. He entered the Bronx New School this year, in first grade. He attended kindergarten in another school with a similar philosophy. His mother is aware of the review and has given her permission for his real name to be used.

Background

Karen: When he got into our school through the lottery, his family wanted him to go here but had some concerns about his making the adjustment due to the length of time it had taken him to make friends, and because he was happy where he was. He had one very good friend at his old school, and his mom felt really badly about separating the boys. She told me that in that relationship, Gabriel tended to function as the older, more skilled member of the partnership: He did the reading (the other boy wasn't into print at that time); he helped with other things, because his motor skills, his writing, were all more developed than his friend's. In the process of deciding if he should change schools, Gabriel spent a week in my class. His mother stayed with him for the first two or three days. He wanted her near him at all times. She began to leave for coffee or for a little while, and although he really didn't want her to, he acquiesced when we pressed him. His father also came one day, and he stayed close to his dad, too. Finally Gabriel decided what he wanted to do about changing schools: He would go a week to our class, and a week to his former class. His parents worked it out with him that he would change schools.

I worked at the same nursery school Gabriel attended when he was about 3½ years old. I knew his mother, who worked in my room from time to time, but I really didn't have a good sense of him.

Physical Presence and Gesture

Gabriel is a slim, maybe even slight, first-grader. He is proportioned small and wears T-shirts and slacks in neutral or dark colors. He has pictures of snakes on several of his T-shirts. He moves quietly from place to place. He usually comes into the classroom quietly. He sometimes comes in with a serious look on his face—perhaps sad or bothered. His face is quietly expressive. Quiet. *Quiet* is the word for Gabriel. He often pantomimes or finds nonverbal ways of getting what he needs, rather than using words. He has many different facial expressions. At times, he lifts one eyebrow and puts his index finger up and says "Aha!" without any further explanation. There are times that he seems to be speaking, but I'm not sure that he's actually producing sound. Some of those times, I don't think he is. But he's very good at expressing himself with words when he chooses to. His speech is quiet and low, but it's very clear and he uses language very well. His vocabulary is extensive: He's very precise when explaining something. Sometimes he might struggle to find just the right word because he is so precise, not because his vocabulary is inaccessible or limited—quite the opposite. Yet he also seems to have the expectation that people will understand him and his actions without any verbal communication or explanation.

Gabriel sometimes works alone, huddled over his work, and can stay with it for long periods of time, doing colorful snake drawings or making lists of things. This was almost exclusively how he worked at the beginning of the year. At other times, and more so now, he works quietly next to other children, sometimes communicating with them, particularly at the puzzle and game table, and then he engages in conversation while he works—constructing multilink snakes, building with bristol blocks or wood blocks. And at other times he can push other kids and tumble on the floor like a very young child. He can talk with the kids constantly when it is time to be quiet, yet his voice is not really heard even at those times.

When I try to notice Gabriel and I haven't dropped everything else and just stuck with him like glue, he eludes me. I get him in my sights, and then he's gone, quietly, he's just gone, and I've never noticed him leaving.

When I was sitting with Mary, preparing for this review, he came near us with his aluminum-foil snake. He held it toward us and was making faces that could be construed as a smile; it seemed a communication without words. Holding something in front of people, making faces, and not saying a word is often his style of engaging with others.

He would come up to me without saying a word and stick his shoe up to me. I would just wait to see what he would do if I didn't respond. He never said a word. I would ask him what this meant, that I thought maybe he wanted me to tie his shoe, but I couldn't really know for sure if he didn't tell me. He would just nod "yes" and smile.

Disposition and Temperament

Gabriel seems to be a little bit moody sometimes: One minute he seems so serious and maybe even annoyed, the next minute a friend can come over to him with a friendly word or gesture, and his facial expression changes, and a quiet, sweet smile spreads over his face. Yet his moods seem quiet and unobtrusive. It's not big moodiness. Nor does he seem to seek attention in his moodiness. It's almost like he wants to stay very small and quiet. His mood can be turned around by the greeting of a friend. He seems to click into the life of the class through his friendships. He laughs easily, when he's not being very serious and unreachable. His laughter is quiet, and his banter with his friends often has a gentle humorous and ironic feel to it. He is big on jokes and riddles.

Gabriel seems to always be figuring things out, to be studying things. Again, he is often quiet and pensive. His pace is also slow, almost like his personal timing is slightly out of sync with the rest of the world. He confuses me—with his quick learning and his slow place. It takes a long time before he commits to something, but once he goes for it, he stays with it. It isn't always clear whether or not he is going to respond to me or others, and the time it takes to wait to find out doesn't always work in a classroom with 25 other kids.

He can be quietly playful. He was sitting and not committing to a center. He then went to work with Play Dough with his friend Scott, who was making cookie-cutter people shapes, all lined up on a tray. Gabriel sat with a ball of Play Dough, and it was unclear what he was making, so I asked him. He told me, with a twinkle in his eye and a subtle little smile, that he was making blobs. There was a lot of humor behind those words. He liked saying that to me. I had the feeling that the boys were also making something else together, but every time I turned to look at Gabriel, he was making blobs (actually just one blob which sat in his hand).

He has an excellent sense of humor, very sophisticated, and likes playing with words. I found this in his folder:

Sam Snake: I hope I'm not poisonous.
Sue Snake: Why?
Sam Snake: I just bit my tongue.

I don't know where these things come from in his folder. He never shows them to me. I have to find them or somebody else has to tell me he's done things.

How I got to know that he was shy: I thought he thought he just didn't have to do things that we were doing. I didn't understand why I was ignored, and I wasn't happy with the way he didn't communicate with me. He told me he was very shy, and it was very hard for him. I believed he was really expressing something important to him that seemed real. I explained how things had appeared to me and said I'd give him the space. He was so clear about this. His explaining this to me turned out to be a help to me in being a better teacher for him. I decided to step back and trust that he was telling me something important. That he could articulate it was so helpful to me.

Lately he meditates. I first noticed this when he was waiting with the rest of the class for me to come back from lunch. They couldn't go in the room since there was no teacher, so they all just hung out in front of the room. I noticed that in the mass of children from my class standing in the somewhat narrow corridor in front of my room, and with the children from other classes walking back to their rooms, Gabriel sat himself down in the middle of all this, folded his legs, put his hands on his knees, and closed his eyes. I assumed that he was meditating, and he confirmed that he was. I said "Gabriel, are you meditating?" and he just smiled at me.

Another time Gabriel was sitting on the rug while the student teacher in my room was talking and passing objects around to the kids. Gabe was sitting in the back, away from other children. He seemed to be listening—He was sitting and snapping his fingers. When the student teacher lost control of the class, Gabriel put his face in his hands, closed his eyes, folded up his legs, and seemed to be aware of his breathing: He looked like he was meditating and centering himself. When the class got back under control, he started opening his eyes and looked at the student teacher. She said, "Get into a group of two or three to share about the special object you brought from home." He immediately started looking around. He looked over my way and seemed to notice that I was watching him and writing notes and sat back down again. Then he seemed to decide to ignore the fact that I was watching him and went looking for his partner.

Connections with Other People

Socially, relating to his peers, he did some things that other children didn't like in the beginning of the year: kissing inappropriately to show that he liked someone in an attempt to make friends, tumbling on the rug during a transition or a meeting, putting his foot out to trip someone on line, always talking with someone on line. He seemed to not know how to make friends and sustain relationships with children. He was obviously very attached to his parents. He didn't seek other adults out very much. He tended to work alone.

At first the kids in the room seemed to think his love of snakes was strange, perhaps a bit too much. They were a little wary of him and what he was about, particularly when he drew his self-portrait as a snake and signed it "Agent Python," or when he would hiss instead of speak. Gabriel took his time making friends. One boy in our class took Gabriel under his wing and helped introduce him to our class, our routines, etc. Gabriel considered this child, Alex, a friend. I heard this from both Gabriel and his mother. It seemed to me that it might have been like the friendship Gabe had in his old school. But although the boys are still friendly, that relationship didn't seem to remain a true friendship. Alex often didn't understand what Gabe was talking about—literally the words Gabriel spoke—and his focus was so often different from Alex's. They no longer spend that much time together. What they seemed to have in common was that Gabriel needed help in becoming comfortable in our class, and Alex wanted to help him and be a friend.

Now, there is no issue about Gabriel being strange. He's an important member of the class, he seems to be respected by the kids for his talents and strengths, and he is also one of the boys. We had a snake for awhile, and he was our expert, and spent time with the snake, and shared his knowledge (and perhaps even more important, his delight) with the class. When Gabriel made snakes from multilink cubes, other kids also began to make snakes from multi-links as well as the transformers they had previously enjoyed. The kids see him as someone who has a lot of accurate information and knowledge. They see him as a child who can figure things out, a child who has strong interests that he stays with for a long time. Gabriel's interest in snakes is so reliable.

Gabriel currently has a best friend named Scott. During the first half of the year, Gabriel did most of his work alone, except for his attempts at friendship with Alex. In trying to broaden his reading to include more fiction, and to help him work with a partner who had strong skills as a reader, I encouraged him to work with Scott. The two paired up around the reading of some early chapter books. The boys seemed to be engaged in this relationship and worked for a day or two, but the enthusiasm didn't last long. Gabriel still liked to mostly read nonfiction, which didn't engage Scott. The fiction Gabriel liked (and still likes) usually had an ironic sense of humor, a story with a clever twist to it. He didn't seem to want to read challenging texts and preferred simple chapter books, which weren't really challenging enough for Scott or interesting enough for Gabriel. When they tried harder books, Scott would assign them homework, which he would do and Gabriel wouldn't. They were both supposed to assign themselves readings for homework, but it always seemed as though Gabriel just sat there and sort of said "yes" to what was asked of him. Again, that quiet, nonanswering way made it impossible to know what he was agreeing or not agreeing to. He didn't do the reading for homework. Scott went on to read more and more challenging chapter books and has incorporated some nonfiction (snakes in particular) into the books he spends time with. Gabriel has continued with the nonfiction and the early chapter books (again, he stays with the same thing). They got bored with each other and stopped being partners.

Gabe partnered with other kids—not as skilled readers, most often, if not always, kindergartners, who loved to be read to. Mostly Gabriel read and his partners listened, or not. I believe Gabe always chose the books and the partners didn't object. The kids he worked with didn't seem to care; he didn't seem involved in whether or not they were paying attention or what they were doing. He sort of took them in and seemed aware of them, but continued to do whatever he wanted without regard for them. I worried that he wasn't challenging himself, wasn't growing as a reader or as a collaborator.

Scott and Gabriel got back together, after noticing that these other partnerships didn't work out. (I really pushed this pairing again.) But they didn't have a focus or energy about their work. Where was their work going? Gabriel wrote about snakes and soccer, but he didn't seem to be really interested. Gabriel on his own would do elaborate snake drawings, adding detail upon detail. When they got back together, Gabe was writing lists of snakes over the course of weeks. I strongly challenged the boys to do something with this list. I brainstormed with them, and they came up with the idea to make a computer list that, when one snake on the list was clicked on, would move the player to a list of facts about the snake. After learning about snakes, the player would then be able to play a game that required knowledge of the snakes. Gabriel seemed as excited by making the list as anything else, but Scott was turned on by the computer idea. The boys started to learn a lot about the computer. This is a project they will do over a long period of time.

Both Gabriel and Scott go to the after-school program together, which has cemented their friendship.

At first I didn't think I would be able to become close to Gabriel. I didn't experience a sense of connectedness and warm feelings from him for a long time. We are now very connected, and I understand that his teasing me and questioning me are an expression of his comfort with me. His affection's now clear. Although he still seems to think of himself as shy, Gabriel is much more outgoing and seems to be very comfortable interacting with many more adults in our school. During a visit to our school by some people from the district whom he had never before met, Gabriel easily shared his ideas and theories about some science work we were doing.

One day, after I read a new picture book (it was independent reading time), Gabriel came over to me with an unhappy look on his face. He told me he needed something new to read; there were no books around the room he wanted to read or hadn't already read. (The kids had just seen some new books I bought but couldn't give out yet.) I looked through some books I hadn't put out and found a copy of *Bony Legs* [Cole, 1983], which I was certain Gabriel would enjoy. James [pseudonym], a kindergartner, was right near us, and I suggested that he might want to ask Gabriel to let him listen in to the book. Gabriel said "yes," and the boys sat down at the art table to read. Gabriel started reading and showed the pages to James as he read. At first James seemed engaged. Every time Gabriel laughed, he turned to James's sometimes without actually looking at him, resting his hand on James's shoulder, as he read a part of the book he really enjoyed. James at some point became uninterested and got up and walked to another table. Gabriel followed after him, continuing to read and enjoy the book as he walked. This same unlikely activity continued from table to table over the course of the reading. At some point Gabriel seemed to become aware of my following him, as he was following James. He just kept on doing what he was doing, only, after noticing me, he put his hand on my shoulder once or twice, to share his excitement about the book. He just kept reading to James, no matter what else was happening.

Gabriel seems to expect people to understand him even when he doesn't explain. One day he was reading a snake book with his book buddy, a fifth-grader, and two other boys from my class. There was a picture of a dead snake, which he said wasn't really real. Then a minute later, he plopped himself back onto the table he was sitting on. Perhaps had he done this immediately after talking about the picture in the book, it would have been understood by the rest of us, but he moved and reacted in his very slow style. When I asked what he was doing, he said he was demonstrating what a truly dead snake would look like. None of us knew that; we all thought he had lost interest in the reading.

Gabriel tends to interact with boys only. I can't picture his working with a girl. He always notices me when I observe him; then he seems to forget about me and goes about his business. He engages with adults on a need-to-engage basis. It's not that he seems to have an aversion to engaging with adults, but he doesn't seem to need that much adult input.

Strong Interests and Preferences

Gabriel learned to read in kindergarten through his interest in snakes. Gabriel always communicated about snakes. His self-portrait was a portrait of a snake. From the beginning, when he spoke, it was invariably about snakes. He always signs his name "Gabriel, Agent Python" (if he leaves any part out, it's the "Gabriel" part, because he knows we'll recognize Agent Python). When the class plays "Duck, Duck, Goose," he plays "Cobra, Cobra, King Cobra." He comes in with lots of snake stuff: books, rubber snakes, different kinds of snakes, a beautiful snake of papier-mâché that his mother made him. Snakes, snakes, snakes.

His first interest in our room, other than the live snake and books about snakes, was the construction of snakes from multilink cubes. In his artwork and writing, his theme is always somehow connected to snakes. He creates symbols having to do with snakes. He has tried to explain these symbols to me: "If it is turned one way, it means one thing, and if it's turned the other way, it means something else. Like this is for snake language and the lightning rods are for energy." I have tried to understand, but I don't. He's so deeply invested in this one pursuit and has really stayed with it. Reading, thinking, drawing—rubber snakes, aluminum-foil snakes, cube snakes, snake staff, his homework folder beautifully decorated in snake letters by his mother.

He's done more interacting and sharing with the class having nothing to do with snakes over time, but the snakes still remain a strong interest. He has shown an excitement and strong interest in science. When we started our balance and motion study, he started figuring things out and would have theories about where the weight needed to be distributed, whether the weight had to be on the bottom, and so forth. He articulated it all. It became sort of a pattern that Gabriel's theories fueled the thinking for the next lesson. He also just loves gym class, and he loves many of our read-alouds. The two series of books we have read since the beginning of the year seem very interesting to him, particularly the *Magic Tree House* series by Mary Pope Osborne [1992].

Gabe, when questioned about perhaps writing a book about snakes, said, "I can't write because I learned these facts from other people's books." He had decided that he himself must create his own knowledge or he would be stealing.

Gabe loves rhyming words. He made up a game, which his mother told me about (he didn't tell me about it until I asked). His game is a game of riddles that rhyme with "The Bronx New School." (Example: What is the school where all the cows go? Answer: The Bronx Moo School. Where is the school the animals go to? Answer: The Bronx Zoo School.) He has made up other activities with rhyming words for the kids to use and loves to tell and create jokes and riddles.

Modes of Thinking and Learning

The first week that Gabriel was in my class, I remember teaching him about the index in a book we were looking over. He had already exhausted all the snake books I had in my room at the time, and I was looking in other books—about backyards, caves, and so forth—to see if we could find anything about snakes in them. I looked in the index and showed him how it worked. He got really excited when we did find the word *snake*. Over the next few days I noticed him looking for the index in several books and using the ones he found. Gabriel was an exuberant learner, very quietly but deeply excited, and thrilled to find new things out. While exploring the index, he noticed that it was alphabetical and that one letter could continue over several pages. He saw this and talked about what he noticed. He clearly enjoys learning. He seems to study things on his own and figure them out.

When Gabe did some pattern work in math earlier this year, the patterns he created with pattern blocks were so intricate and complicated that he and I had trouble documenting them on paper.

During our balance and motion study, he constantly developed theories as he worked and experimented with the material provided. He tested his ideas over and over to see if they held up. Gabriel could articulate his thinking and his questioning very clearly. Testing his theories often became the class focus for the next lesson.

As a learner, he tends to stick with and focus on particular areas of interest to him. Once he finds something he likes, he stays with it. Gabriel's enthusiasm about snakes has drawn others into this particular interest of his. He only chooses to pursue things that interest him; for example, his computer project about snakes. He spends a great deal of time on some of his illustrations, which can be very detailed. He goes back to the same themes in his work over and over, adding more and more detail.

Gabriel still often chooses to read a lot of nonfiction, sometimes about snakes, and sometimes on other topics, very often with a scientific bent. His tastes in reading seem to be growing. He has begun to ask for new books and is enjoying a wider range of fiction. He seems to enjoy a story with an ironic sense of humor or a clever twist to it. He still loves the chapter books we've been reading with the whole class and is an attentive and enthusiastic listener and participant in class discussions about these books.

He told me that he is shy, and knowing this has helped me to understand that it will take him time to feel comfortable and to settle into his work. He needs to feel accepted as he is and needs his own time and space to try new things and to express himself fully.

Integrative Restatement by the Chair

This is a complex child. Karen has done such a good job of helping us see him as she has come to see him over this year. One of the things that kept coming up was how interior Gabriel is, how much is going on on the inside. This, then, makes it hard for others to see him. On the other hand, he is someone who is engaged and connected. One way that he connects to others is through something he is engaged with; interests like snakes, books, humor are connecting places. It is not person-to-person that the connection is made, but through another avenue, as when he put the foil snake or the shoe in Karen's face.

Gabriel's nonverbalness or tendency to be *quiet*—a word that kept coming up—was put right next to his capacity with language. Karen described him as very articulate, as someone who knows words and knows how to play with words. His rhyming jokes are a wonderful example of that. In a certain way, he is a linguist exploring language. But he doesn't necessarily always feel a need to use language to communicate. He uses lots of other ways too to express himself, and he expects that he will be understood.

One of the questions Karen put forward was whether it is appropriate to ask Gabriel "Where are you going with this and what is this about?" with regard to something he is engaged in. Is that a useful question for Gabriel and is it important for the teacher to understand what he is doing at all times? This seems to relate to that interior aspect of Gabriel. So much is going on in his head. He is working so much through. Karen described him in many ways. My list includes: scholar, listmaker, collector of information, jokester, thinker, theoretician, scientist, linguist. That range gives us the sense of a complex person.

Time is not an issue for Gabriel. It may be an issue for those working with him. In our fast-paced world, it feels as though he moves to a different drummer. That pace is not necessarily accepted or easily read by others. It is part of what makes Gabriel stand apart, harder to get a handle on, at least initially. He lets things unfold, as Karen said.

Gabriel has a deep, abiding interest in snakes, but there are also lots of other interests that Karen named alongside of that one. There has been an unfolding of those interests as the school year has progressed. His interests seem influenced by the culture of the classroom as well as by the children he is connecting to.

In Karen's description of Gabriel's physical presence and gesture, I couldn't help but think of the way he moved—quietly, in and out, there and not there—as snakelike. The kind of elusiveness that Karen was describing felt so much like the movements of a snake.

And Karen described Gabriel as shy. He describes himself as shy. Yet the description raised for me the question of how Gabriel defines *shyness*. There seemed to be no need to show other people who he is or what he is, as if his definition of *shy* is equated with the desire to be left alone to be who he is.

We heard about this 7-year-old meditating, and I was struck by the resourcefulness of using meditation in the face of noise and confusion. His ability to center himself in that way seems extraordinary.

The dead-snake imitation stood out to me. There is so much going on inside, and Gabriel is responding to what he has internalized in a physical way by enacting it. He lies back, trying out what he thinks a snake's dying would be like, not necessarily for anyone else to see or with concern for what others understand about that.

There are many ways he has pursued his interest in snakes and his interest in language. He is not interested in writing stories at this time, but he creates lists. And he holds high standards for writing: It has to be his own. Can you really copy this information about snakes even if you put it in your own words? That is a high standard! As Karen stated toward the end of her description, for Gabriel the need is to create knowledge for himself and the process is important to him.

Control of his own learning is a large theme running through the review; another is the importance of continuity and the importance of supporting Gabriel's interests over the long term and into next year. There is a lot that we can begin to say about the standards Gabriel holds for himself and about the standards Karen holds for her teaching of Gabriel and about the school standards necessary for supporting Gabriel.

RESPONSE: FROM THE INCREDIBLE TO THE POSSIBLE

Elaine Avidon and Mary Hebron

At the end of the description of Gabriel and the chair's summary, we made time for questions, comments, and recommendations. In a multilayered way, the conversation moved back and forth between the implications teachers in the review circle were seeing for their own teaching practice and the support they wanted to give Karen with regard to her focusing question.

The first response of the teachers, new to this process, was around the extent of Karen's knowledge of the child and her ability to describe him so fully. One teacher stated her appreciation of the depth of Karen's knowledge in this way: "Your descriptive review is incredible. You have all this detail to put into understanding this child. I don't think there will ever be another teacher that he will ever have that would have that much on him. It's *incredible*." These teachers seemed initially to believe that what Karen had done in knowing and portraying Gabriel so well was beyond the capability of most teachers. As another teacher commented, "I don't think you're going to get that many teachers that would be so attuned to his likes, his preferences. I mean, it's very difficult to zero in on each student so much. I think he's very lucky to have you. Very, very lucky."

The teachers were also amazed at Gabe's knowledge: "As you presented him, I would have put him in fourth grade almost. If I hadn't seen his work on the paper and you were just describing a child, I would put him more fourth- or fifth-grade age level." And another teacher stated: "The list of snakes is incredible. I mean, to see a first-grade child go down and look at it the way he has . . . he's got everything in order, all the way down the line. That's incredible" These comments revealed the expectations the teachers held for children and the possibility for rethinking those expectations in light of the description they had heard.

Another dimension of the discussion was teachers' placing themselves alongside Karen in recognizing how well she was accommodating Gabriel in her classroom: "Gabriel is definitely in the right environment in this room. Karen has focused on him to make sure that he has an environment where he can be productive. He sounds like he's growing very comfortably within the room." They noted the places she was providing *enough* in validating Gabriel's interests and his approaches to learning and to the world: "What struck me was that you noticed his intensity, his focus, his attention to detail and how you are providing for him opportunities to do that, to return to things. You give him time. I was very struck by the room he's finding in here to be intense and focused."

The opportunity to hear a child described through his interests and strengths, as well as to hear how the teacher provisioned her classroom in support of those interests and strengths, made both the child and teacher seem unique and incomparable at first. During the review and in the week following the review, that discussion continued. Teachers articulated ideas that arose from the description of teaching and learning they had heard. New understandings were made and new possibilities for their *own* teaching became evident. Those understandings were further articulated in the reflective responses written as a final assignment for the course.

During the seven sessions of the course, Theresa Clapp, a relatively new first-grade teacher, worked at understanding the purpose of observation and documentation. The review of Gabriel made clear the value of structured conversations that draw on one's observational knowledge of a child. She wrote: "I would be a better teacher and I would see more of my children if I were involved in this type of positive reflection and dialogue on a regular basis."

The issue of time, so present in Gabriel's review, was also of importance to Theresa. In her final paper, she wrote:

> Observing and documenting Dayne [pseudonym] has clarified something I always knew but made me anxious. Children need time. So many times I have told parents that their child needs the gift of time, but yet I do not listen to my own words of wisdom. . . . Dayne has shown me that some children might do better if they had the same teacher for more than one year. It has taken almost the whole year for Dayne and me to get to know each other. I wonder what I could learn from Dayne if he were in my class next year.

Yangnae Elizabeth Thorsten struggled all term with what the child she was observing was learning. After the review, she wrote:

> I used to think Susan [pseudonym] was not learning much because she was on the same topic, even after we had worked with the family unit and moved to other units. Was I wrong? Susan knows more about family units—human and animal—than anyone else in the class.

The clarifying both Theresa and Elizabeth do for themselves here—the idea Theresa considers about years with one teacher and the reevaluation of curriculum as units that Elizabeth hints at—are deeply connected to their ob-

servations of Dayne and Susan. The distinct articulation of these, we suspect, is a result of their participation in the review of Gabriel.

The role of the teacher in provisioning, supporting, facilitating, and extending a child's learning was a central idea in this part of the discussion. The
complexity of teaching practice was acknowledged as teachers sought to re-
define the role with respect to a child who is a self-starter, someone who does
not seem to need the teacher. They recognized the importance of Karen's stance
in working with Gabe. One teacher said: "I feel that Gabriel is not a child
who you need to give to, but a child you need to step back from and allow to
do for himself." The stance of "stepping back from," and the knowledge and
trust that implies, were impressive to teachers who are aware of how narrowly teaching can be conceived when you believe "you are supposed to be
the teacher even when the child thinks he is teaching himself." The description of Gabriel opened up new ways of understanding teaching. The notion
of teaching as "joining with" and "following after" children took on real
meaning in this review (see Weber, 1997). We acknowledged Karen's giving
children the room to let her follow them and providing time and place to teach
themselves, emphasizing the critical importance of this in Gabe's learning.

The teachers recognized how well Karen valued Gabriel's interests and
how her classroom gave him the opportunity to pursue them. They suggested
ways in which his inquiry into snakes might be used as an entry point to
writing stories and how his strong theoretical and analytical ability could be
engaged in investigating various scientific phenomena. They continued to look
for ways the teacher could engage the child and extend his learning. Through
the portrayal of this one child, the teachers were beginning to see the importance of recognizing a child's interests in supporting him in his teaching of
himself as well as for what it tells the teacher about supporting him in other
aspects of his education.

Following the review, Michelle Rogers Doyle, a prekindergarten teacher,
wrote that she wanted to remember "how important individuality is, and
that children's differences have to be valued and supported. . . . I'd like to
remember that it is okay that students don't always have to be engaged in
particular groups." One week later she noted that the most useful idea that
she'd taken from our class was to "let my pre-K kids be kids more and to
not be so controlling." And in her final assignment, as if speaking to herself,
she wrote: "I've learned that some children really stick with one strength or
area. And that this is okay." She told us also of talking about these ideas
with the educational assistants who worked with her in the classroom, trying to help them see the value in allowing children to engage in one area over
time, trying to help them understand this idea.

Karen's review of Gabriel moved Elisa Grier toward articulating some
of her concerns about provisioning for children. In her final paper she won-

dered: "What is not enough and what is too much? How does one take the observations and turn them into something meaningful and worthwhile that will benefit the children and their learning?" In reviewing her experience of the course, she likened herself to her children who needed encouragement to "step out of our comfort zone and experience new things." She asked herself: "What are the beliefs that are driving what happens in my classroom, causing me to value/devalue the abilities and strengths of children?"

The issues of time and *enough* were also of concern to Marilu Ragno, a first-year teacher: "Children are complicated, yet we need to give them the opportunity to work out their own theories/ideas, and that leaves the question of what is enough to provide an opportunity for natural growth." In another writing, she considered these matters for both her children and herself: "Just as I need the time to organize and discuss what is happening in the classroom, so do the children." Like several of her colleagues, Marilu returned to the issue of the adult role in the classroom raised during the comments and questions following Karen's descriptive review. She indicated she wanted to do more talking about "teacher, facilitator, and provider," and she connected this to "trust"—to the ways she viewed her children.

The review, then, raised questions about the very nature of schooling and the role of teacher and school in the child's education. One teacher acknowledged how child-oriented this review was compared to how school-oriented the focus often is. Teachers showed a willingness to reconsider expected behaviors and outcomes in light of the recognition of what a particular child needs in her or his education: "He sounds like a child with a plan. . . . It looks like there's definitely a well-thought-out process he's going through to do his work. . . . He doesn't want to be bothered with the words [to explain what he knows] . . . because this is for him, it's not for you." Classroom activity and curriculum were being rethought in this conversation to include a child's ownership of her or his work and the right to pursue that work for her or his own purposes. Another teacher responded to the value Karen places on this child's approaches to his work and the trust necessary to believe learning is occurring even when the conventional visual work is not produced: "I'm just impressed with his process and that you're not concerned with his product."

As the discussion evolved, teachers addressed the value *trust* has in teaching—a value that came through strongly in the review—and the difficulty of establishing trust. One teacher stated it this way: "It goes back to trust over time. It takes a while to develop that trust. And it takes a lot of warmth in a new environment." Respect and trust were evident in the ways Karen described Gabe and in the insights we gained into her teaching practice.

As well as supporting and challenging the teachers in the course, the descriptive review, in bringing forward what is possible for a child in a public school in New York City, raised some troubling issues. Luz Real, a teacher for 12 years, was relatively quiet during the go-round following Karen's description of Gabriel. After the review, we spoke for a moment as she stood with a colleague in the doorway of a classroom across the hall. She told us that she had never seen classrooms like these with *so much* for children. On her response sheet that afternoon, she noted that things had clicked into place for her that day, that "What we learn about one child can help us understand and work with other children. . . . Gee, it took me a while to really see this!" In her final piece, she acknowledged aspects of her own teaching that do not allow children to be visible:

> In making children more visible, I need to be less restricting . . . I do not allow the opportunity for the children to do that. I do not allow the . . . children to be selective, nor do I let them build on their creativity. Allowing independence and creativity will allow me to observe and assess the children.

What, though, can such an acknowledgment mean when it is far from the fabric of a school, when there is limited support for the sorts of changes implied in Luz's recognition? Lesia Wilder, another participant, wrote:

> As long as teachers and their classrooms need to be predetermined before the students enter the class, as long as restrictions and mandates are placed at the state and school levels around curriculum and room arrangement, how can I ever really know, be allowed to know, my kids?

The matters raised by Luz and Lesia do not go away. Yet the richness, or thickness, of Karen's description brought Gabriel as a particular child into view. Convening the review in Karen and Gabriel's classroom—among a cacophony of books, creatures, art and building materials, and an array of Gabriel's and other children's work—allowed us to visualize Gabriel within the lived circumstances and contexts of this classroom.

And for many, it made the possibilities *real*.

AFTERTHOUGHTS

Karen Khan

Looking deeply at Gabriel brought up questions about my practice and about how to implement my beliefs. Is my practice consistent with my beliefs? Is this right for all children? What is the teacher's role? Who am I in class?

Quiet. How many times and in how many ways did I use that word? It really had been confusing to me. When not looking deeply, my impression was that perhaps he wasn't doing much—it was hard for me to see all that he was doing because of how he does things. Now I see that it is his essential nature to do all the many things he does in this quiet manner, and I can keep reminding myself to embrace what he does, how he does it, and who he is. Because it is not clearly visible to me doesn't necessarily mean it isn't happening. Because it is not the way I expect things to go, it doesn't necessarily mean it's not the/a right way for things to go.

I notice that this work has reminded me, in a very concrete and grounded way, of something I've known for a long time but haven't really understood. That is, that children need to try things on in their bodies, in their hands, in their imaginings, in ways that grown-ups maybe have forgotten. When Gabriel collapsed over the table, trying on being a dead snake, it likely wasn't just to tell us that the dead snake wouldn't have looked like the picture in the book. It was more than that—more like he was just feeling being a dead snake for a minute. I don't really understand it, but it feels right and important. Not important just for Gabriel, but maybe even more important to remember for the kids who, unlike him, don't also have the language to describe and explain the things they know and the things they're figuring out.

He's got so much going on inside—such a deep interior life—and he connects in class through his snakes, through books, through his love of rhyming words, and through his humor. Is it so important to understand it all? Is it maybe more important to just see it, acknowledge it, and say "yes" to it? Does it all have to be demonstrated in school, when so much goes on inside him and at home? How much is *enough*? His work and thinking go so deep, perhaps there is no way for him to express it all and have it all be seen at this point in his life.

I see how much I know about Gabriel, how good I feel about the work we've done this year. Sharing in this way with others is important—important to the kids, important to me. Time seems not to be an issue for Gabriel, but time is an issue for me. Taking the time to look deeply and having community to speak it out loud in and puzzle it through with is so important. In looking deeply, seeing, accepting, and valuing Gabriel, the space is created for me to look deeply, see, accept, and value other kids and their unique processes.

I notice my inclination to "follow after." I want to notice it and stay with it and develop and refine it, because it feels like my natural way of working. I want to find ways to do it that feel right for my kids. Maybe I need to let myself stand outside the circle more (because it's where I feel I really am much of the time). I know what that feels like, and that's really okay, so I can have it be okay for my kids.

My science area has been slowly growing over the last three years. It is now in a far corner of my room. It's moving to a more central location. This work, along with some other work I've been doing, suddenly helped me notice its place in my room and where it really needs to be.

Share these notes and thoughts with others—family, teachers. Gabriel's mother is very anxious to read about this work. I don't yet know who his teacher will be for next year.

And now it's time to stop. I think I've done *enough*.

CHAPTER 3

A LETTER TO PARENTS AND TEACHERS ON SOME WAYS OF LOOKING AT AND REFLECTING ON CHILDREN

Patricia F. Carini

Fall 1993

Dear Parents and Teachers,

I have chosen a letter as the way to talk with you about looking at children and reflecting on what you have noticed for the reason that letters can be personal in tone and rather informal. And that fits with what I want to say about observing—an attitude or way of looking that I prefer to think of as *attending to children with care*. Parents and teachers are interested in children. They are with children a lot. Through that continuous immersion, parents and teachers possess thick layers of working knowledge about children. Parents and teachers care *for* children and they also care *about* children. Parents and teachers share the responsibility for educating children. And yet, often teachers' and parents' knowledge of children is neither recognized nor valued.

This letter describes an exercise that is meant to do just that: to value and recognize your interest, caring, and knowledge and to build upon it for the benefit of children. The exercise I propose asks teachers and parents, or others with children close to them, *to form a habit of regularly re-viewing them*—that is, calling them to mind; picturing them in particular settings or locations; remembering them in a variety of postures and moods; listening with an inner ear to their voices. The purpose of this re-viewing is the deepened recognition of children. It is meant to give you, the important grown-ups in a child's life, a way to recognize fully how much you already know and understand. It is meant, too, to expand those understandings and to create a context of memory, ever growing and deepening, that will inform your own responses to children as individuals.

If your experience with this exercise turns out to be something like my own, you will also find as you visualize a child in your mind's eye—or listen to the child's remembered voice and words—that there are blurs and gaps in the picture. Some of these will make you wonder, reconsider, and take a closer look. In this way, for me, recollecting leads to more attentive looking and listening. It is also important, though, to keep in mind that the purpose of attending isn't to scrutinize children or even to "figure them out"—and certainly not to change them into someone else. The purpose is simpler and more ordinary: to be more sensitively attuned to who they are and are becoming, so that, recognizing them as persons, we can assist and support their learning better.

To do this exercise, cast your inner eye on a particular child. If you want to re-view several children, perhaps all the children in your family, or a group of children in a classroom, it usually works best to do this one at a time. At least in my experience, if I try to do several at once, they blur or one child takes center stage and calls the tune for others. Then, instead of seeing each child as who that child is, I find myself comparing them according to what stood out to me about that first child who caught my attention. What does work is to develop the picture of one child, allow an interval of time, and then move on to others. The first few children will take quite a lot of concentration; as you form the habit of attending carefully, you will find yourself noticing more and remembering more. As your memory strengthens, you will grow more attuned to subtler and broader aspects of children's expressiveness. As you notice more, *and attend to what you notice more consciously*, the picture of a child will form with greater ease, and your capacity to keep a number of children in mind at the same time without blending them will increase.

As you are recollecting a child, also form the habit of making notes to yourself about what you are remembering. The notes are raw material that you can go back to later to review in preparation for a parent–teacher conference or in order to present (or write) a portrayal of the child. Other raw materials you might keep along with this folder or journal of notes are photographs, drawings, or other things that child makes, or even, if you wish, audio- or videotapes.

Another help in recollecting a child is to think of the child in a variety of settings and locations. Every parent knows how surroundings and time of day influence a child; so do fatigue or illness. Teachers are often aware that a child who is free and open outdoors on the playground may look less so in the confines of a classroom or even seem subdued or withdrawn. Also children (and adults) have favorite places to be and other strong preferences; for example, feelings about how quickly or slowly they want to start or end the day or an activity; how many people they want around and how much time they need to be alone; how long they can sit in one place and concentrate on the same thing and how much variety and change they can comfortably tolerate, and so forth.

The following paragraphs use headings of the *Descriptive Review of the Child* as a sort of organizing device for recollecting. Use them as they seem helpful, but please don't feel bound by them. They are meant to prime the pump of memory, but not to be confining or predetermining.

Thinking of a child's *Physical Presence and Gesture*, be attentive to what stands out to you immediately. Then, take note of size and build, but also of style of dress, color preferences, prized possessions, and so forth. Visualize how the child moves, with attention to pace, characteristic rhythm and gestures, and how they may vary. For example, you might think about how the child tends to enter the classroom or the child's pace at home first thing in the morning or at the end of the day. You might think, too, of how much space a child occupies, where the child tends to position him- or herself in a group, and so forth.

Locate the child in motion, physically engaged, both outdoors and indoors. For example, you might think of what the child likes to do outdoors (such as bike riding, exploring, sports, etc.) and notice to yourself the energy, pace, and gestures involved. Do the same for active indoor play, such as dress-up, block building, and other construction. Then think of the child quietly occupied; for example, drawing, reading, observing, conversing. What pace and gestures are characteristic in these occupations? Think about where the child seems most at ease and how you can tell that is so; then take it other side round and think of where the child seems least comfortable or most constrained.

Other slants you might take on the child's presence include the voice, its inflection, volume, and rhythm; characteristic phrases and ways of speaking; the expressiveness of the eyes, hands, and mouth; where the child's feelings can be read (and how easily); where and when energy flows most easily and smoothly; where energy seems to be concentrated; how tension shows itself; and so forth.

Attending to expression makes a natural bridge to the child's *Disposition and Temperament*. You might start by reflecting on how the child usually greets the world. Or to say that a little differently, you might think of how you would describe the child's most typical attitudes toward life.

With these characteristic feeling tones at the center, picture to yourself the sort of emotional terrain the child covers in the course of a day and also according to a variety of circumstances: Some children (and people) tend to maintain an even, steady emotional balance; others are quick to laughter and quick to tears; still others are likely to be inward turned and unlikely to display their feelings.

Think, too, about what the child cares for deeply and what stirs deep feeling. Similarly, reflect on what goes against the child's honor or sense of rightness or justice and where the child has deep loyalties and strong personal commitments. Reflect, too, on how these deep feelings tend to be expressed.

Connections with Other People are not easily separable from disposition and temperament. First, gather in your mind some examples of the child in the company of other children. In the classroom or at home, think about the location of the child in relation to the larger community of children. That is, reflect on where you usually see her or him; how she or he goes about making a place for her- or himself; how she or he tends to move into a new group or to respond to unfamiliar children.

Picture to yourself the range of the child's relationships with other children; for example, think about any children with whom the child has formed a close, enduring relationship, but also think of how the child falls in with more loosely connected groups that may form around games or other classroom or neighborhood activities. Reflect on what the child's role is within friendships and small groups; with brothers and/or sisters or other close relatives; within larger groups.

Give some attention to how the child responds if difficulties arise in a group or with a friend or if she or he, or another child, is in distress or left out, and so forth. Also think about when the child prefers to be alone or left to her or his own devices.

Now you might shift your attention to the child in relation to you or other adults. Think first of the child's characteristic responses and ways of connecting with adults and also the range of these. Picture, for example, how the child greets familiar adults and the kind of contact the child establishes in the course of the day. For example, if there are adults who are sought out, reflect on what draws the child to them; if there are others who are ignored or avoided, think about what keeps the child at a distance.

Think, too, about the child's preferred ways of being with you or with other adults and what the child expects back from you. Another point of reflection might be the way the child negotiates the transition from one adult to another. Yet another might be your sense of what makes the child feel safe, trusted, respected, and secure with adults (or not).

Now give some attention to how you and other adults tend to welcome the child and generally respond to him or her. Think about how easily you or other adults recognize and value the child and how you or others express that to him or her. If the child is hard to see, give some thought to what keeps the child hidden from you or others. Reflect, too, on what adult responses, interests, and ways of being hold the child's interest and win her or his respect and, alternatively, which kinds of responses or attitudes are likely to put the child off or lead to anger or conflict.

Children, like adults, tend to have *Strong Interests and Preferences* that are absorbing and longlasting. From my experience, these are likely to offer much valuable insight in terms of the child's entries into learning and particular talents to be nurtured. I like to start by making a list of all the things I know a child really likes, such as particular foods (or eating in general!), colors, people, animals, places (indoors or outdoors), and a parallel list of what I know the child dislikes or finds repellent. Quite often when I look at these lists, patterns emerge of which I wasn't previously aware. Think, too, about the ways the child expresses these likes and dislikes and how likely they are to change or to be sustained.

A next step is to make a list of any questions, wonderings, or curiosities that have stirred the child's mind and imagination, giving special attention to those that persist or are recurrent. Here, too, it is interesting to look for patterns among these—for example, connections and contrasts—and also for range. Reflect, too, on how these questions and interests are expressed; for example, in play, in choices of books or films, in conversation, in drawing or construction.

Closely related to this, picture the media and the play that most capture her or his attention. I find it helpful to start by recalling what the child is likely to do if she or he has choice and plenty of time; for example, listening to stories, reading books, building with blocks, making "small worlds," drawing, writing, painting, junk construction, sand or water, video games, the natural world, games and sports, making large-scale forts or houses. Here, too, lists are often useful and again usually yield patterns and give a good sense of the range of play and media in which the child finds satisfaction. I often start this listing with favorite stories and books, television programs, and movies, and turn next to play, games, and activities that are absorbing.

Other interesting points of reflection are the kinds of props that are part of a child's preferred play and activities (dress up clothes, boxes, miniature figures, balls, wheeled vehicles, etc.); the ways that play or activities may be linked to particular seasons or times of day; or the role the child tends to assume in keeping group play and activities going and developing. Sometimes, too, there are particular figures or especially interesting topics or themes featured in the play a child prefers; for example, superheroes or knights or battles or space or dinosaurs or ninja turtles or olden times or disasters or fairy tales or . . . (this list is virtually endless in its possibilities).

Think, too, about what seems to you to be really satisfying and fulfilling about these kinds of play, interests, and activities. And reflect, too, on the standards the child observes around this play; for example, what makes it go right, what spoils it, what rules or customs other children have to observe in order to be part of the play.

In my experience, the child's preferences, interests, and choices are windows to the child's *Modes of Thinking and Learning*. Through these windows it is possible to glimpse how a child goes about making sense of the world and her or his own experience. Or, to say that a little differently, from noticing those world themes that fascinate a child, it is possible to intuit fields of study that will have a strong appeal. In a parallel way, attention to play— as a sort of thinking space of the child's own making—yields insights about the child as a maker of knowledge.

A good place to start is to think of things, ideas, or media for which a child has an inner sense or "feel"; for example, machines or music or language or people or throwing a ball or animals or drama or number or color or paint or the piano or building or . . . (again the possible list is virtually endless). Another way to approach this is to reflect on what the child has always done or does with great ease.

Think, too, about how, through what situations and experiences, this "feel" or inner sense is observable to you and others. Give some thought to whether the child recognizes these talents. This is important to consider since often people take their greatest strengths as givens and, although they rely on them, are not aware of them. I don't personally think that it is always a good idea to point these strengths out to another person, since for some that could be inhibiting or embarrassing. I do think, though, that having a sense of where children stand in relation to their own abilities is useful to a parent or a teacher. Then it is a matter of judgment, based on your other knowledge of the child and the nature of your relationship to him or her, to make the decision on what will best support and assist the child's development of these strengths.

Looking in another direction, think to yourself how the child gains a firm understanding or internalizes knowledge or is inclined to figure things out. For example, there may be an inclination to map or sketch or draw or construct or graph. Or, equally, a child may rely a lot on a strong capacity for observing and remembering. Or perhaps the child gets to know something by talking it through or dramatizing and enacting it. There may be interest in taking things apart and putting them back together; or looking at things or ideas from many angles; or counting, ordering, and creating patterns; or discovering what makes something happen by trying different combinations;

or looking things up in books; or studying pictures or photographs . . . (again, the possible list is virtually endless).

Since we all have many ways of figuring things out, spend some time reflecting on when the child is likely to prefer a particular approach and when that may be discarded in favor of another. I have noticed, too, that usually there are observable connections among the range of approaches. For example, a 5-year-old child of my acquaintance, much interested in nature and natural objects, was a close observer and an astute connector of events. ("Grown-ups . . . mow down the dandelions because they grow bumblebees. I know. I saw them together and they were both yellow.") While the conclusion is faulty, the logic is sturdy. He was also an able tree climber, using the trees as an observation point that gave him new and different perspectives on the world.

Sometimes, and especially from children's questions and wonderings, it is possible to glimpse what I think of as a sort of bent or inclination. Some children incline toward imaginative, poetic comparisons with an eye to surprising likenesses between objects or events that on the surface are quite different. To offer one example, I once overheard a child of about 3 say softly, to herself, "rain" as she observed her mother's long dark hair to fall back, catching the light and shimmering as it flowed. Both the comparison and the image that captured it were apt. Or there may be a philosophical, reflective, and speculative talent, or the child may have a religious or spiritual bent. There may be an attraction to the big picture and big ideas, or the child may be adept at seeing the outline or structure that holds things or ideas together, or there may be an attraction to textures and small detail. There may be an experimental or problem-solving slant on the world and an interest in causal relationships.

However, it's important to keep in mind that in life children draw on all these and more. So, even if there is a strong bent in one direction, don't overlook others that may be there. One of the things about us humans is that we are complicated. Given that complexity, in my experience, creating types or categories of thinkers and learners tends not to do a child (or adult) justice or to be especially helpful in the long run to the parents and teachers responsible for that child's learning and education.

From this bigger picture of the child's ways of making sense of things, you might focus in on the narrower piece of the child learning something specific; for example, a task or skill. I often find it useful to think first of how the child positions her- or himself as a learner. Some children (and adults) tend to plunge right in or take some other "I'll do it myself" approach. Some children (and adults) want a lot of time to observe and to practice privately on their own. Some of these same persons value the chance to sit alongside someone else doing the task and follow along, sometimes asking questions.

Some children (and adults) want one-on-one instruction; others shy away from any direct contact with a teacher. Some children (and adults) like working on something new in a sort of social, cooperative group; others like to be on their own.

Again, the picture that emerges is complex. Much may depend on what is being learned and much may also depend on the degree of trust that exists between a child and a teacher or among a group of children. A way to get at this complexity is to think of how the child positions her- or himself when the task or skill to be learned is self-selected; next to that picture, reflect on how the child positions her- or himself when the task is assigned or has a strict time limit or is in other ways pressured. The contrast in these circumstances contributes nuance to the portrayal of the child as a learner.

Other slants you might try include picturing the child's responses when mistakes or accidents happens, when it is necessary to rework or do something over, when there are interruptions, when the situation is highly competitive, when the child has options about leaving and returning to a task as compared to a start-to-finish expectation. Or you might think of specific skills the child has easily mastered and those that have been more difficult, giving particular attention to surrounding circumstances and other factors that have helped or hindered the child.

Thinking again more broadly, reflect on the subject matters or fields of study to which the child gravitates; for example, science, history, literature, art, drama, music, geography, math. Note to yourself what seems to make these attractive and also how the child engages with these modes of thinking and learning. Think, too, about how these interests might be supported, deepened, and expanded. It is also worthwhile to give thought to the future and the learning opportunities that need to be sustained and others that should probably be made available as the child grows older. If there are disciplines the child finds boring or actively dislikes, reflect on those with particular attention to what seems to distance the child.

Finally, reflect on the standards the child tends to hold for her- or himself and how these may vary depending on circumstances. Think first about the child's own pride of work and in what places and circumstances that is visible and observable. A useful way to approach this is to think of times and pieces of work that have been really pleasing to the child as well as the converse—times and pieces of work that have been displeasing.

In a more general way, reflect on what seems to influence the value a child accords to his or her own work, when the work and learning are the child's choice. Think, too, of how that may be the same or different when the child finds the task to be mastered boring or distasteful or hard. Taking a slightly different approach, call to mind any situations that would allow you to glimpse how outside expectations and standards affect the child's learning and self-evaluation. It is also useful to give thought to how the child's standards mesh (or don't) with external standards held at school or at home.

What I have outlined above asks for a lot of thinking and reflecting. It isn't necessary to do this all at once, nor is it important if there are sections under each heading that don't ring any bells. Ignore them. Equally, this is an outline and there is a lot that isn't touched on. Add in anything that comes to mind—including other headings, if that seems useful. Remember, this is an exercise and an organizing device. Use it only in the degree that it is helpful to you in picturing the child and expanding your understandings of him or her as a person.

As a conclusion to this exercise, and especially if the picture of the child has become very full and complex, I find it useful to write down words or phrases the child brings to mind. Some of these turn out to be images; others are simply vocabulary that seems particularly apt for describing the child. Quite often, among these, there are ones that seem especially to capture the sense of the person. I remember, for example, a teacher's description of a child's way of moving *and* his way of thinking as "quick-silver"; or an image of a child's warmth and clarity that was made vivid by likening her to her own drawings and paintings, in which there was often a suffusion of yellow light or a figure was seen through a transparent surface. I mention these because one of the yields of doing this kind of exercise is the discovery of a vocabulary that is *particular* to the child: not jargon, not labels, not categorizations or stereotypes, not empty generalizations applicable to virtually anyone and everyone.

I find this kind of recollecting of children refreshing and renewing of my faith in our humanness. I hope you will, too. It is always easy to criticize and find fault with children (or other adults), to point out what they can't do and how problematic they are. It takes more time and patience to paint a fuller picture in which the person is understood to be not the sum of unchanging traits but in process, in the making. Understood as active and open-ended, each of us is at any moment in our lives, and in all taken together, a complex blend of failings and virtues, of strengths and vulnerabilities. It seems to me that this is what makes us interesting and what makes education (and not merely training) a possibility. I hope you will find the time it takes to look at children (and adults) this way worth the patience it requires.

I won't give this letter a formal closing, but simply extend my best to you and to all the children you attend to with care.

CHAPTER 4

THE ROLE OF THE CHAIR: JOINING WITH ANOTHER TEACHER

Betsy Wice

Frederick Douglass Elementary School is a neighborhood public school in North Philadelphia. I'm the reading teacher there. Cheryl Haeberlein is a classroom teacher at Douglass, my colleague and friend. Though our teaching styles and histories are different, we both like to talk, in detail and with care, about teaching and about our students. When Cheryl came to Douglass several years ago, she turned to me for advice on fifth-grade curriculum. I, in turn, came to rely on Cheryl's calm strength in setting up a classroom that felt safe for all of us. I continue to depend on her steady kindness to help me get through the tough days at Douglass.

Cheryl began joining us after school at weekly meetings of the Philadelphia Teachers' Learning Cooperative (see Streib's "Context" in Chapter 5). She volunteered to present a child in a descriptive review, and I offered to serve as her chair. I expected that the planning process and the review itself would give us time together outside the busy school day—time to look more closely at our teaching and at one of our students. Andre (pseudonym) was our choice for the review. He was an 11-year-old whose active behavior often exasperated us. He wouldn't stay in his seat. He "popped" other kids in the head. He'd call out responses without raising his hand.

Cheryl and I met for two planning sessions, which we tape-recorded. In going back over the transcripts of those tapes, I've been able to see power in this kind of disciplined conversation. To prepare a descriptive review, you end up steeping yourselves in the child's work and gathering stories. You find yourselves reaching for the right descriptive language, setting aside official terms of category and judgment. This effort produces a space for thinking about teaching, which can change the way you look at classrooms and enlarge the way you imagine school.

MEETING ANDRE BY READING HIS STORIES

I was glad Cheryl had brought a lot of Andre's writing and drawing to our first planning session. A child's work is my preferred way in to seeing him. The work stands still. The classroom is always in motion. And Andre particularly is often in motion. Sitting down at my dining room table spread with Andre's work made me feel more comfortable. Lynne Strieb joined us. Her long experience with Prospect also helped to make us comfortable. We also had in front of us Pat Carini's "Letter to Parents and Teachers" (see Chapter 3). Cheryl had already made preliminary notes, following the outline of the descriptive review process.

Cheryl began by stating, "I find him very creative." To get a feel for what she meant, I read aloud Andre's recent Valentine story on love:

> Who I love is Sonny. She has a body that no other girl could have, especially them legs. They are hot. I wish I could see Sonny in my school. Even those hips. As soon as you see Sonny, your eyelids will pop open. You will freeze like a popsicle. That's the end of my story about love.

Cheryl apologized that it wasn't typical of him. I suggested, "It's part of him." "Yeah, it's part of him," Cheryl conceded. This phrase, "*part* of him," indicated that Cheryl and I were already joined together in an enterprise that assumes the complexity of the student. We were tacitly agreed that we wouldn't be able to pin Andre down with a few definitive adjectives. We had set aside two hours of our busy teaching lives to *begin* to find out who Andre was.

Andre's most recent story lying on the table was "Tilea and the Cyclops." Again Cheryl started to apologize.

Cheryl: I guess I was in a silly mood this morning when I put their journal work on the board. . . . I don't think this is necessarily his *best* and most *creative* stuff either. He had done some other stuff that was really wonderful, but unfortunately I'm not sure what happened to it.
Betsy: I just want to get the sound of his voice.
Cheryl: Okay.
Betsy (reading): "Once upon a time there was a boy named David and his sister Tilea. Tilea was a smart girl who never says a word in her

classroom. The strangest thing about Tilea is that you can hear a snail but not her. She talks very, very, very low. So, one day in the castle, a big castle you can ever imagine, and there was a tall, strong man that lived there with little soldiers. He probably can be the whole army because he was 11 feet tall and had a big head. His head was bigger than 40 boards [?]—"

Cheryl: —40 bowls.

Betsy (continues reading): "—40 bowls put together. So, one day the king wanted to have a war against the 11 foot tall giant and his little soldiers.

The next day came and they had a war, but the king's men lost. Then the king said, 'We need a strong man or woman.' David said to Tilea, 'I'm not going to fight that giant.' Then Tilea said, 'You're a punk.' Then Tilea said, 'Well then if you don't, I will.' And her brother said, 'Repeat that again?' And she did. But little did she know that the 11 foot man had a fake eyeball. He was really the Cyclops. So the next day, Tilea came to the king and said, 'I will fight the 11 foot giant.' The king said, 'You and what army?' Tilea said, 'Me, myself and I.' So, she went out with a sling shot, and she said to the 11 foot giant, 'I will fight you right here, right now.' Then the giant said, 'You and what army?' Tilea said, 'Me, myself, and I.' Then he tried to swing his giant sword. And the sword hit the—"

Cheryl: —rock—

Betsy (continues reading): —"the rock, and the rock broke into tiny pieces. Then she swung her sling shot around and around, and hit the giant with the rock at his forehead. Then the giant fell down and never got back up. They picked Tilea up and the king said, 'You and your family can come and live in my castle.' And they lived happily ever after."

Betsy: He just sat down and wrote that?

Cheryl: Yeah. Mmmhmmm.

On the audiotape I feel I can hear Cheryl thinking, reconsidering. Andre's piece of writing might have value outside the official system, that zone where a piece can be evaluated by scoring it according to a rubric. As we continued to look through the papers spread before us, I used a valuing term that would be coming up again and again in our conversation.

Betsy: This drawing is *interesting* to me.

Cheryl: The one with the unhappy face?

Betsy: Yeah, he put the same one in the Smith Playground story.

Cheryl: Oh, wow!

The picture had caught my attention because the sun was wearing "shades." I had been amused by the hip look to the traditional piece of scenery and by the possible irony that the sun could be blinding itself. Rereading the transcript of our planning session, I realize that Cheryl was interested in the face because it looked unhappy. At this early stage of our descriptive work, she assumed that the reason we would look closely at a child's picture would be to explore his emotional side. The very headings of the descriptive review promise a look beyond the narrowly academic. She was assuming that by understanding the whole child, we would be closer to solving his classroom problems.

The concern about emotional problems also lay behind Cheryl's remarks a little later:

> Well, fortunately, [writing and drawing] are two things that he will be able to *focus* on. I find that Andre is extremely *active*. I find that he has . . . I think he has a really quick mind. But it just doesn't seem to be focused. . . . I mean, sometimes his ideas are really good. It's just they're not *appropriate* to whatever it is we're trying to do in the classroom. . . . I correct him a lot for his behavior. . . . He wrote on one of his papers one day, "I hate myself," so I don't know exactly what's going on there.

At this point I must have felt that we were heading toward psychological speculation that wouldn't help us:

Betsy: I think probably what we should do is go through the headings for the descriptive review. And out of this, I think what we'll get is a focusing question.
Cheryl: Oh, out of this (*points to the descriptive review format*)? 'Cause I didn't know what it was, and I was really nervous.

From years of following the descriptive review process, I had faith it would help us get to know Andre. Lynne, who had been listening to our conversation, steered us back toward what can be observed. She read aloud the advice on language use, "'Make the language as vivid and descriptive as possible,'" and added, "Like if you have examples and details that illustrate— like if you say he's active, you could have specific examples of when and where he's active." Cheryl considered this:

> It's very hard. I was sitting at lunch time, and I was thinking of how I was going to . . . I don't even know if I have the right vocabulary to describe him.

Later Cheryl would gain confidence that she did have within her a capacity for the descriptive language that would capture Andre's uniqueness.

But at this point Cheryl was working hard to understand the decorum that rules this new descriptive world. Again, Lynne helped us along.

Cheryl: I do find him—I don't know, can I say—extremely *creative*.

Lynne: You have examples of his work, so that you can say what it is in his work that makes you feel that he's creative. It's not that the word *creative* is a bad word, but it's empty if it doesn't have something—

Cheryl: —to connect with it?

Lynne: —backing it up to, specifics—

Cheryl: Okay. As I said, I don't particularly find that this work is his *best*, but I think there's lots of *interesting* imagery in here.

Here the word *interesting* perhaps helped Cheryl switch from our school district's assessment mode to this other, descriptive mode. In the fall Cheryl and I had met with the other fifth-grade teachers to understand the Pennsylvania Holistic Writing Assessment. Like all rubrics, it is designed to rank something on a numerical scale (5 is "best," 1 is "worst.") But that writing assessment also gives opportunity for the scorers to describe the work they are reading. They have to be attentive to the writer's story structure, imagery, and language to arrive at a score. Cheryl's remark about "interesting imagery" gave me an entry point, using the Tilea story we'd just read together.

Betsy: Yeah, I think this is full of good, creative stuff. If we had time to sit and describe it line by line, I could be more specific, but, just the way he says it. Like that "Me, myself, and I" and "you and what army," the way he uses those quotes, and for creating, building a story that's kind of a fable or a biblical story, the way he's using story elements, repeats them. He really knows—he's a writer, he really knows what he's doing.

Cheryl: He did do that—

Betsy: I think—and the way—oh, the way he made the Cyclops in disguise, that he had a false eye so it didn't look like a Cyclops—

Lynne: Yes, that's wonderful.

Betsy: So he's taking a known myth and changing it and making it very up to date. And, oh, when he talked about that girl Sonny.

Cheryl: What did he say?

Betsy: "Your eyelids will pop open. You will freeze like a popsicle." The way he went from that pop in the eyes popping open, to the word *pop* in *popsicle*. In a way, maybe that's like what you were saying about how one thing will lead to another with him. But how he can use it. I mean, it's not like he was sitting there daydreaming about popsicles and left the story off and went into his head. But he used it.

Cheryl: Yeah, I see.

What is it that Cheryl saw here? Quite possibly, an inkling that there might be positive—"creative"—power in a quality that first appeared to be purely negative. The planning transcripts show this idea growing for Cheryl, until she said (in the second session two weeks later):

Oh, the negative behaviors do seem to be very much a part of who he is. And I think that that's—it frightens me in terms of, if we want to squelch that part of him, I hope it doesn't stymie his creativity. . . . That all seems so intertwined that I just hope we don't interfere with him.

FINDING THE WORDS TO PICTURE ANDRE

At this point we started working our way through the headings, beginning with *Physical Presence and Gesture*.

Betsy: How is he when he comes in, in the morning? Do you have a picture of that in your mind? What he looks like?

Cheryl: One way to describe him is projected motion. Sometimes he'll just sit for a minute or so, and not start unpacking his things. But usually he's everywhere in my room.

As the process pushed Cheryl to put words to her real and thorough knowledge of daily classroom life, she began to qualify her absolute statements. "Projected motion," yes. But also, there's "sometimes," the minute or so of just sitting. Cheryl continued to see Andre with more clarity and complexity as she drew this picture for Lynne and me:

Cheryl: I do have him slightly isolated from the rest of the class to kind of remind him to calm down. But also because in the back of the room, there is a little bit more space there where he can move his chair from his desk. He was crouching, sort of, in his chair. Not just sitting there today. But he was definitely interested in the class. But he was—he just doesn't seem to be able to sit.

Betsy: By the way, that's a great word, *crouch*. *Crouch*. That's the kind of stuff that makes it unique to him.

Cheryl: Okay.

Lynne: That's right.

Cheryl: The time when I see something other than this is pretty much, as I said, if he's involved in something like his writing or his drawing. He tends to be very *focused*—

Betsy: So when he's focused, how is his body? In fact, I was going to try to look at that last week when he was working on a drawing in my room, but then I realized that all I could see was the box he got behind.

Cheryl: Right.

Betsy: Is he like, is he bent over it?

Cheryl: He does, yeah. There's an intensity there.

Betsy: He gets his head in an angle? I'm trying to picture how he would look when he's writing.

Cheryl: I can't remember.

Betsy: Well, we'll watch. We'll watch. Because that would be part of his gesture, how his shoulders are and how his head is.

In the above interchanges, I see Cheryl joining with me in a careful attempt to see Andre at a specific moment and to capture that image in words for others to see him, too. Cheryl's admission "I can't remember" propelled a search that began for both of us the next day in school. As she said two weeks later:

> You know, I love this because it's really taken—I have to look at the child a lot, and I had two full pages worth of these little scrawled notes to myself.

This urge to get another look became rooted in Cheryl. She went back to look more closely at Andre, and she also began to look more closely at her own teaching decisions. She called into question an earlier choice she had made in assigning Andre his seat.

Cheryl [in March planning transcript, two weeks later, when were discussing relationships with other children]: But I don't see Andre being close with anyone. Now part of it might be—so *interesting*. I hope I haven't ostra—well, I kind of have ostracized him, because I tried to separate him from the rest of the class, because he just does sort of create such a commotion, and normally, when I have two kids sitting together, they kind of bond and I wonder if that's done something then, you know. Now let me just write this down. But I just . . . oh, now I feel like this horrible teacher who keeps doing things to this child.

Betsy: If you're wondering about it, this is something you could say in the presentation.
Cheryl: Yeah, I'm wondering if I'm hurting him by keeping him apart from the class.

Cheryl used the word *interesting* not to signal a search for an underlying psychological disorder but as a marker for her own awareness of complexity.

In our first planning session Cheryl groped for words to describe Andre's physical presence:

Cheryl: He's petite. He's light-skinned. His hair is very curly, but it's probably an inch and a half or something. It's not very wild or long hair, but it's cut fairly close to his head. He's got a longer face. Should I take a picture of him?
Betsy: Well, it's good to do it with words.
Lynne [quoting from the "Letter to Parents and Teachers"]: "Be attentive to what stands out to you immediately, then size and build," which you've done, "then style of dress." Is there a particular way he wears his clothes?
Cheryl: I don't know if there's a way he wears his clothes. The other day, down at the library—this has nothing to do with everything.
Lynne: You can give us a good example. I can tell already.
Cheryl: Well, I'm not sure.

Lynne's reassuring coaxing prompted a telling anecdote that we returned to in the later planning session when our focusing question began to be about freedom and restriction. But the anecdote might not have seemed "appropriate" for the upcoming descriptive review if Lynne had not pressed Cheryl for examples about his clothes.

Cheryl: The other day down in the library, he had this jacket. The jacket has a belt, so he tied himself into his chair. He says, "Oh look, Miss Haeberlein, I have a seat belt on." [laughter]
Betsy: That's *creative!*

The pressure to describe Andre's clothes led Cheryl to look more closely at what he wore in the days to come, which led to another reassessment. This is from the March transcript:

I do find him a child who is full of contradictions. The way he dresses. It's very somber and neat, and yet when we describe him, the child's like a burst or a flash of energy. It's just sort of an explosion almost, which contradicts the way he dresses. With his behavior, and I don't know enough psychology to understand this, but at times I think that he is doing things deliberately to get attention. When he hits the children, when he makes fun of children, I think he wants their attention. And yet, sometimes in the classroom, he's almost invisible. When he comes up to my desk and drops a paper off, or when he is sliding on the floor down an aisle, or when he's hiding in the closet.

Reading the transcript, and returning to the first session, I'm struck by how often we talked about language:

Betsy: Anything special about his voice?
Cheryl: It's kind of chirpy.
Betsy: That's a good word.

A little later, when Cheryl was describing times that Andre slipped out of his seat and disappeared into the coat closet:

Cheryl: Um, I'm just not sure if there's a pattern there. I'll just find him in the closet.
Betsy: I remember this myself from last year, that he can do a lot of his stuff without you being aware he was doing it.
Cheryl: Oh, yeah. Someone else did call him "sneaky." I wasn't sure if that was going to get down to it.
Lynne: See, that's one of those words you would want to—
Cheryl: It's loaded.
Lynne: It's loaded, yeah. It's a generalization.
Betsy: But there are other ways to say it. You can say it more specifically, that he can be planning and executing—
Cheryl: Well, [the preparation period teacher] said—
Betsy: Okay. He can be planning and executing something without other people in the room being aware of it until it's already executed. Is that saying the same thing?
Lynne: Well, you can say even, that one teacher described him as "sneaky" and—
Cheryl: Well, actually, it was *interesting* because I did start paying a whole lot more attention to his behaviors and who initiated things. And I think that just clued me into his behavior perhaps a little bit more.

Here, Cheryl noticed that a closer look at language can prompt a closer look at classroom events. A little later in our planning, Cheryl used language to see a quality that holds true across conventional boundaries:

It says, "emotional tone or color." I would think *vivid* and *bright* are both very good words. Vivid in terms of his energy. There's a liveliness there. Vivid in terms of his thinking and connecting ideas and his insights. Vivid in terms of his vocabulary and his ability to use the language.

Here Cheryl was working on an underlying unity to Andre's force in the room: that physical energy which often causes classroom problems is connected to an intellectual energy which fuels a notable talent. Cheryl appreciated this aspect of our planning for the descriptive review. It could help her see positive and negative aspects to the attribute "energy." Later in that first planning session, we were enjoying several of Andre's notebook papers, filled with unassigned writing and drawings, which had appeared on the teacher's desk from time to time. We saw another aspect to the attribute "sneaky."

Cheryl: He might have gone up to, you know, sharpen his pencil, and one of these papers is on my desk. Or he's up hitting somebody and it's on my desk. Or he's supposed to be getting in line, and it's on my desk—

Betsy: That reminds me of the other side of when he starts trouble and you don't know when it started. It's sort of like he can get something onto your desk and you don't know exactly when he did.

Cheryl: Oh, yeah. Exactly.

Betsy: This stuff shows up on your desk. It's sort of the way he can move across a room without making a whole lot of noise, and your attention's not on him, and then all of a sudden he's somewhere else. He's one of those kids who can do that.

Cheryl: That's really good.

THINGS GET MORE COMPLICATED

Later in the conversation we moved onto the heading *Connections with Others*. Cheryl remembered something that happened during lunch hours when she let a group stay up in the classroom with her. As the conversation progressed, Cheryl used *interesting* in a spirit of intellectual delight. These discrepancies in Andre's appearance and behavior, and these surprising and often funny writings—these are a pleasure to explore. Looking more closely at a child and his work has turned out to be intrinsically worth doing.

Cheryl: It's real *interesting* because he's off by himself, and then I'll look up, and the desks form into a new grouping back by him, you know?

Betsy: People will collect by him.

Lynne: Now, see, that's a really interesting thing. So that would be a good thing to have—
Betsy: Yeah. How does that happen?
Cheryl: But I don't see him necessarily as a leader.

As Cheryl reflected on the contradiction here, she thought of another time her assumptions were jarred. Again, the word *interesting* seems to signal Cheryl's detour to notice something she initially didn't think worth mentioning.

> This is *interesting*. I'm sorry, it might not be interesting for this, but maybe it is, I don't know. Apparently Keith [pseudonym] lives close by Andre, you know? And I see Andre and Keith as being really similar. I thought they were going to be best friends. But I don't see them being as much buddy-buddy as I really anticipated because I thought that buddy-buddy thing was going to turn into another problem.

In our second session Cheryl returned to her mistaken assumptions about Keith and Andre.

> I would think that they would be really close because there's really a lot in common. Because they're both creative kids, because they're both fairly petite kids, because they are—I don't know—they're both light-skinned and active. And yet, I don't see anything between them.

We moved on to *Modes of Thinking and Learning*, a heading that perplexed Cheryl in our first planning session. Now Cheryl realized she had interesting things to report. Here is a recollected observation that contains several unexpected aspects:

> I saw him quietly reading this book about the life of Christ. [Later he wrote a quick summary of it, and in the summary] there was almost a superhero quality to the things that he wrote down, I think, that wasn't the religious or staid kind of slant that *I* was giving the book. But he saw something much different than that. He was really—he was mesmerized by that book. He sat there, and I'm thinking, as long as he's being quiet, he can sit and read this book the whole time. But we were reading one of those *Weekly Readers* or whatever by Scholastic. And it was about Palestine and Israel and fighting over disputed territory. . . . So I'm thinking, he's not paying one little bit of attention, and I'm saying, "Well, this is really an important area because this is important to a lot of religious groups. And this is

where Christ supposedly lived," that type of thing. The next thing I know, he is piping up, from behind his book, because it's a big book and he's a small kid, so he's almost kind of hidden by it, but he's saying, "Well, isn't that where the Garden is then?" I'm thinking, he must be reading about the Garden of Gethsemane, except again it's interesting because in his summary, he didn't even mention one thing about the Garden of Gethsemane, and I don't even know if it was mentioned in that book. But almost from nowhere, he's making the connection from present day, and what we're doing in class, to the life of Christ 2,000 years ago. It's just—well—it's real interesting the way his mind works.

Reading the February and March transcripts, I think I see another assumption beginning to crumble in Cheryl's thought. When we first glanced at the collection of Andre's work that she had been able to bring to our meeting, Cheryl apologized that most of it wasn't his *best* work. Much of it had nothing to do with her official writing assignments. Again, the word *interesting* helped give Cheryl permission to explore something she hadn't originally planned to include in the review.

Cheryl: This is bizarre, I think, how I got a lot of this stuff (*looking through papers*).
Betsy: Talk about this. This is interesting stuff.
Cheryl: This is—all this stuff shows up on my desk—
Lynne: Ooo. That's so interesting.
Cheryl: —periodically. And then I'd say, "Okay, well, you gotta write me a story." He wrote two dynamite stories about a soldier, because we were doing some things with the American Revolution, a soldier who died and his ghost still haunts this house. I forget what that other story was he wrote, but it was a really good story. I'm thinking "Wow!" and I showed it to [a student teacher] and then told Andre, "Now I have to get you a book and I want you to write me some stories and we'll keep them in the book." And he'd say, "I can't find the book." "You can't find the book?" Like once it's for a purpose, then it's—
    [We leaf through the bunch of loose-leaf papers that got left on Cheryl's desk, noticing and enjoying lively details.]
Lynne: So how do you get these?
Cheryl: He put them on the desk.
Lynne: When? Are you there at the desk?
Cheryl: No, I'm walking around. But now I haven't gotten any of them since I started asking for them.

LOOKING PAST THE SYSTEM TO SEE THE CHILD

A lot was going on in this conversation. Through our attention to the unofficial work, Lynne and I were affirming its intrinsic value and leading Cheryl to call into question the artificial boundaries of the official curriculum and also the partialness of the official grading system.

> A couple of these pictures do seem to be about Space. Their science curriculum right now is looking at Space. But I think these were even done before Space, when we were probably still in Energy.

And in the March session:

Cheryl: It occurs to me when I look at his writing that he's really very gifted and he should have a pretty good Language Arts grade. There's a lot of creativity. I think he tells a story well. I don't find a whole lot of grammatical or spelling errors in his work. And yet I was really curious to find out what a low grade I gave him, because he doesn't necessarily always hand in the assignments that I ask him to do. And yet obviously, your table is filled with pieces of his writing that reflect a really very talented child.

Betsy: It's interesting. The official stuff doesn't always happen, so the columns in the grade book—

Cheryl [excited]: That's really interesting because one of the other things I told him to write, this *Bony Legs* [Cole, 1983] story, I was almost disappointed with. I only gave him a C because it was very flat. But that was one of the things that I was attempting to grade. His Future Story was another thing I was intending to grade, and that was when, everyone else is "I want to be a doctor," "I want to be a lawyer," and he's writing "I think the world might explode and I think we might be living on Jupiter." I don't even know that they're representative of what he's able to do, you know? So, I'm again grateful for this whole process, especially with this child, because it gives me more insight into him and what he's doing.

Reading Cheryl's remarks in this part of the transcript, I wonder how she has changed the way she sees her classroom assignments and her grade book. I also see Cheryl questioning the routines of the school day when we moved to the heading of Modes of Thinking and Learning. Cheryl had worried that she had no information for that heading. Lynne made a suggestion: "Could you make a list of any questions, wondering, curiosities?"

No, gosh, I almost wish that I would have some type of recorder being able to go all day because, as I said, it is this free-association thing he does. They are really a lot of times interesting, but like "Come on, Andre." If you were walking with him in a different environment than in school where you're trying to teach a lesson to him and a bunch of other children, he'd probably be fascinating. But in school it's just like anything pops into his mind and he wants to—he probably would really want to get into a discussion on one-on-one.

And a little later:

Cheryl: Well, I think it's broad, expansive thinking. Learning. I think he's like a sponge. I think he takes in a lot of stuff. He can be in some squirrely position, under his desk, looking for a pencil that he put in his shoe, but he's taken in almost every word that I say.
Lynne: See, that's an important aspect to gesture, too.
Betsy: I think this labeling [in his unassigned pictures] is interesting, too, about the way he thinks. Look at this picture of his room, and the picture of Outer Space. He puts in all these labels with arrows pointing to the object. He wants to make sure you understand just what each thing is and where it's placed in relation to each other thing.
Cheryl: That would be again, exact, or would you think, very meticulous in some ways.
Betsy: Yeah, there's something about "*this* is what I mean, *this* is what I mean." He wants you to know just how his room is and just how Space is.
Cheryl: I guess I was more—
Lynne: You were worried. Now you're not worried.
Cheryl: Less worried.

Again, it seems that our common effort to find exact language had led us to look closer at the work and at Andre. Cheryl may have surprised herself with her descriptive power—in drawing us the verbal picture of Andre under his desk and in characterizing Andre as "meticulous" in his thinking. Cheryl had not given up all her worries—about the upcoming presentation in the descriptive review, about Andre's mental health. But our work together during this planning session had given us a way to talk about Andre that drew on things we teachers can see and know for ourselves.

A little later, Cheryl stopped to consider an unofficial part of that day's testing session.

Cheryl: There was this *interesting* thing, though I don't know if it's that relevant.

Lynne: Say it.

Cheryl: They were really funny this morning because it says, "Have you been taught to use this calculator?" And I'm going through, half the class is saying "yes," and half the class is saying "no." So I am having a fit. I'm picking up the book at the end to see who's saying what. So—especially because I taught a lesson in it before I gave the calculators out. So, his contention was that he didn't learn from me, so he was going to put down "no." And I said, "But that's not what the question asks. The question says, 'Were you *taught* to use calculators?'" And he's saying, "But you didn't teach me. My mom taught me at home." And I'm saying, "That's not what it says." But anyway, semantics—

Betsy: That hooks up with what you said about you'd think he'd enjoy puns. Because he does like—

Cheryl: (*excited*) Oh, right, right, right, right.

Betsy: He wasn't taught to use a calculator because he learned at home from his mom. That doesn't qualify as the educational system dispensing this knowledge.

Cheryl: Yeah.

GOING OUT ON A LIMB: NEGOTIATING LABELS AND DESCRIPTION

As we kept going back to Pat's "Letter," Cheryl gained the confidence to introduce a subject she'd been troubled about all along. Cheryl had read the caution to avoid labels like "hyperactive."

> I think this is a little bit important. I'm not sure how much. I am concerned that he's hyperactive.

Cheryl went out on a limb to breach the decorum of the descriptive review process. What made her so bold? I think it was mostly the depth of her concern, but also partly a growing trust that Lynne and I would not jump down her throat if she uttered the taboo word. Cheryl would not easily abandon her strong hope that a drug such as Ritalin could cure this constant activeness that was disrupting her class. But she was also committed to working with Lynne and me to think about Andre in the context of the Philadelphia Teachers' Learning Cooperative (PTLC) and the Prospect processes. Cheryl had come to our planning session with a hunch that her teaching philosophy put her at odds with most of the teachers who come to PTLC on Thursdays. Cheryl's sense of this came through when she wondered about activities to keep Andre from getting out of his seat during a whole class lesson.

Cheryl: You guys. Your philosophy is a little different than mine, so
   maybe you could see this as okay, but I don't want to just say, "You
   can start drawing if you get bored in class." [*At that point, Lynne
   jumped right in.*]
Lynne: I'd have a lot of trouble doing that, as a matter fact.

In her ready response, Lynne joined with Cheryl and with all teachers who see their job as taking charge of their classroom. In the strong light of specific talk about actual practice, the line between "traditional" and "progressive" begins to fade.

Over the course of the two planning sessions, Cheryl, Lynne, and I had been partners in a *shared* quest to describe Andre. When I picked up a paper to read aloud, Cheryl was right there next to me, leaning over Andre's familiar handwriting, ready to supply the correct reading of a word (such as "bowls" and "rock" in the Tilea story). Also, Cheryl and I had for many months been partners in a painful disappointment. There were so many children assigned to her class who were academically so far from being able to do fifth-grade work. Every day there were so many distractions and disruptions keeping us from teaching. Adding to our pain was another awareness: There were quite a few able students who seemed bored with the review work. Andre's disruptions crystallized our disappointment with our teaching work. Here was an able student who felt free to get up during a lesson and tap a classmate on the head. Our shared pain about this difficult teaching situation linked up with Cheryl's strong feeling for Andre as a person she deeply cared about.

Cheryl: I am concerned that he's hyperactive and I don't know—I get a
   little bit concerned, I think, because he gets into so much trouble
   because of his behaviors, you know, the impulsiveness. I think maybe
   for this child that a little bit of medication might be good if it gets him
   out of trouble and he can focus on doing these important things. I was
   trying to tell that to the mother. So the next day he came to me, and
   we weren't even in the classroom yet, and said, "You told my mother
   I have to go to a doctor because of my behavior." I said, "Well, that's
   not exactly what I said, Andre. I said, 'If you need glasses to help your
   eyes see better, if there's a problem and you need glasses, then it's an

okay way to go to a doctor. If there's something wrong with you, you have to go to a doctor to help you feel better.' I said, 'I think that's a good idea, that you're just not bad.'" I think this was right after he did the whole "I hate myself" thing, which, I don't know, now that I think about it, he is kind of manipulative, if that's what you call it, I don't know. But I don't think that that "I hate myself" thing was manipulative. I think that was coming from his frustration.

Lynne: His frustration was—?

Cheryl: Being corrected because he was doing these things that are very natural to him, you know.

Lynne: I—I would really, for this particular purpose—[to Betsy] Don't you think? Would you steer away from? Don't you think?

Betsy: Well, there's not much we can do about it, for one thing, because it might or might not happen that he will go to a doctor, and the doctor might or might not prescribe some kind of medication. But within the scope of what we're doing, to try to learn more about the way he is, it doesn't really—it's kind of—we don't really know.

Cheryl: Right, and it said not to label him as hyperactive, so I tried not to use that term.

Lynne: But you've described a very—I mean, you've made a very vivid picture—

Cheryl: Of an active child.

Lynne: Of an extremely active—

Betsy: —emotional—

Lynne: I mean, you hadn't used the word *impulsive*. That was the first time I heard you use the word *impulsive*. But if you can give some examples that describe that—

Cheryl: Well, I happen to think it's impulsive that he hits the kids on the head.

Lynne: Oh, so you have had some examples.

Cheryl: Well, that's my—

Betsy: He'll pop a kid on the head without there being—

Cheryl: —thinking of the consequences—

Betsy: —no chain of events that preceded it.

Lynne: And he doesn't think of the consequences. Yes.

Cheryl: And also the fact that he's out of his seat constantly. I don't think it's deliberate "Ooo, Miss Haeberlein's reading to the class, I can probably sneak into it." I think it's just that he pops up.

Betsy: The word *pop* seems to be—it came up in his writing, and it came up in our talk about him. The way the word is.

Cheryl: You're really good with that.

Betsy: A pop is a kind of a spontaneous thing—something inside of him
  that's a popping quality.
Cheryl: I think that's really insightful.
Betsy: Where are we now?
Lynne: We're thinking. I guess I wanted to ask you about something
  different—like how does he do his math? Subject areas?

Re-reading the transcript, I sense that the three of us had come through a
difficult patch. We had shifted away from the term *hyperactive* without
denying Cheryl's real and painful experiences with Andre. Again, the discipline of preparing together for the descriptive review had helped us move
forward.

GETTING WHAT YOU NEVER ASKED FOR

Cheryl had been concerned that she wouldn't have enough to say for the
heading Modes of Thinking and Learning. During our second planning session, we returned to Andre's writings and began to see some connections with
anecdotes Cheryl had been telling. Cheryl and I were reading Andre's report
on colonial settlements, about Puritans seeking freedom from England, and
then Roger Williams and Anne Hutchinson seeking freedom from those
Puritans. This outward motion resonated with a question Andre had raised
about a Chinese folktale ("The Prison of the Jars"). He had wanted to know
more about the spirits who were roaming loose in the story. The word *tan-
gent* occurred to Cheryl.

> He can appear to be, and he isn't exactly, technically on task. And
> yet, mentally, he's right there with you, and processing it, and going
> beyond it to ask these questions that aren't exactly related, but
> they're related in his mind, in a sort of divergent way that his mind
> thinks.

We looked again at Andre's picture of Outer Space. We returned to a
remark Andre had made one day while gazing out the classroom window,
looking down at the neighborhood: "I wish I didn't live here. I wish I was
a spirit. I hate these dirty houses. I hate these dirty streets. I hate these bomby
cars." The remark resonated with Andre's retelling of the death of Jesus:

> Then the next day, they put his body inside a tomb. Then the guards
> were blocking the tomb. Then it blew open. A spirit came out and
> told the two women that Jesus was alive. . . . And then he went up in

the sky to heaven with the two spirits, and God, Jesus's father. And you should love Jesus just the way I do. The end.

Cheryl was struck by the drama of the verb *blew open* and Andre's choice of the term *spirit(s)*—not *angel(s)*. I was struck by the gracefully penciled handwriting in the final sentence.

Betsy: This is what's nice about having the actual papers. You know, we could retype it but then it would lose . . . the way the "t" goes below the line.
Cheryl: Very flowing.
Betsy: Yeah, I mean, when you said his handwriting was neat . . . there's something else beside neat. I don't know.
Cheryl: We've gotten this whole sense of freedom and a sense of being out there and roaming free and not restricted and no limits and no boundaries, which again, going back to that contradiction thing—we were saying he likes his world very ordered, very neat.
  In his drawings, everything is very exact, very precise. His writing, even physical handwriting . . . his personal being is very well-kept looking. He likes things ordered and structured, yet here he is with a great desire for . . . thirst for freedom, for being beyond perhaps where he is.
Betsy: When you said handwriting, I can't help looking again at the really graceful letters at the end of the Jesus story. It's almost like he sharpened his pencil.
Cheryl: I don't know.
Betsy: I don't know.
Cheryl: It does look a little sharper. You're right.
Betsy: It's really lovely. Like he's thinking of . . . it's not just a superhero idea anymore. Do you know what I mean?
Cheryl: A more spiritual quality to it, you mean?
Betsy: Well, I don't know if that's reading it in.
Cheryl: "And you should love Jesus just the way I do." I don't think that came from the book. And considering I didn't even ask for this. What it was, was the homework assignment, which was just to read anything for 15 minutes and tell me a bit about what you read.

As Cheryl and I kept talking, we realized that we had plenty of material for the imminent descriptive review with PTLC. We could even arrive at a provisional focusing question for the meeting. We framed it this way: "Cheryl is looking for ways to give Andre's mind and spirit freedom to roam without his disrupting the learning of others."

NO NEAT CONCLUSION

This story will not have a neat ending. Our planning did not guarantee an exemplary descriptive review the following Thursday. Our colleagues' rich supply of recommendations did not end up changing the classroom into an entirely new place. (They never do.) But I do know the whole process got both me and Cheryl thinking a bit differently about Andre and the classroom. At the end of the descriptive review, we were doing a critique of the afternoon's work. Cheryl told us, "For me, I would like to say this was really an incredible experience, examining him so much. I mean, I might've been fond of him, and see that he—I mean, I felt that he could read well and write well, but it's just when you really start looking at it so closely, you see all kinds of layers and connections, and all kinds of things that just didn't appear to me before."

CHANGING THE CONVERSATION

In the two years since the descriptive review, Cheryl and I have grown closer as colleagues. We often lunch together in her room. Sometimes colleagues join us. Our talk feels like an oasis. Douglass School continues to overwhelm us with challenges, but at least we can discuss our morning and our kids without invoking a litany of blame and disparagement.

I go back and listen to the tapes of those planning sessions, and I hear the seeds of many of our lunchtime conversations. I hear Cheryl's rueful humor, so different from the stiff diction of the detached professional. We talk about students we share—about the interesting details in their latest batch of drawings, about Andre and how he ended up a lot more social in his sixth-grade year with Cheryl. ("Hey! His desk is right in the middle of the other kids' and it isn't a problem anymore.")

Our classroom world feels roomier.

PART II

TAKING A DESCRIPTIVE STANCE

We invite you now to the descriptive review of Victoria, a fourth-grader in the Philadelphia public schools. Tara Shaw, the teacher who presents the review, had just begun to participate in the Philadelphia Teachers' Learning Cooperative (PTLC) and was excited about the possibilities of learning to use the Prospect processes to describe children and their work. We present here an edited version of the planning session with Tara, Lynne Strieb (who served as chair), and Betsy Wice. We then provide a full, though edited, transcript of Tara's description of Victoria, along with the questions and recommendations section of the review. We want to demonstrate how the questions and recommendations continue the description of the child, by drawing out more stories and observations and by providing a fuller understanding of the classroom and school context in which the child and teacher work.

In Chapter 6, Margaret Himley explores the values and philosophical assumptions that inform and motivate Prospect's work. She explains how the descriptive processes emerge from within the philosophical tradition of phenomenology, with its insistence on inquiry that aims to understand a child, or a work authored by a child, or a teaching practice in its fullest expression of meaning. The descriptive processes are importantly, then, about language use, about attending *to* and *with* language, and about the hard, ethical work necessary to describe children in all their complexity and thereby to accord them—*all of them*—the status of person.

In Chapter 7, Ellen Schwartz, in collaboration with Anne Martin and Karen Woolf, provides an introduction to the many publications written by classroom teachers associated with Prospect. This is not an exhaustive account or a traditional literature review, but rather an introduction to the ideas, values, and styles that characterize this body of work, a guide to reading Prospect publications. You should expect many voices, close description of actual classrooms and real children, and a deep valuing of human capacity, in writing that relies on story and journal and that produces not answers or solutions but thinking space. And you should expect classroom teachers, committed to a descriptive stance and individual capacity, at odds with systems of assessment.

CHAPTER 5

VICTORIA

FIGURE 5.1. Tubman on Stage, by Victoria

CONTEXT

Lynne Strieb

Tara Shaw was new to the Philadelphia Teachers' Learning Cooperative (PTLC) when she did the following descriptive review of Victoria. She had learned of the group in a Philadelphia Writing Project course and had received our schedule the first time I sent it out over the Writing Project listserv.

The Philadelphia Teachers' Learning Cooperative

The PTLC began in 1978 when the Advisory Center for Open Education, a teachers' center in Philadelphia funded by the school district, lost its funding. At the center, I had been part of a group of educators who met on Thursday evenings for dinner and discussion of educational issues, and we didn't want to stop those important discussions. We decided to meet every Thursday at participants' homes and to create the Philadelphia Teachers' Learning Cooperative with no outside funding. In 1972, the Advisory Center had begun its association with Patricia Carini and colleagues from the Prospect School. From the beginning of PTLC, we wanted to continue that association with Prospect, and many of our members attended summer institutes there. We had no idea whether the group would even last past the first six weeks, but we continue 20 years later. In fact, this year the Spencer and MacArthur Foundations funded a three-year study of what we have learned about teaching in urban schools over these past 20 years.

During our second year we decided to print our schedule so that participants could plan which meetings to attend, and I have been doing that job ever since. We create that schedule every six or seven weeks, about four each year, out of our own classroom stories. We continue to meet every Thursday, September to mid-June, from 4:30 to 6:30, with refreshments preceding each meeting. The only cost has been for postage or refreshments. Through the years we have met with top administration of the school district to voice our interests and concerns, have sponsored talks and conferences for teachers, and have taken public positions on educational issues. All these activities grew out of describing. Many of us have helped classroom teachers, school administrators, and university students and teachers to begin to take a descriptive stance by facilitating descriptive reviews in their settings.

Most of our members are elementary classroom teachers. There is also a school counselor, a teaching and learning facilitator, and several retired educators. Of the eleven people who participated in the review of Victoria, eight were elementary school classroom teachers, one taught in a parent cooperative nursery, one was a reading teacher, and one was a teaching and learning facilitator. Three participants, including Tara, were new to the group that year.

Many kinds of teachers' groups meet throughout the country. Some choose to discuss readings, others choose a topic like aspects of literacy and look at children with that focus. Still others are associated with courses in schools of education. From the beginning, we knew we wanted to use the descriptive processes developed at the Prospect Center because they not only gave us a way to focus on children and teachers and their work, but also provided frameworks for discussion of wider educational issues in ways that allowed each participant's ideas to be heard and each person's perspective to be valued. Groups who use the descriptive processes developed at Prospect use them in response to local issues and around specific children, curriculum, and teaching practices.

Tara Shaw

Tara majored in education at Temple University and was taking courses toward her permanent certification. This was her fourth year of teaching in Philadelphia, and she was taking advantage of many of the professional development opportunities associated with the school system.

Tara attended her first PTLC meeting in November 1997 and became very interested in the way we describe students and their work. She decided to do a descriptive review of Victoria because she found her writing fanciful and because she noticed that most of the descriptive reviews had been about boys who needed a lot of their teachers' attention. She wanted to describe a girl and a child who never got in trouble.

PTLC members were impressed by Tara's enthusiasm for teaching and her deep commitment to the children she taught. She showed this by the way she talked about their classroom lives and the things she did with them in school and voluntarily after school, such as taking them on Saturday and holiday trips into Center City Philadelphia to see movies, baseball games, and historic sites and inviting them, with parents' permission, to visit her at home. This is a common practice among the newer, younger participants in PTLC.

Tara's school is a three-story square stone and brick school built in 1899 on one of Philadelphia's narrow streets of row homes with porches. Tara's school includes a day-care program, Head Start, and kindergarten through fifth-grade classes. Its 400 students are all African American. Tara is White and 26. During this year, Tara taught 34 fourth-grade children with no assistant.

The School District of Philadelphia

It is important for this descriptive review of Victoria to say some things about the Philadelphia school system because it affects children, parents, teachers, and schools in important ways. The system is not mere background. Accountability based on test scores now has a determining influence on what teachers do. Like Tara, all teachers entering the system must find their way into and through it.

Before the current superintendent of schools arrived in Philadelphia, there were five subdistricts, each with its own district superintendent. There are now 22 clusters across the city made up of at least one comprehensive high school and the middle and elementary schools that feed it. Although the reorganization is spoken of in terms of decentralization, Philadelphia is as strongly centralized, hierarchic, and monolithic as it was before this superintendent came. Our union is also centralized, hierarchic, and monolithic, echoing the organization of the school system. Teachers are assigned to schools from the central administration building. When Tara was assigned to her school, she did not "shop around" or apply for schools where she thought she'd like to work; her principal did not interview her ahead of time, because she had no say in who arrived at the school on the first day. As of this writing, summer 1998, there has been no alternative school movement in Philadelphia. The formation of charter schools, based on a single philosophy and with principals able to assign staff, independent of the school system but answerable to it with regard to assessment, has just begun. The school district's mandates, including the standards and curricula that were developed by the central administration with some teacher and parent input, are enforced from the superintendent, through the cluster, down to the principal, who then feeds them to the teachers who are supposed to enact them.

One of these mandates is the testing of children in grades 2, 3, 4, 8, and 11, using the SAT-9. Because each elementary school's rank in the system is based only on its fourth-grade test scores, fourth-grade teachers have been under a lot of pressure from principals, who are pressured by cluster leaders and the superintendent of schools to do well. During the year in which Tara's descriptive review was done (1997–1998), there were 14 schools in which the number of children scoring "below basic" on the test rose when compared to their 1996–1997 scores. Those schools were publicly targeted as needing improvements and were investigated by a committee of administrators, parents, and community members who then made recommendations for improvement. The staffs were threatened with transfer to other schools if improvements were not forthcoming at the end of 1998. Tara's school had not been targeted during this 1997–1998 school year, but targeting was a threat that hung over her during the entire year.

Tara works in a system that ranks and orders schools from top to bottom and publishes the rank orders in the newspapers. Children in the system are viewed through the lens of achievement according to test scores. In Philadelphia, as in the rest of the country, "academic excellence" means ranking according to test scores. The Philadelphia Teachers' Learning Cooperative has a very different view of children, and Tara responded to this difference. During the planning meeting and in the descriptive review session itself, Tara continually expressed surprise and delight at how much she had learned from describing Victoria, in all her fullness and complexity (and not by comparing and ranking her), always followed by the wish and intention to describe all of the 34 children in her class in this way.

PLANNING THE REVIEW

Tara Shaw, Lynne Strieb, and Betsy Wice

At 3:30 P.M., a time when most elementary school teachers are exhausted from the day's work, three teachers meet around a dining room table to prepare a descriptive review. Tara is Victoria's fourth-grade teacher, Lynne is a first-grade teacher and serves as chair for the review, and Betsy is an elementary reading teacher who has been involved with descriptive processes for years. Tara has participated in three descriptive reviews at PTLC meetings, but this is the first time she will be presenting, and there is a lot to think about—working with the review headings, gathering stories and observations, thinking carefully about the words used to describe Victoria, and forming a focusing question. The following is an edited transcript from the meeting in February 1998.

Lynne: We can go over the procedure a little first. The headings for the review are Physical Presence and Gesture, Disposition and Temperament, Connections with Other People, Strong Interests and Preferences, and Modes of Thinking and Learning. And we like to include a floor plan of the classroom and a time schedule. That gives a little more context. Another thing is that you want to give lots of examples. If you use a word like *creative*, you would want to say, "for example."

Betsy: One of the other purposes of a planning meeting is to think what kind of question you'll want as the focusing question. Then, when people are listening to your presentation, they've got something in the back of their minds, like a place where they're going to end up. And at the end of the review, we offer recommendations, if you want them, of things you might want to do or think about, and that will have to do with the focusing question too.

Lynne: I thought it might be good if you want to describe Victoria now generally, and the three of us could use this hour to think about what you'd like to focus on in the descriptive review. One more thing: when you talk about her interests and her ways of thinking and learning, you'll want to have some samples of her work with you.

Tara: I'll start with Physical Presence and Gesture: To me, she's just a normal child. She is a kind of middle student. She does some things real well and she struggles with other things. She's very pleasant. She's very sweet-natured to the other children. She doesn't really have any arguments, like some of the other children will say, "He's talking about me" and stuff and that doesn't really happen with her. She doesn't tease anybody or doesn't seem to actually have a problem with anybody. She just comes to school and does her work.

I want to do Disposition and Temperament next: She does express herself well, I think. She'll write in her journal. Sometimes she'll write about little problems in her journal, and then she'll end it and it's over. I think she does express her feelings in her journal. She stays after school for the homework club, and there she's a little more animated since there are fewer children.

Lynne: What is your homework club?

Tara: It started out with just one boy. I was staying late anyway. His mom works at the corner store near the school, and she was having trouble helping him with his homework, so she asked if he could stay in school and if I would help him. Now it's up to about 10 kids and their brothers and sisters who wait for them. But it's good, because it gets a lot of the kids who wouldn't work together working together. And she's one of them.

She has a pretty even temperament. She doesn't really have ups and downs. She has a lot of friends in the classroom. She sits at a table with three boys and a girl who's hearing-impaired. Victoria's a big help for that girl, and that's one reason I put the girl next to her. Victoria's a pretty good person about not teasing her. Also, the boys at her table are boys whom for the most part she gets along with. She doesn't have any kind of problem with them. When they have to do group projects, they all work together.

She's average size. She's not the tallest girl, not the shortest girl—but right in the middle. She dresses fashionably. She uses her hands a lot when she's talking. She'll put them in front and she'll say, "Well, you know what I mean. You know what I mean." She does that a lot with her hands. Let's see, her voice—it's a little bit hard to think about all of this stuff off the top of my head.

Lynne: That's why Pat's "Letter to Parents and Teachers" [see Chapter 3] can help you plan.

Tara: Yes, because when I was thinking about this, I was only thinking about her academic kind of stuff, not this. Her Connection with Other People: I think she's a little bit more mature than other children in my class. She and her mother do a lot of stuff together. She lives with her mom and stepdad. She also has an older brother in high school who goes to Engineering and Science, and he's a really smart kid. Her stepfather works in the post office. Sometimes her parents stop by either after work or on days off to see how she's doing, so she has a lot of support, and they're a really good, strong family.

Sometimes, too, parents aren't an ally with the teacher, but her parents really are, and we agree on a lot of stuff. So that made it easy, for example, when I called home to say "She's distracted, but not by anybody." She had had a week when she was just distracted and wasn't getting her work done. Her dad said, "Well, you know, I see she does this at home. I have to call her name three and four times, and it's like she doesn't even hear me." Since she started staying after school with me, though, that distraction problem went away.

I have a kid who always gets everything done and gets it right, and everybody wants to be his partner. And I have a kid that never gets anything right, and nobody wants to be his partner. But she's just sort of a middle ground kind of a student—though the more I look at her, the more I see some really good things about her that I never really saw.

Lynne: It's amazing, isn't it?

Tara: I wish I had this time to look at all my kids this way, because I'm sure there are other kids that I'm not sure I know.

Lynne: But once you do one descriptive review, you start to process it in your head, even if you can't write it down or think about it. It's amazing how you start to see other children more fully.

Tara: And friends: she's friends with everyone in the class. She doesn't have any problems.

Lynne: Does she have a special friend?

Tara: I'd say "no." When they choose their own partners, some kids always gravitate to the same person. She'll just choose somebody. Sometimes she'll just choose to work alone, depending on who's left. She'll work alone rather than with someone who she thinks won't get the job done.

Today she had to work with someone, and she erased the girl's name and said to me, "I erased her name because she didn't do anything." She said, "She didn't even want to sit next to me. She said she wanted to play with the other girls. I erased her name." She knew that she had done it right, and she said, "It's not fair for her to get the same grade I did, because she didn't help me." She is very self-motivated like that. And the other girl had no problem. She said, "Well, I didn't really do anything; she's right."

Lynne: See, now that's a really good example. You said that she chooses to work alone and that she likes to get the work done. That's a really good example of how she likes to get the work done and is self-motivated.

Betsy: Also, when you used her words, I could hear someone talking. It was not what I expected.

Tara: She'll say it in a way that is not fight-y or full of attitude. She just told me that the other girl didn't do anything. She didn't come up to me and say, like some of the kids will do, "They're not doing anything. Make them work." She just didn't. I knew the girl hadn't helped her. I could see that they weren't even working together. Had it been another girl besides Victoria, the other girl would have been, like, "No, I helped her. I did it." But the kids know that there are kids who never lie, and Victoria's a very truthful person. If she does something wrong, she'll tell me if I ask her about it. If she's talking a lot, for example, I'll say, "Victoria, was that you talking?" She'll say, "Uhm no, not any more." The other kids would say, "No, it wasn't me."

Lynne: That's another nice example.

Tara: She's just really pleasant. And since she has started staying after school, I have seen a big change in her work. Before I would have said her work was satisfactory. If she hadn't started coming after school, she would have been satisfied with the minimal work, just enough to get done. Now I see her really paying attention to what the particular question is or something like that.

Victoria gets along with most people in the school, like the other adults, the staff, the teachers. She does not like gym. I remember Gill [a teacher in PTLC] once saying that gym's such a competitive thing. I think, too, that because my class is so big, it's hard for the kids to wait their turn. It's really hard. They want to get there, and the gym teacher has different activities and he'll make them all sit and only two kids at a time can get up and run around the gym and do that. Victoria will tell me she doesn't like gym and she'll wear nice clothes on gym days, on purpose, I think, so that she doesn't have to do it.

When Lynne asks about Victoria's Strong Interests and Preferences, Tara talks about Victoria's pleasure in writing fantasy stories and in talking about the things she does with her family, such as going to the movies and museums.

Lynne: Have you seen her outside at recess? Do you go out with the kids?
Tara: Sometimes, sometimes. When I interviewed Victoria for this review, we talked about things she likes to do, especially during free time and at recess. I said to her, "Sometimes I notice that you just walk around. Sometimes you play with the girls and sometimes you won't." She said, "Sometimes the girls will get into little arguments about whose jump is next, and it turns into a big fight, and it's not fun any more." She said she'd rather walk away and be by herself.

That led us into talking about her being alone. She said she likes to be alone, sometimes she'll just read different things, sometimes she'll just draw. Pretty much solitary activities. Sometimes she'll want to come up and eat with me. She likes to come back up to the room at lunchtime, and help wash the board, sweep, grade papers, or even just set up—and not have to sit in the lunchroom.

Victoria does like to do her best. At the beginning of the year, she was hesitant. She isn't what I would call a top student, but I honestly think that she does things that are like the top students. She's very intense in her work. For example, when she's thinking about what she's doing and she makes a mistake, like in writing, she'll keep going. Some of the kids, when they make a mistake, that's it. But she'll write the whole story. She'll use invented spelling, and then later she'll go through it with me, saying, "Well, I know I spelled this wrong. But I had to get it out." When she is frustrated, she just goes through it, because she figures she can go through it again and work on it more.

If I hadn't taken so much time looking at her, I would have never picked that up. That's why I was saying I wish I could really look at all my kids like this.

It's neat, too, comparing what she was like in first grade to what she's like in fourth grade. In first grade she was really social, like a social butterfly. And now she's more happy, more content, to work by herself or with one other child, not with a big group. But in first grade, she was always with the most talkative girl group, and she was one of the most talkative girls.

Lynne: Can you tell me how old Victoria is?
Tara: She's 9.
Lynne: Should I summarize this a little bit?

In the summary, Lynne reminds Tara of the words she's used to describe Victoria, such as *intense in work*, asking her to think of more examples of that intensity and suggesting she look closely at Victoria when she works by herself, when she works with other children, when she's with good friends. Lynne and Betsy propose areas where Tara might do more observing as she prepares for the review.

Betsy: Do you know if she has a best friend or a close relative that she sees a lot? Like sleep-over dates?

Tara: Yeah. She has a best friend in the other fourth-grade class. A little girl named Sharita, whom I also had in first grade.

Betsy: Do you see her and Sharita together at lunch?

Tara: No, because they don't let the classes sit together. At recess, yes. At recess they would be together. Since her parents work, Victoria sometimes will go to Sharita's house or sometimes she'll go straight to her house. Usually she has a key, but she won't stay home alone. Sharita lives right down the block.

Lynne: As far as beginning to think about the way she thinks and learns, one of the things you said is that she's very motivated, that she likes to get the work done. She's *focused*, it sounds like. If that's the wrong word, you have to correct me.

Tara: No, I think that's good. A couple more things are coming to my mind now. She'll just (*blows out*). She'll do something like that, like a sigh. She won't just say, "Oh, Miss Shaw, help me. I don't know how you spell that." She'll just shake her head and keep on, or else I'll see her erasing it. But she has to be stuck on something other than spelling because she's not one to fix spelling mistakes right away.

Lynne: But she does then correct them? Because some kids write through it and then they won't bother to go back.

Tara: Yeah, if we go through it. We're getting ready to write books for the kindergarten, so the class is really excited about that. We had a committee that made up an interview sheet and voted on an interviewing committee. One of the requirements was that you had to be a fast writer. You had to be able to write fast and neat, because we decided that the kindergarten kids would probably be excited and talking and have a lot to say. Victoria wasn't chosen, but she wasn't upset.

Lynne: So she didn't do the interviews?

Tara: No, no, she's not one of the interviewers, but that didn't upset her. She kind of goes with it. That's another gesture—that (*sigh*).

Betsy: You mentioned, not today, about that medical stuff that she's interested in.

Tara: You mean being a doctor?

Lynne: Does she like to talk about illnesses? other people's illnesses?

Tara: I don't know, I have to really look at that about her.

Lynne: Right.

Tara: I think I would like to add that in my class there are kids who always raise their hands, who always want to answer questions, but she's not one of them. If I ask her, even though she doesn't have her hand up, a lot of time she does know the answer.

I wish she was more vocal and more active, because I think she is just as bright or just as smart or talented as the "top" kids in the class, and it might help her to move from that "solid-kid" category.

Lynne: When you say "top kid," what do you mean by that?

Tara: I have a boy who will write something, and he'll write a page, and it's perfect. He'll go back and check his own work and look up words in the dictionary, and he won't ask me for help at all. Then when it's done, he'll say, "It's done." I think about kids like him. I have a boy and a girl who are really top kids who just catch on quickly. If you tell them something one time, they never forget it. With Victoria, I have to repeat a lot, and that's like a lot of my kids. But then there are the kids who understand a little bit more, kind of higher-order thinking. And I think she could be like that, where she will get everything right. I see that sometimes in her reading comprehension. She's not getting certain things, but she could. I think she's very capable.

Lynne: You might want to find out and describe more aspects of her reading. What kinds of books does she choose if she's given a choice? Does she read at home? When she's with a book, what does she look like? Does she seem relaxed? Is she sounding out the words? Is she reading quietly? Is she in a relaxed position or a tense position? Is reading comfortable for her? What does she get out of it? I'm trying to think of all the range of questions about books and describing how you'd do it. Is there a time of day when they choose books to read? It would be interesting to find out what she finds interesting.

Tara: I think she's always picking *Magic School Bus* [Cole, 1987–present] books. That's because I just got a bunch of new ones, all shiny. I think she loves books. She's a book lover.

Lynne: When you say that, describe it as fully as possible, because that's really interesting.

Betsy: If she draws, is it with pencil or marker?

Tara: Colored pencils.

Lynne: Bring her drawings as well.

Betsy: Let's start thinking about what particular focus we might want to explore?

Tara: Well, one question I have is, "Do you think it is pushing her too much to be in the upper echelon?"

Betsy: That's an issue we see with many children.

Lynne: Pushing children.

Betsy: That's a great question, because that's not just about her, it's about all of our work, particularly in the situation where the school district has a definite take on it. They'd like us to get as much as we can out of the kids.

Lynne: "Children Achieving" [the motto of this administration]. You know, too, words like *top echelon*—I would like to think some more about those words, too. Words like *pushing* and *ranking*.

Betsy: And you're worried about pushing?

Tara: Yes. The academic difficulties she has are normal, and the more she practices reading, the more she does different things, the better she'll get. That's what kids do when they read. So is it pushing if I expect her to be even better, or will she just get there naturally over the normal school year?

Betsy: So do we have a focusing question?

Lynne: Well, part of the focusing question might be, "How can you get to know Victoria better, and then once you've gotten to know her better, how can you find ways to support her interests, aspirations, and standards—all of this in a system that emphasizes 'academic excellence.'"

Betsy: I think it's good.

Tara: And should I bring examples of work?

Lynne: Yes, writing books, her journal, some stories she did, pictures she's drawn. These are always wonderful to have. And a class schedule—it can be really rough—and a floor plan, because these really help people. You'll want to show people where her seat is and how your room is arranged. I think the focusing question is good.

Class Schedule

8:45	Children prepare for the day
9:00	Journal writing, small groups, writing workshop
9:20	Math
10:15	SAVE anti-violence program
11:00	Teacher preparation time (Children go to gym, computer, science)
11:45	Lunch
12:35	Silent reading
12:55	(Monday) Homework pack;

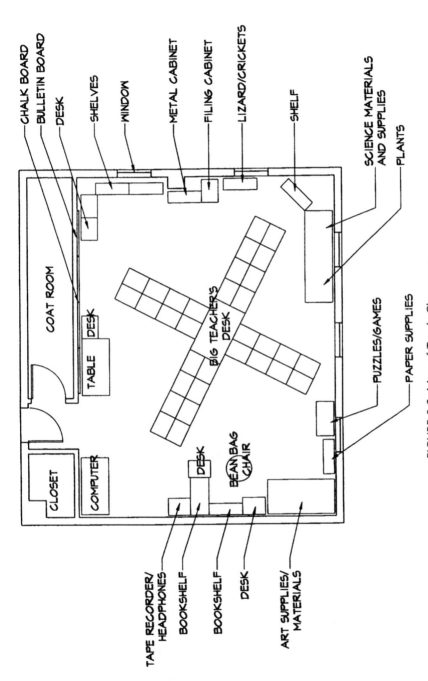

CHALK BOARD
BULLETIN BOARD
DESK
SHELVES
WINDOW
METAL CABINET
FILING CABINET
LIZARD/CRICKETS
SHELF

SCIENCE MATERIALS
AND SUPPLIES
PLANTS

COAT ROOM
TABLE
DESK
CLOSET
COMPUTER

BIG TEACHER'S DESK

DESK
BEAN BAG CHAIR

PUZZLES/GAMES
PAPER SUPPLIES

TAPE RECORDER/
HEADPHONES
BOOKSHELF
BOOKSHELF
DESK
ART SUPPLIES/
MATERIALS

FIGURE 5.2. Map of Tara's Classroom

(Tuesday-Thursday) Reading/language arts is from
12:55–1:15
(Friday) Math strategy pack, five-step math problems,
math journals
1:35   Reading/language arts
2:15   Social studies/geography
2:35   Prepare for dismissal
Friday mornings there is a spelling test and a math speed drill.
Friday afternoons from 2:00–2:35 is choice time.

DESCRIPTIVE REVIEW OF THE CHILD

Tara Shaw

Participants

Karen Bushnell, grade 1, Douglass
Lisa Hantman, grade 4, Hunter
Molly Hasheian, grade 2, Greenfield
Rhoda Kanevsky, grade 1, Powel
Tamar Magdovitz, Shawmont Parent Cooperative Nursery
Gill Maimon, grade 1, Pastorious
Connie Major, teaching and learning facilitator
Marcy Morgan, kindergarten, Wilson
Tara Shaw, grade 4
Lynne Strieb, grade 2, Greenfield
Betsy Wice, reading teacher, Douglass

Focusing Question

Part One

"How can you get to know and support the interests, aspirations, and
standards of a good, solid student who does her work reliably and
well, who calls to mind words like *creative* and *imaginative*, but who
doesn't stand out in a system that emphasizes 'academic excellence'"?

Part Two

"What are some ways of continuing to make children visible in the
classroom?

History and Background

Tara: I chose Victoria because I wanted to look at her more in depth.

I have had Victoria for two years, in first and now fourth grade. It's really interesting when I think of what she was like when I had her in first grade and compare that to what she's like now. She will be 10 in October. She lives with her mom and her dad and her brother, who goes to Carver High School for Engineering and Science.

Physical Presence and Gesture

Victoria is about average height and weight in comparison to the rest of the girls. In terms of gestures and mannerisms that I see, she'll sit at her desk and she'll hunch over all of her books and her notebook. I don't think it's so much that she doesn't want people to look at what she's doing, but that she's just so one-track. She's thinking about what she's doing, and it's like she's in her own world. So she'll hunch over her book and put her arm around it and lean into it. When she talks to people, she talks with her hands. She does a lot of motion with her hands. When she reads, she'll put her head in her hand like this (*demonstrates*) and she'll lean on her desk. And she'll sigh.

If I want the class's attention, usually they have to sit up straight or put their heads down or fold their hands. She usually puts her head down. She doesn't fold her hands. She usually puts her head down.

Victoria dresses fairly trendy, more so than the other children in the class. A lot of the other girls admire her clothing. I don't think it's a particularly expensive type of clothing, but she's very neat and she's always in matching type of sets and shoes. Today we had a play to go to in town, and she had these socks that were red with all these frills around them, and all the girls kept telling her how great her socks were. She had all this leopardskin print around the cuffs and the collar, and all the other girls were, like, "ooh" and they were a little bit jealous, I think.

Another thing about her is that she has a sense of herself that other children don't have in the classroom. Her mom is a hairdresser, and a lot of the kids' parents go to Victoria's mother to have their hair braided, and Victoria loathes braids. And she has longer hair. Part of her hair is braided in the back, but that's it. And it's all her own hair and there are no extensions or anything like that. The kids are always saying, "Well, how come you don't let your mom braid your hair? She'll do it for free!" And she'll say, "I hate the braids! I hate braids!" She'll just like wear it back like in a ponytail-type of thing. I said to her, too, "Your mom could braid your hair," and she said it takes too long, and it hurts, and she's just not having braids. You can't sleep with them. She's really confident about it, that she hates the braids, and everybody else is thinking "that's the best thing—her mom's a hairdresser." But she's really adamant about no braids.

Disposition and Temperament

Victoria has a very calm voice. She's a very even, calm person, with an even temperament. She doesn't get angry easily. If there's a problem with the class or with someone else, she doesn't yell or get upset, she just says, "It wasn't me, I didn't do it." That ends it, because everybody knows that that's her way. She never gets in fights. She never has any physical confrontations, and if somebody says, "Victoria did it," she'll just say, "Well, you know I didn't do it." And that just ends it. The kids just back off because they know she doesn't lie about things and they don't really challenge her on that. And, again, this is something else I wish the rest of my kids would do—you know, say one thing and it was over.

Victoria does have a quiet confidence that will come out when she states something with a lot of force. If she's getting pressured, she'll just sigh and she won't tell me that she's having trouble. She won't sigh real loud, but I'll see it sometimes, and I'll hear her and she'll just erase and start again, so she's got a lot of persistence.

If there is a misunderstanding, she'll talk about it rather than make it a bigger problem, escalating it to something bigger than it is. She's not confrontational. She'll just state her feelings very firmly and with confidence, and, to her, that's how she ends it. It seems that she holds feelings inside, but it's almost in a good way. She'll wait until she's thought about it and then bring it to me. When she has a problem, she'll alert me. Like if she feels that someone was picking with her or bothering her.

This goes along with how she likes to be alone. I didn't notice this so much when she was in first grade. Then she seemed to be very social, more outgoing, than she is. She's pretty outgoing, but she also can be very quiet and almost shy. She has many friends in the classroom. She's very well-liked by the children, boys and girls, but she says to me that she just likes being alone.

Victoria told me once that she likes to be alone, even at recess, because it gives her peace of mind, time to think about what is going on later or about something that's bothering her. She said that it is good for sorting things out in her mind.

Victoria's not a tattletale. She just kind of minds her own business. In turn, she doesn't like anybody to say anything about her, and nobody does. Here's an example. At the beginning of the year she would eat sunflower seeds all the time. I banned them from about the third day of school. I'd look in her desk after school, and there would be nothing but seeds. It would really irritate me. So I told her every day, "No more seeds." But the thing is that other kids will tell on anybody, but nobody will tell on Victoria. It's very rare that somebody comes to me and says, "Victoria's doing this or Victoria's got seeds in her desk." It's just that they know she's got seeds, and they leave her alone.

She's special in class because of some of the behaviors she shows, especially like wanting to be alone. A lot of the kids in the class don't want to be alone, don't want to work by themselves. She's just very confident and sure of herself that she likes to be alone, she likes the person she is, she likes the private activities that you can do alone.

But that's when I think that people will confuse her strength for wanting to be alone as a weakness, let's say, because it doesn't bother me that she wants to work alone, but I think some people will think, "Well, if we're doing a group project, she should be working in a group." But if her reasons are valid as to why she doesn't want to work in a group, of course I'll let her be.

Connections with Other People

Victoria started staying after school with me at the homework club, and I have noticed that her grades have improved. She has always seemed to like school, but since November she just really loves school. She hasn't missed a day, and after school she's a little bit more assertive and she'll help other kids that come in, especially little brothers and sisters. If she gets her homework done, she'll help other kids that are waiting for their brothers and sisters with their homework, so it gives her a little bit of a leadership role.

If she has a problem, she'll wait to speak to me in private. If something's bothering her and if she feels it's something she doesn't want to let slide, she'll tell me after school at homework club.

I watched her at recess, and usually she doesn't play with the other girls. Usually the girls jump rope and the boys play ball and run around, and usually she just walks around the schoolyard looking at all the other children. I see this sometimes when I have recess duty. She doesn't really get that excited about recess. For example, if I tell the kids they're going to miss recess, they're very upset, but Victoria is just like, "Oh, well." It doesn't really bother her.

And it's not because she doesn't have friends. She told me one of the reasons she doesn't like recess or she doesn't play with the girls is because they fight all the time over silly things like who gets the next jump, who's turning the ropes wrong, and she says it seems silly for them to fight and waste all the recess time. So she'd just rather walk around and see what everybody else is doing.

When I was thinking for this descriptive review about her interactions with other children in the classroom, I thought about her best friend, a girl named Sharita. They live half a block away and are always at each other's houses. Victoria goes to Sharita's house after school until her parents get home. Until this year, they've always been in the same class, so I was thinking: What would Victoria be like if Sharita had been in the class this year? Would things be different? Would she be more talkative than she is if Sharita were here?

I was talking with her about who she felt she could work with best in the group, because some girls and boys just partner right up with their friends. But Victoria will see whoever's left and see who she could work with. A lot of the time she'll tell me she'd rather do it by herself because whoever's left are people who aren't that reliable, and she likes to get her work done and she likes to get it done right. She's afraid that if she's partnered with someone else, they'll play and keep her off-task.

When I was talking to her about that, she mentioned some of the children she thought she could work with, and one of them was this boy who's *always* in trouble. He might be the smartest boy in my class, but he's always in trouble. I was surprised and said, "Oh, you think you could work with him?" She said she could work with him, but it's a shame he's so bad at school. They do partner up for some things and their work is good—totally excellent. I think she knows what he can do. She said it's a shame that she can't work with him more, because any time she works with him, she gets excellent, excellent grades.

The other thing is that she sits next to a girl (who sits in seat 31) who is hearing impaired. I put Victoria next to her because I figured that Victoria would be the best one to help her. Victoria helps make sure that she stays on-task and that she's getting her work done, and Victoria can do it in a way that the girl doesn't think she's doing it to copy off her paper or see what she's doing or getting too much in her business. This girl gets very territorial about someone looking down at her paper and seeing what she's doing.

Victoria has a pretty good reputation among the other kids as a fair and even person. When I think about her, I think, "Well, she's not very assertive" and then I think about how she says to other kids, "I said I didn't do it," and that ends it. So I think she is very assertive in some of the comments that she makes.

Since she's been at the homework club, she is staying on-task during instruction time and getting her work done. Sometimes she'll work with the group and sometimes she won't. Some kids always gravitate to the same people, but she'll kind of float from group to group to see who she decides to work with that day. She gets along with the children in the class.

There's a boy who sits at seat 6, all the way in the corner, who is sort of away from everybody. We had a leak in our classroom the other day. This part of the ceiling fell down all over the books over there in the corner, and everything was all wet. I asked him to sit in seat 31 because that girl was absent, and all the boys at that table went, "Oh, no, don't put him here. You can't put him here." They were afraid he might misbehave. Victoria just shrugged her shoulders. You know, it wasn't a big deal, and I was surprised. They got along really well, and I thought for a second I'd have to move him from that table.

Though Victoria is very confident, she's not petty about things. She doesn't hold things. Other kids, if somebody did something to them two weeks ago, they'd think about it every day until they could get some kind of revenge. Victoria will say, "It's over. It's no big deal."

Strong Interests and Preferences

Some of the things Victoria likes to do at home are reading, drawing, playing on the computer. She has a computer at home.

After school she plays with Sharita. They'll play dolls and school and board games like "Monopoly" and "Life," and they'll jump rope. Sharita has three other sisters, so there are a lot of girls around. Victoria also said she likes Sharita's house because there are so many girls.

Her activities during free time: I asked her what she would choose, and she said, "The logs, the Lincoln Logs." But when it came time, she chose the computer. The computer's a big draw for the kids. But she has one at home, so she's not all that impressed with it. She uses it at home a lot to type stories and to play games. She says she does educational kinds of things, those games that are just for fun.

We had a field trip today to see *Freedom Train* at the Annenberg at Penn. I tried to watch her reactions to drama. She was sitting two seats away from me. She was looking up to the lights, and her face was just lit up, and she liked it. It was a lot of singing and a lot of clapping, and it was all about Harriet Tubman, and she just really, really liked that. She had wanted to sit next to Sharita, but she came in late, so she couldn't sit next to her. I was hoping that I could see them in action at the play, but she just really, really enjoyed that dramatic thing.

Another thing I could say is that she wants to be a doctor when she grows up. I asked her about that again, and she told me she wanted to be a doctor. I said, "What about an actress?" She said she thought about it, and she thought she wanted to be an actress, but she decided that she really wanted to be a doctor. Some of my kids change every other week what they want to be. This goes back to her assertiveness and her confidence that she wants to be a doctor, and she has said this to me a few times.

Modes of Thinking and Learning

With her language and her word choices Victoria seems to pick up what people say in the context of how it's said, and she remembers it and then incorporates that into her stories and even into things she says to other children. When I looked at the story she wrote, she wrote things like "in good hands" and "at the stroke of midnight."

Now she's into the "once upon a time/happily ever after" stories. Her writing is a lot of the fantasy lately: a lot of the princess, once upon a time, happily ever after type of stories. She's very creative in her writing in that she doesn't do so much "Well, I went to the zoo" and personal experiences. And she's very intense about her writing. She does a lot more thinking about that than the other kids. She might not have as much written, but she does probably 10 times more thinking. I'll see her sitting at her desk, and she's hunched over, and she's not writing, but just thinking about what she wants to say. When I first looked at her writing, one of my concerns was that maybe she wasn't writing enough or wasn't organized. But now that I've really looked at her, it is organized. She'll explain it to me when I go through it, and it's quite organized. She'll take time in her writing. She seems very methodical about other kinds of work, too, like with the group work, she'll try and get everything done. She wants to get her work done, and she wants to get it right.

She's a pretty good reader and she said her favorite books are *The Berenstain Bears* [Berenstain & Berenstain, 1978–present] books, because they remind her of her older brother and her. She just said to me the other day, "Well, it's like you and your sister. Your sister is always irritating you, but deep down inside you love her and you don't want anyone to do anything to her. That's how my brother and I are." That was kind of interesting.

Victoria's not finishing all of her work, but it's not because she doesn't try or she doesn't understand, it's just because she's taking her time, especially with science projects. And, again, it's the same thing. She's really taking her time to do it. The other kids get done right away, and they want to have free time and do something else. She's still doing it because she's thinking about how she wants it to look. I think she sees the big picture and she's always stopping to see if her work matches the picture she has in her mind.

When we're learning new things, she'll sit up straight and she'll listen. I can tell when she doesn't understand because her forehead gets crinkled up and she'll tilt her head. If I say it another way, that'll usually help set her straight. She'll also ask questions and tell me when she doesn't understand.

For example, if she's doing a writing project at her desk, she won't necessarily tell me she needs help, but if we're learning a new math skill or something like that and she doesn't understand, if it's the whole class, she'll raise her hand and say, "I don't know what you mean." So then I do it in another way.

It's almost a contradiction, some of the things she does with her learning. She'll go through some things, like I said, very step-by-step, but not in other things, like in the drawing, where she's seeing the big picture, and in her writing.

When we do this five-step math problem—where we take apart a problem and break it down into facts, the question, the strategy, the problem, and the final solution—she has the hardest time writing out the strategy. She can do the problem, she can draw the picture, make a pattern. But then when it's time to go back and write what she did, she'll say, "Well, I drew a picture," and she thinks that's good enough. "Well, then explain, how did you make your picture, what did you do, and how did you decide that you needed a picture?" It's almost like she thinks it seems silly to write about it when she did it already. We're trying to get them into that open-ended math type of stuff, and we've been doing this since the beginning of the year. It seems to be that she has the most trouble in school with these five-step problems. Sometimes she'll choose to work with someone that can explain it to her a little bit better.

When she doesn't understand something, if she's having trouble, she'll look at her book, she'll look at her paper. She knows something isn't right, and she'll just, like, keep looking at her paper, trying to figure out how to fix it. Look at her book, back to her paper—she'll go back and forth. And again, she won't ask me to help her. I was thinking about how I could describe it. It's like the best I can do is to say that she understands what she doesn't understand. So if I'm near her, she'll point to something and say, "I don't know what I did." I'll try to talk to her and say, "Well, what *did* you do?" She'll say, "Well, I know it's wrong, but I don't know why." I wish some of the other kids understood what they don't understand, so they could be more specific when they're telling me about something they are having trouble with. Like she can point to something and tell me, "This part isn't right. I just know it." She has a feeling or a hunch, but she can't explain it exactly to me. The only time she'll ask me for help is if I happen to be near her. She won't raise her hand and ask me to come over. If I'm next to her, she'll just say, "What's this?" or "I know there's something wrong."

Sometimes when I watch her, she'll be looking at her paper, like a drawing, and she'll say, "Well, this isn't what I wanted it to be like" or "I should put more or add this." But there are other times, like with science, when she's more step-by-step or methodical. Like we just did a science experiment in class and it didn't work the way it's supposed to work out. She was the one telling me, "Oh, well, that was because you broke up the Alka Seltzer." We had put Alka Seltzer and vinegar together in a balloon and she said, "What probably happened when you broke up the Alka Seltzer, you took away its power." So then we had a big discussion, you know, like—does Alka Seltzer have any power? (*laughter*)

And another thing. All the other kids were just like, "Oh well, it didn't work." You know, most of the kids were a little disappointed that it didn't work, but she was just like, "Well, I know why it didn't work."

In science, she always asks the "what-if" questions. She wants to know what happens if—what if she does this, or what if she changes around my procedure and does something different? Could she do that? What would happen if she did that? This goes again to that big picture. Then in other things she's very step-by-step, so it's kind of a contradiction. She's not all one way.

I also took her to see *Amistad*, and we were walking by the Liberty Bell and things like that. She calmly looked in and saw it and she didn't like say, "Oh, my goodness, that's great" or anything. She just kind of looked and took it all in.

Lynne: Tara, could you sum up how you see Victoria's strengths and vulnerabilities?

Tara: Again, some of her strengths are her ability to be creative in her writing; the confidence she has in the kind of person she is, the kind of child she is; her confidence that she'll get the work done in the way she wants it done, in the way she knows she'll get a good grade.

She's concerned about grades, but she's not *concerned* about grades. If she feels like she's done a good job, then she knows she's going to get a good grade. I always ask them to evaluate how they felt they did on a project or what grade they think they should get. We do a lot of the work that's involved in class assessment things, and she's very good about explaining why she feels her grade should be advanced or her grade should be proficient and she's very honest about it: "Well, our group didn't work so well, and it's the last time I'm going to work with these people." That sort of thing.

I think her vulnerabilities are that other people will be confused about what her strengths are. I thought a lot about that when I was doing this review, and I'm concerned that somebody could come in my class and say, "Victoria's an average student," and then will rank the kids top, middle, bottom. They could label her a "middle" kid. But when I look at Victoria, I think she's just an excellent, excellent student. She might not catch on as quickly as other children and her grades might not be as good as other children, but she just has a real talent in areas that other children don't have. As I was saying to Lynne, I think maybe in two years, she'll just blossom, and a teacher will be, like, "This is the best student I ever had" and I'll think, "That's because she was in my class."

But I worry that in other classes, when she's not assertive and she's one of the quieter ones, she'll be sort of bypassed because, you know, she's *reliable*. She's a reliable student. She'll do what you want her to do, she won't cause any trouble, but because she's not so outspoken and talkative and assertive in that way, some teachers won't think of her when they're thinking about what students they want to do special things. She won't come to mind first. And I think that the more I look at her, the more she should be one of those.

I think I covered everything in my notes.

Lynne: Did you bring some of her work?

Tara: Yes, I have some of her writing, some of her science and speed drills, a spelling test. And this is a spelling test that she got 100 on. She told me she's so happy, that's the first 100 she ever got this year.

Lynne: Let's pass some of the work. There's also a picture she drew about the performance today.

RESPONSE: QUESTIONS AND RECOMMENDATIONS

Rhoda Kanevsky

Tara completes her description of Victoria. While she has been talking, the teachers who are participating in the review have been listening attentively. As we listen and make connections with Tara's story of Victoria, a lot of us are writing down questions, some for clarification, others for expansion of things Tara has said. Lynne, as chair, has been taking extensive notes, as she listens for recurring themes and for contrasts or what appear to be divergent elements in the description. Now she looks over her notes and gathers up some of these ideas to make a brief restatement or summary.

Integrative Restatement by the Chair

There was a large cluster around Victoria's keeping to herself and being private: She minds her own business, children leave her alone, she likes working by herself, wants to be alone at recess time, speaks to the teacher in private, would rather do things by herself. Her gesture while working is hunched over, arm around her paper, leaning into it.

Yet Victoria is not isolated. She chooses to work with young children in the homework club and willingly worked with a girl who needed help hearing and focusing, with a boy with whom no one else wanted to work, and with a boy who is "always in trouble." She seems reliable and steadfast. The children admire her clothes. Though she works in groups when necessary, she has good reasons for not working with other children—for example, they might keep her from getting her work done. She has a very good friend in another class with whom she spends lots of time after school.

One aspect of her being alone is that she is quietly confident, sure of herself and self-contained. She has limits, and when children cross those limits or accuse her of doing something she didn't do, Victoria states her case with force. There are no physical battles, but problems are ended quickly: "It's over. No big deal."

Thinking and pondering were another cluster. The thinking was often paired with her wish to be alone. She likes to be alone at recess to think, to sort things out, to get peace of mind, to look at what the other children are doing—taking it all in. She thinks about what she is doing while she is writing, to organize her writing, and that takes a long time. In math she persists in thinking without asking for help even after Tara notices that she has run into difficulty. Her thinking in science contrasts with many of the other children's in the class because she tries to explain some of the phenomena; she tries to make sense of what happened. She also thinks about "what would happen if" they were to change a procedure, looking at an experiment from more than one point of view, from several angles.

There is a sense of the whole. She has an idea in her mind and, especially in drawing, she wants to get the whole thing down, to make it look the way she has thought it. It takes her a long time to do this. The sense of the whole causes her difficulty when she must work quickly. It also causes difficulty when she must figure out problems using a five-step procedure (something she is asked to do in practice for the SAT-9.) She can get the answers, but has trouble breaking the problem up into the steps it took to get there or explaining in words the strategy she uses.

Victoria likes writing fantasy or fairy-tale stories rather than stories about personal experiences. But when she reads, she connects some of the stories up with her own family.

Questions

Following her integrative restatement, Lynne invites questions and comments from the PTLC teachers who are participating in the review: "Okay, let's take about 15 minutes for questions for Tara. Maybe we want to think about some of Victoria's interests and standards."

A conversational space opens up, as teachers ask questions and Tara responds. In the process, the story Tara told is mirrored back to her from many perspectives. She hears where parts of the story aren't clear to the listeners and what remains elusive. She hears connections the listeners have made, which join material from one part of the description of Victoria to material that appeared under another heading.

Imagining Victoria from Tara's description, teachers are also drawing on their own work with children. As Tara listens to the questions others raise, her memory is jogged. Responding, she tells more stories about Victoria— bits of remembered conversation, a happening in the classroom, new things that further focus the picture of Victoria. Together in dialogue, Tara and the group of teachers build a fuller, more nuanced, more detailed description of Victoria. At the same time, the teachers are learning from each other and from Tara.

Lisa: I want to know more about Victoria as a reader. Is she a good reader? Does she like it? Is she comprehending what she's reading rather than just deciphering?

Tara: Yes, I think so. I have them read on tape, and once when she was about halfway through the story, I asked her some questions about it: "What themes are in the story? What other kinds of stories have these themes?" She made a connection between two stories she had read, and said that one of the stories reminded her of her own neighborhood, with its trash and littering and graffiti. She said, "This is just like the story about a tribe of cave people. The people that we live with are living with the same problems as then."

Rhoda: What does she read? What level is she at? And what kinds of writing happen with the reading?

Tara: She's reading at a fourth-grade level. If she's reading on her own, she'll choose some chapter books, like *Goosebumps* [Stine, 1992– present]. That's a big thing. She has it now in her desk, and she'll pull it out every so often. Sometimes she'll choose some of the easier books that we have in the classroom that she wants to read and get through real quickly, like *The Night I Followed the Dog* [Laden, 1994]. And Dr. Seuss, she loves Dr. Seuss.

Some of the writing she's done has been free-writing, where they have a choice, rather than writing a summary or a book report–type of thing. They're working on books now for the kindergarten classes, and that's something she's really excited about doing.

From Tara's responses, we learn the kinds of books that Victoria enjoys and that she makes connections which relate what she reads to her own experiences.

Other questions asked by Betsy elicit responses that add further facets to our understanding of Victoria's modes of thinking.

Betsy: I was thinking about the papers Victoria did that you passed around earlier. There was one in particular that caught my attention, the "before" and "after" picture assignment that shows a weather front moving through on the beach. The question asked is, "What changes took place when a weather front moved through on the beach?"

Tara: I got this from the principal for SAT-9 test practice. The answer is supposed to be about the "after" picture, but Victoria really looked at the "before" picture.

She wrote, "Some of the changes are on the 'before' picture. It is all clean. In the 'after' picture, it looks like a tornado came through. This picture [the 'before' picture] looks like a beach. Why is a fire hydrant on the beach and the phone lines? They shouldn't have houses on the beach anyway. They can have a fire. Anything can happen."

I think she did a pretty good job on this, but then when you have to go by the rubric that they give you, she wouldn't get a good grade. She'd just be "partially proficient." On the rubric are answers like, "The electricity is cut off."

Betsy: Yes, she seems to have stood back from the assignment. She's saying, "Well, those houses really shouldn't have been built on the beach anyhow." Not part of the assignment. I guess I'm wondering about other assignments she's completed where she's considering it in a larger picture than was assigned.

Tara: Yeah, like in the science experiments that we do. She seems pretty good about that. She can say what happened and she can go back and say, "I think this happened, because of a reason." We did a lot of water and balloon experiments, and she's good about that kind of thing. Even in her mind, even if we don't actually do the experiment, she can think, "Well, if I did it, this would happen." Other kids can't really picture it.

I ask another question related to the big picture, which opens up another line of thought.

Rhoda: Is it that she has an internal picture of what she's doing that she isn't always—

Tara: —right, that she's not getting down on paper. It happens sometimes when she's having a problem when she's drawing. When the children were drawing the play we had seen about Harriet Tubman, the other kids finished their pictures quickly and had lots of stuff going on in those pictures. Victoria just had some of the curtains and one character. She said, "But there's so much more." She said she just felt the drawing didn't look like it looked in her mind.

Rhoda: She said that?

Tara: Yes, she said, "I know that Harriet Tubman was on the stage, and the slaves were on the stage, and some props. So this [drawing] isn't the way I want it to look like."

I told her that I wanted to take it today, but she wants it back so she can work on it. She'll take it home and she'll finish it. She'll do it because she feels like it's not done. She'll finish something for herself.

Rhoda: Okay, she knows more in her head and sees larger things than she actually gets down.

Through these questions and Tara's responses, we begin to understand that Victoria not only uses personal experiences to make sense of a problem, but also seeks causal relationships, pressing for reasons about why things happen. We see, too, that the question "What changes took place?" appears to have made little sense to her, because her response indicates that her attention was caught by what seemed to her inconsistencies in the "before" picture. A fire hydrant and phone lines don't belong on a beach. Attending to this inconsistency, she enlarged the frame of the problem by relating it to her own experience of the actual world, and so exceeded the limits of what the test was asking. We learn from this example, too, that the picture Victoria has in her mind's eye is a standard against which she measures her own work, and that that standard is nameable as *wholeness* or *completeness*.

Pursuing Victoria's inclination to reason things out, I try to understand why Victoria has difficulty with the five-step math problem that Tara had described.

Rhoda: What doesn't she catch on to?

Tara: I don't know, because she's usually very methodical and will go step-by-step. The math problems on the SAT-9 have five steps: question, facts, strategy, computation, and drawing, which means either a picture or a pattern.

Rhoda: What does "strategy" mean?

Tara: They have to explain how they're going to attack the problem. They have to say that they are going to add or subtract, or they're going to draw a picture, or use a pattern to solve the problem.

Rhoda: So Victoria has trouble putting her strategy into words?

Tara: A lot of kids do. They just skip the third step. Victoria will do everything. She'll get the answer. She'll get the right answer. But if I ask her to explain what she did in words, she'll just say, "I drew a picture" but not say how the picture shows her thinking.

In the five-step math problem, it seems that Victoria doesn't understand the purpose in going back and putting into words something she has already completed—and completed correctly.

Karen puts into words what is becoming clearer to us about how Victoria's thinking jars against the kinds of tests relied on for assessing student learning.

I keep wondering what Victoria's attending to. I look at her work and contrast what she's attending to with what the school district is wanting her to attend to.

We begin to grasp with greater clarity why Tara is concerned that Victoria will not do well on the assessments the district uses and that other teachers will not recognize her strengths as a thinker. Victoria can figure things out for herself, but her way doesn't match up with the SAT-9. Victoria's capacity to draw on her experience of the world and to reason things out from that starting point isn't tapped by what the tests test.

Another line of questioning builds on the picture we have of Victoria's social strengths and visibility in the classroom.

Lisa: So is there an opportunity in your class to have class discussions about the stories you've read? Is her hand up often? Is she joining into those discussions?

Tara: No, not if we're in whole group. She won't raise her hand unless you ask her and the groups are small enough that everyone would have a chance. Then she would say, "Well, I don't think that's what happened." She answers really confidently in that sense, but she's not a hand-raiser. But if you ask her, she knows.

What emerges is a confident, self-reliant, self-contained child, who knows her own mind and who is comfortable with herself and others. Tara adds, "She likes the person she is. She likes the private activities that she can do alone. She has a real talent in areas that other children don't have."

Through the following questions, we learn other things about Victoria's relationship with Sharita (her best friend) and Tara.

Gill: I'm interested in her loyalty to Sharita even though they are not in the same class. I'm wondering about other ways she's maintained consistency or, as Lynne says, "steadfastness," in those friendships. And are there ways, too, that she hasn't remained consistent? Ways that she was outgoing and she's not outgoing anymore?

Tara: This is the first year they've been separated. After homework club, she'll go to Sharita's house until she gets picked up. The more I think about this, the more I think I should let Sharita come into my homework club, even though she won't have the same homework. Maybe it's because they're apart from each other this year that Victoria's not so talkative or as outgoing.

Next year I want to put them back together. There are things at school that keep them apart. If we're with the other fourth grade, she's with Sharita most of the day.

Connie: I was trying to get a feel for whether or not she has a need for teacher approval or if it's the self-approval that's enough for her.

Tara: Sometimes I think it's both. She might feel closer to me than the other kids, because she'll spend a lot of time with me after school in homework club. But that may be true with a lot of kids who stay after school for homework club. And the one reason I took her to see *Amistad* was because we were doing a project and she had worked the hardest on it. But at school, I talk to her a lot more than other teachers do or other students even do.

Sometimes the questions can give the presenting teacher new insights. After answering the questions about the close friendship between Sharita and Victoria, Tara begins to wonder if Victoria's self-contained behavior now might have to do with her separation from her longtime friend. She begins to think that it would be a good idea to put Sharita and Victoria together again next year. We also learn that Victoria's relationship with Tara is furthered through regular contact in the homework club and that because Victoria works hard in class, she has even more opportunities to spend time with Tara.

Through other questions, we learn more about interests Victoria now has in taking care of animals in the classroom and more about her role in the classroom.

Tara: She has a big thing with the pets now that she never had before. She has asked to be the pet person for the lizards and turtles.

Lynne: Oh, this is a new interest. Tell us more about the pets and how you know she's interested in them and what she wants to do.

Tara: I don't feed the lizard because you have to feed it live crickets. You've got to take a big packet of crickets and throw them in there. Victoria will look at the lizard, and when she gets her homework done, she'll ask me, "Can I feed the lizard?" This just started happening in the last couple of days. I said, "Do you want to be the pet person?" She said, "Yeah, I think I can do it." I said, "And the turtle, too. You have to clean his water all the time."

Tamar: Are there other jobs you have? Do you have jobs in the classroom?

Tara: Hmm, I'm trying to think of all the jobs. Messenger. Somebody to take care of the books, to make sure they're nice and neat.

Tamar: How are the jobs assigned? Do the kids just choose?

Tara: Randomly. Sometimes I let a kid who comes in early on Monday to be the person who puts the jobs up. They'll go with whoever they think can do the job. Like the messenger has to be someone who doesn't get into trouble in the hallways. I have one kid who does all my attendance circles. I have another kid who answers the phone. When we get a call from the office, the kids know they have to say, "Good morning, room 210, may I help you?" Attendance has to be someone who hasn't missed a day of school. The telephone person has to be somebody who's nice on the phone.

Tamar: Does Victoria get jobs?

Tara: Oh, yes. She was doing the books for a while, because she was staying with me after school so much. But now she's telling me she wants to be the pet person. Because of where she sits, she also does the door. Some kids will take five minutes, opening and shutting the door, looking down the hallway to see what's going on. But Victoria will go up and do the door fast.

Before we make recommendations, the chair gathers up the questions and makes a brief restatement of the new material that has been added to the description of Victoria, some of which has not been mentioned before in this edited account.

I'm not going to summarize fully now because it's late, but some things were added and expanded on.

Some more interests: Victoria's interested in becoming the pet person. When she has free time, she sometimes goes to the math manipulatives. She loves to make things out of popsicle sticks with glue, and she plays "Connect Four." She returns to drawing and the computer when she can.

In addition to contrasts about seeing the bigger picture and trying to do things methodically, there's a contrast too in the way she speaks in the larger group and the smaller group. She uses words she's read. Tara gave two examples of that, where Victoria's used words she heard other people saying. And she can think abstractly: "what if?" and "if this, then that." Tara compared that with some of the other children who have trouble thinking about something if it isn't there in front of them.

Then we talked about her standards, or at least some of the standards that surfaced a little. She has a standard for completion. She perseveres. She relies on her own observations and knowledge of the world. She likes to figure things out for herself.

When she can't carry out what she has a picture in her mind to do, she's willing to go back and work on it until she satisfactorily, or at least to some degree of satisfaction, meets that picture that's in her mind. She sometimes sees more than she can get down.

We learned more about the classroom and about her relationship with Tara. Tara is both her teacher and her friend.

We have expanded our picture of Victoria as a thinker, a self-sufficient problem solver, a productive and respected member of her classroom, and a child who can sustain long-term relationships with other children and adults.

Recommendations

On the strength of Tara's description of Victoria, enlarged now by what has emerged from the dialogue, the participating teachers are ready to offer recommendations. The recommendations are intended to move Tara's thinking along in the directions she has framed through her focusing questions for the review. Following her lead, they are offered in the spirit of encouraging what she has already initiated that is working well for Victoria and offering new possibilities supportive of her strengths.

The recommendations are not prescriptive or intended to fix or change the child. Often they are about new activities or materials for the teacher to try out, new approaches for involving the child in her own learning, or other ways of expanding her learning opportunities. Typically these changes and enrichments in the classroom surround have potential benefit for other children as well.

Because the recommendations follow from the dialogue among the participating teachers and the teacher presenting a child, this part of the process has a reciprocal benefit, offering everyone involved the opportunity to rethink the kinds of learning surround a classroom can provide. For everyone in the room, the process calls forth their own students, their own classrooms, their own strengths and vulnerabilities as a teacher, their own painful experiences, their own hopes. It is entirely possible that each person may come away from the session with a new way of thinking about her or his own teaching, or with new ideas about an approach to a perplexing classroom situation.

For example, the review of Victoria has made me wonder about one of my first-graders, who also seeks to understand how things happen. He has a picture in his mind of how things work and how they should look. He tries to get the "whole" down, but he gets frustrated because his pictures and writing don't capture what he is trying to convey. Hearing about Victoria made me resolve to help him become aware of his learning strategies so that he can realize they are his strengths.

Each time I participate in a review, another layer is added to my understanding of children and classrooms in general. Thinking about recommendations during the review clarifies my ideas about what is possible for children and classrooms. I come away from the review with new energy to reimagine ways to make classrooms, including my own, more responsive to individual children.

It is useful to note that sometimes recommendations contradict each other. That's okay. Participating teachers are each drawing on experiences and perspectives very much her or his own. Equally, not all recommendations will make sense to the teacher, nor will they necessarily suit his or her situation. This is a time for the presenting teacher to listen, consider, gather ideas together, perhaps even decide to do further observations. In the spirit of the descriptive process, the presenting teacher quietly listens to the recommendations without comment and later chooses the ones that appeal and that seem possible and desirable to implement.

Lynne: Now we should give some recommendations. I'm going to say the focusing question one more time: "How can you get to know and support the interests, aspirations, and standards of a good, solid student who does her work reliably and well, who calls to mind words like *creative* and *imaginative*, but who doesn't stand out in a system that emphasizes 'academic excellence'?"

And the second part is, "What are some of the ways of continuing to make children visible in the classroom?"

The recommendations begin with a cluster of ideas about supporting Victoria as she becomes more aware of her strengths, while at the same time helping her become more test-wise.

Karen: This might be heresy, Tara, but if you see her as a big-picture person, then let her go through the math problem without checking off the steps. I think it's more helpful for her to stand back and look at the completed problem and then she'll be able to say what she's done.

Tara: Are you talking about changing the order of the five steps?

Karen: Yes, let her finish the problem. If she has to stop, then everything else is lost. Like when kids are writing: If they have to stop to worry about spelling, then everything else is lost. It seems that maybe she's getting lost. Maybe other kids are, too. That's why these things are so difficult. It's not a natural thing to stop and say, "I did this, I did this."

Tara: That's a good idea. I'll try varying the order.

Lynne: I want to just step in here for a second. I forgot to tell you, Tara, at the beginning, but usually the presenting teacher doesn't respond to the recommendations. It would take a really long time. Sometimes, too, the recommendations directly oppose each other, so we just let them sit.

Karen: The other thing is I would like to see you respond to her more in writing. What would happen if you responded to her more in writing? During the review, I kept wondering what she attends to, and writing is a way of helping her focus her attention into some areas that she may need to be looking at, like details and things, for the SAT-9 tests.

Connie: Maybe she could write sometimes for younger children, say second-graders. Maybe for somebody who's afraid, she could write "Five Easy Ways to Feed a Lizard." Or she could write "Everything You Need to Know About Life in Fourth Grade." Or maybe, "Hey, Turtle Lovers, This Is All You Need to Know."

Betsy: I'm thinking about helping her get her voice stronger in the large group, like by staging a debate or having her be a panelist or maybe stage a press conference, with the whole class as audience. Or maybe Readers Theater, with books like *Yellow Bird and Me* [Hansen, 1986] or *Gift Giver* [Hansen, 1980]. They're colloquial novels about teenagers, with lots of pages full of conversation. Kids like to take part in the dialogue, and the teacher can narrate the "he said" and "she said" in between parts. It's useful to do this with kids who have trouble speaking up. It also helps with their punctuation in their own writing, getting aware of where the quotation marks are.

Lynne: I think that a person who has a picture in her mind of the way it should be needs a lot of time to get it looking the way she wants it looking. I'd like you to think of some ways for Victoria, and maybe other kids, too, to have more time to do that. It would be wonderful if you could carve out a little more time, though I know that clashes with the tests coming along—

Tara: —yeah.

Lynne: It's the anxiety we all feel, and as the children get older, it gets harder. But I'm thinking that she really needs some time to do more drawing on her own.

Rhoda: You have a terrific relationship with Victoria, Tara, as I guess you probably do with all the kids. And I was really impressed by the comment you made on the assignment when she's raising questions about the phone lines on the beach: You said, "Good things to think about." I think that she might need to have several conversations with you about what it is she's doing in this assignment, about what her strategy is in this, and about how strong that is—even if she isn't necessarily getting at what was in the examiner's mind.

Karen: Play the game.

Rhoda: That's right, play the game. Show her what the strengths are in what she's really thinking and doing, but then talk to her about playing the game. About what it is she has to do when she looks at that question and how she has to maybe just focus on that and maybe put herself in a different place for it. To make her a little more kind of test-savvy, at the same time that she's not denying her own strengths as a thinker, which are considerable. I think your recognizing that is wonderful, but it's going to be squeezed out of her unless she gets a good sense of that strength plus that terrific personal strength she's got.

   I would just like her to see what a powerful, powerful figure she is. Her social skills and the profound way other kids know that about her. That gives her a bigger voice somewhere along the way if she can find her strengths.

Gill: I'm thinking, actually, that one of the side effects of the wonderful relationship that you have with her, plus the fact that you know her so well, is perhaps that she doesn't have to express as much to you on paper. If you're her primary audience, she may be reverting to a kind of a shorthand. So I think one good suggestion is to find other people for her to write to, like Connie suggested. Maybe, too, you could set up some kind of correspondence with her, with you in the guise of another character. Maybe leave notes for her, asking her questions, signed as this character, not as Ms. Shaw.

Tamar: First, I think the word *integrity* most describes Victoria. I hope you'll stress that if she holds onto that, she's going to be a great adult. Second, you should keep doing what you are already doing—which is showing her how wonderful she is. Give her responsibilities, like working with kindergarten buddies, perhaps peer tutoring, and give her responsibilities that will have titles. Third, in terms of testing, she's the kind of kid that if she were asked the question "There are three cowboys and three Indians, how many are there all together?" She'd say "There are zero because they'd never be together."

Tara (*quietly*): Exactly, exactly.

Tamar: And you need to help her to psych out the test. I wondered if she were losing details. Maybe you could give her a small notebook to keep notes in while she's reading or doing a project or doing what she's planning—things that she wants to remember to write down for later. Find things that she's real passionate about and encourage her. Pets could be one. Send a note to her next teacher and let the next teacher know what you find special about Victoria and then encourage her next teacher to send a note to the teacher that will come after her.

Tara (*quietly*): I like that.

Lynne: I have one that has to do with making children visible, and not just Victoria. It goes along with my other recommendation about giving her more time. My experience is that I see children best when they have some choices, when they can choose what they're going to write about, for example, rather than when they're doing a workbook or assigned writing of some kind, when their values and interests show through. Certain materials allow kids to show through, like drawing, or construction, or work with lots of different materials, like magic markers, crayons, oil pastels.

Rhoda: And save the work. The work itself is a way of making the kid visible. Save the work. What the children do. Then you can talk with them about the work, especially about a few significant pieces, and that gives you ideas about what other interests children have.

Lynne, as chair, gathers some of these recommendations together, noting there were suggestions about writing and drawing, especially about giving her more time and more choice in those activities; about teaching her how to play the testing game; about making her voice more visible in the classroom; and about supporting Victoria more explicitly in her own awareness of her many strengths.

At the end of the recommendations, the chair asks the group to critique the entire session as to how well the review maintained the integrity of the child and respected confidentiality.

Rhoda: I wanted to say that I really enjoyed hearing Tara's appreciation of Victoria, especially in all those social situations that she described. I enjoyed seeing her room.

Lynne: That was so helpful. It was so helpful to have the context first.

Betsy: As a group, at PTLC, we've been looking for a way to get at this question about where we stand in relation to these tests, particularly fourth-grade teachers who are under this huge pressure that the whole school's reputation rides on how their kids do. It is really interesting to me how the recommendations ended up falling out about a lot of different ways to deal with the test—some very explicit about "playing the game"—but others about her real interests and ways of encouraging that. So that it isn't either–or—either you've got to be part of the system or you've got to buck the system. It's about working within the system.

It is really helpful to me for thinking not just about Victoria, but for thinking about so many of our kids. We see strengths and we know they're not going to show up on the printout or we wish it would show up more than we fear it will.

So it has been very useful to describe Victoria, particularly because she's such a strong kid that we basically aren't worried about.

AFTERTHOUGHTS

Tara Shaw

It was very interesting to read the full transcripts over and over again this summer (July 1998). My initial thoughts were that I didn't seem really clear in the planning session. It seemed slightly disjointed and not fluent in that I don't think things came together. It was as if I was putting a lot of questions out. However, as I reread the planning session, I noticed that it does start to make sense because I was trying to organize all my observations and make sense of the review. And my thoughts, the things I said, were my initial reactions. So I think the planning session was very strong. I had a more defined focus after the session, and that helped me when I went back to observe Victoria more. Lynne and Betsy were tremendously helpful, especially in terms of my developing the focus and essential question of my review.

There are a few things that really stood out for me in the planning notes. It seemed that certain things came across to me as being very "loud." I kept thinking about those issues.

Children Who Enjoy Being Alone

It seems teachers want children to be able to work with others as a group (i.e., the idea of teamwork), yet some children prefer to work alone. Where does a teacher set the balance? What is the appropriate balance, and should the teacher really decide it? Victoria has a strong self-identity that is very positive. Her family nurtures it. She isn't needy in the sense that she wants me around her all the time. She is very sure of herself and who she is. I think this is so unique and wonderful. It doesn't seem to be a trait valued within the school district, but I value it. I've described it as a "quiet confidence." I think she likes being alone because she likes the person she is. I don't think others would recognize this as one of her strengths unless they really knew her. So I'm left with the questions of possibilities: Is it possible to teach this "confidence" or do children just have it? How would you teach self-love? Is this necessarily important for me as a teacher? Do I invest time for this? How does this relate to self-esteem? How do you nurture this trait?

Being Specific About Confusion

Victoria is very specific in explaining things she doesn't understand. Again, this is an overlooked strength, one I didn't fully appreciate until I did the review. It makes it much easier for me as a teacher to make clear what is unclear. I always try to have my kids be specific. In that way I try to guide their confusion so that they can begin to identify at what point they started to have trouble. My questions about this issue are: How do children process information? How do they connect what they learn? How do they know they are confused? Are there signs? How does prior knowledge become important?

Specificity of Examples

I felt this was important, because maybe I should have had more specific examples. Going through the planning session was good, because I do use words like *bright* and *creative* and *excellent* to describe students. The review really showed me that I need to qualify and substantiate what I mean when I use such words. The examples also give a fuller and more vivid picture of the child. It also raises questions about when I use these words and when I don't. Why do I describe some children as "creative" or "bright" and not others? What makes a child "creative" or "bright," and what are the criteria? Who sets such standards for creativity? Do I presume to because I'm the teacher? This mostly is my issue, one I'm still trying to work out in my own mind.

Pushing Academic Excellence Versus Other Strengths and the Issue of Top/Middle/Bottom

These two concerns really stood out the most for me when reading the transcripts and thinking about the recommendation that Victoria be more vocal or assertive. My answer is both "yes" and "no." I'm not sure if pushing her to be more vocal is appropriate or respectful of her identity. What if that's not her nature? Should her nonacademic strengths be overlooked because she is not a straight-A student? I'm thinking Victoria is on her own timeline and she will know when she is ready for new things. I keep coming back to the nature of schooling. A great many schools are limited in their resources of so-called extras (music, art, drama). Might this be an area where Victoria excels? I think she would.

I watch her a lot more carefully now after going through the review with her. It brings back the question of what makes a top/middle/bottom student. How can all the multiple intelligences be nurtured so that all students have levels of excellence? How do you break a child out of that self-perception? What are realistic expectations? Students know when they have been labeled and tracked. It also brings up the issue of what is valued within the classroom and by the teacher. It seems to me that going back and reexamining the review has given me many more questions. In a way, it's good for me to look at what issues and concerns are being raised. But at the same time, I'm overwhelmed by not being able to answer them all, or knowing where I should start. It's almost harder to go back and reflect on the review, because I feel there are ways I should have been more organized, ways I should have been more clear, ways I could have helped Victoria more effectively. A huge implication is that I must do this review with all my students, so I can "see" them in another way, see the strengths that are not so obvious.

Actual Review Presentation Issues

One thing that came up is about voice and audience. Other people in the group kept bringing up audience, by asking who Victoria's audience was. The implication for me is to vary the audience, not only through writing activities, but also so that her voice will be "louder" to others. I find the idea of "voice" interesting because of people's perceptions about the word. Again, the implication for me is to give her opportunities to use her "voice" in different settings.

The second thing is about the SAT-9 test. This is a big deal in Philadelphia, but I am struck by how unimportant it really is to me when I think of student progress and performance. I still worry and get stressed out when I have to give it, but I never use the results for grades or report cards. I think the work we do in the class is much more authentic and important. Another issue, which was raised by a student, is that they don't get the tests back in a timely fashion.

And the third thing is about family and friendships. I think Victoria's family structure is so strong and tight that it has shaped and defined her self-identity. She knows where she belongs and what her place is. Gill also mentioned her friendship with Sharita. I think it would have been very interesting to see them together in the same class. Victoria strikes me as a very loyal child. (I am taking them both to a Phillies game on July 4, 1998, and they are staying overnight, so I will see them together.) Lynne and Gill also used the word *steadfastness*, which I love. This describes Victoria in a lot of ways.

Finally, a lot of people discussed Victoria's writing and gave great, helpful recommendations. They stayed true to the nature of my focusing question. It was almost an overload of ideas. They were all so great, but I couldn't do all of them. I wanted to, though. It's difficult to try to fit everything in that I want to do.

Looking back on the review, I realized what a wealth of knowledge I have about this one child. It's so amazing to me to look back and through my thoughts and show her work. People not only see what I see about her, but they also *see* Victoria.

CHAPTER 6

DESCRIPTIVE INQUIRY: "LANGUAGE AS A MADE THING"

Margaret Himley

I guess I can't pay enough attention without language. I don't mean the kind of language I'm using now, where I'm talking spontaneously, but language as a made thing. That work of making causes me to look harder, to see if I've said what I really feel. Have I done justice to the world I'm attempting to describe? And I have to look again at my description and that process brings me closer.

—Mark Doty, poet, 1995

Many voices. Edited transcripts. Stories layered into other stories. Details and specificity. A hybrid of descriptive review alongside narrative essays alongside theoretical argument. Ideas that ring both familiar and strange.

A reader might legitimately ask, What is this? Is it teacher research? Or case study? Or ethnography? Why this open-ended format, with so many voices and rough edges? What will I learn? Is it worth my time and effort?

The body of work produced by Prospect over the last 30 years does not fit neatly into current categories of educational research or method, so we want to locate the work theoretically, emphasize its value, and explain the book's nontraditional format. This book, like a good conversation, is full of different voices. It achieves coherence through a grounding commitment to disciplined description and collaborative inquiry.

DESCRIPTION AS METHODOLOGY AND VALUE

Nearly 30 years ago, Prospect committed itself to observation and description as the grounding for teaching practice and inquiry. Under the leadership of Patricia F. Carini, an extensive network of educators in various sites—from preschool through university, from New York to California—developed the phenomenologically-driven methods for *disciplined description* that are now known collectively as the Prospect processes. Grounded in the particulars of actual children and real classrooms, these processes animate, open up, and move forward the thinking of teachers and parents about children, classroom activities and curricular choices, and the larger challenges facing public education. They do so by producing imaginative, engaged, and richly detailed understandings of children and classrooms.

The purpose of the Descriptive Review of the Child, for example, is not to fix or explain that child, but to make the child more visible by coming to understand him or her more fully and complexly as a particular thinker and learner.

The descriptive processes do not provide research results or new curricula or "solutions" to "problems"; rather, they develop in all of the participants the habits of mind—*the stance*—of careful observation and description. Teachers and parents become, as Carini says, disciplined students of childhood.

Descriptive inquiry is a powerful resource. While children should be at the heart of schooling, it is ironic, even tragic, that they often become invisible as individual learners, as people with particular strengths and interests, within the pressures, constraints, mandates, institutional discourses, and daily demands of schooling. It's hard to see children in all their complexity. It's hard to connect with them. It's hard to value their difference. All too often they are reduced to test scores or categories, like "stars" and "handfuls" (or even "double handfuls"). Furthermore, as Margaret Howes (an educator and member of the Prospect board) once said, sometimes teachers find themselves frozen in relation to a child or a classroom situation, stuck in a way of thinking that isn't productive or perhaps even really clear to themselves. Doing a descriptive review with other teachers and parents *unfreezes* them, allowing them to see the child or situation from many points of view, to have new ideas and images to work with, to flesh out meanings, to imagine possibilities—and so to get the teaching going again. Rich in phenomenological detail and depth, this kind of working knowledge moves teachers and teaching along.

PHENOMENOLOGICAL PREMISES

The core concepts in the Prospect philosophy are set out in Patricia F. Carini's first monographs, entitled *Observation and Description: An Alternative Methodology for the Study of Human Phenomena* (1975) and *The Art of*

Seeing and the Visibility of the Person (1979). Carini begins here with a critique of the emphasis on models in the educational reform movements of the 1960s and early 1970s, models constructed in the absence of rigorous theory. Her critique hinges on the tendency of such theory-free models to do nothing more than concretize current beliefs about teaching and learning. Carini turns to other genres and other traditions in Western thought for a more disciplined inquiry into knowledge-making in schools, and specifically for more nuanced understandings of how children grow and learn. Among those traditions are phenomenology, art, story, oral traditions, and literature more generally. Whitehead and Merleau-Ponty are major influences on Prospect thought. Other thinkers who figure prominently include Owen Barfield, Raymond Williams, Isaiah Berlin, and Heinz Werner, as well as John Dewey and other progressives in American philosophy, social theory and action, and education.

Carini's thinking draws from phenomenology, a branch of philosophy that originated around 1905 with Edmund Husserl, who understood human consciousness as active, not passive, in making meaning. He argued that we do not just receive the world, but engage with it, and in that active encounter produce what it means. In extending the phenomenological project, Merleau-Ponty described human existence as it is lived at that point of encounter, at the lived point of world and consciousness, where there exists a dynamic relationship of the person and the world. What phenomenology offers then is a particular take on what knowledge is or can be, as Linda Martín Alcoff (1998) explains:

> It is only because being is always in the world, and not apart [from] or over the world, that we can know the world. But it is also because being is always being in the world that our knowledge is forever incomplete, caught as it is inside, carried out within the temporal flux, and incapable of achieving a complete reduction. (p. 14)

Thus knowledge is understood as always unfinished, incomplete, emerging, and partial.

Phenomenology provides the basic tenet of descriptive inquiry: "Before it is possible, let alone desirable, to abstract and isolate the elements of a phenomenon according to the principles of logic, we must first conduct an inquiry that brings us closer to the phenomenon—if you will, *into* the phenomenon—in all its complexity" (Carini, 1975, p. 5). Thus the phenomenological process, as a method of knowing, involves immersion in direct observation of a small number of instances over extended periods of time within their natural setting.

A similar premise underlies qualitative research and participant–observer ethnography and relates to what Bissex (1980) calls the "enlightened subjectivity" that serves as the premise of her case-study method. The purpose of this research is not abstraction or generalization, but extended, active, layered, perhaps startling intersubjective engagement with others. In *GNYS AT WRK*, for example, Bissex (1980) concludes, "I found in the end that generalizations, as they distill meanings, may also dispel them by abstracting away the very particulars that gave them life" (p. vi). The point in this approach to knowledge is to study individuals "in the act of learning" (p. vi), with all that implies about drama, action, and motion.

Yet all too often positivist assumptions slip back into qualitative research. The details produced by the researcher become *data* that get transformed into *conclusions* and *applications*. The movement in the research again is toward abstraction, though perhaps grounded in empirical detail and told through anecdotal or narrative evidence. The object of study—the child, the classroom, the text—comes to be accepted as directly and even fully knowable. The language used to describe persons or events, to develop analyses, and to represent the work later to a larger audience goes unquestioned and risks reinscribing conventional categories of thought and assessment. All too easily the results of this research may come to confirm conventional knowledge rather than challenge it.

These are the very risks that Prospect wants to avoid.

Disciplined description as inquiry aims to come to understand, albeit partially, a child, a work authored by a child, or a teaching practice in its fullest expression of meaning. At Prospect a founding premise guards that aim: that however close and careful the description and however full the meanings achieved, these understandings are necessarily partial. That acceptance of limitation is paired with a critically important and consequential conceptualization of person and self: that the child, as the object of study, is finally not reducible to predetermined categories nor explainable (or predictable) in the way events in the physical world may be. In an early monograph, Carini (1979) says it this way: "When all the traits, causal agents, and classifications of behavior and personality have been categorized, the person has fallen through the net of abstractions" (p. 7). Thus the processes, by forgoing prediction and explanation and judgment, produce a context of meaning and significance for a different aim: to recognize and remember and revalue the richness and complexity of human beings. This imaginative engagement with others/otherness produces the ground for teaching practice and is the goal of doing descriptive reviews.

During the Prospect processes, for example, a group of people, through a series of formally structured rounds of description, offers observations and descriptive comments about the child or work under study. These are recorded by those involved in order to identify clusters of ideas, themes, and points of confluence, and to craft language that is more and more precisely evocative of the particular child or work. These notes serve, too, as the basis for further and fuller reflection on the language that was used in the process.

Saying and seeing remain reciprocally intertwined. Again, to cite Carini (1975): "As the observer grows more immersed in the phenomenon observed, the power to articulate in words and other representations grows ever finer and more particular . . . so that in the example of 'anger' a complex of words specific to its particular expressions emerges to supplant the global concept of anger" (p. 22). The point is to use language to resist easy or conventional explanations of a child or work, to use language to produce precision and particularity.

When teachers and parents first encounter a descriptive review, or when they first listen to a teacher or parent present a child or a child's work, they are often amazed at how much teachers know about the children in their classroom and how powerful that knowledge is when gathered together in a review. The child comes to life as the teacher describes the child and tells stories about that child. But it's not a mystery: Descriptive accounts depend, to return to Patricia Carini's phrase, on "human capacity, widely distributed." It is the fundamental human capacity to observe and describe and narrate that enables us all—teachers, parents, and researchers—to imaginatively engage with others, to see continuity and complexity in others, and to enlarge our understanding of the possibilities for teaching others.

"WORD-WORK": ATTENDING TO/WITH LANGUAGE

From my perspective, this means that the Prospect processes are importantly about language use: not the spontaneous language Doty refers to in the epigraph to this chapter or the way teachers may swap stories or trade classroom strategies in the hallway, but the kind of talk—or "language as a made thing"—that is formally prepared in order to describe others with careful precision and full respect for their uniqueness. This descriptive language refuses to place people and events in predetermined categories of thought, categories that oppress us all with their conventionality and totalizing impulses. Descriptive language draws us into a shared humanity, as judgmental language does not, and invites us to connect with others in many ways. Disciplined by structures and summaries, driven by story and image and detail, this kind of descriptive language produces the kind of engaged understanding that renews possibilities for action.

Following Toni Morrison, I call this "word-work." In her lecture to the Swedish Academy upon receiving the Nobel Prize for literature in 1993, she spoke angrily against "the systematic looting of language [which] can be recognized by the tendency of its users to forgo its nuanced, complex, mid-wifery properties, replacing them with menace and subjugation" (pp. 15–16). She decries the "obscuring state language or the faux language of mindless media," "the proud but calcified language of the academy," and other "dead languages" that police our thoughts, thwart our intellect, and preserve privilege (pp. 13–16). She challenges us to return to language use itself, as we grapple with meaning, provide guidance, and express love:

> The vitality of language lies in its ability to limn the actual, imagined and possible lives of its speakers, readers, and writers. . . . It arcs toward the place where meaning may lie. (p. 20)

Morrison is talking about narrative and the power of narrators (like herself) to render, portray, and reimagine the meaning of our lives. But as Prospect proves, we can all use language this way, given time and structure and opportunity.

THE VALUE OF THE PERSON

Through description the person becomes more visible and real education begins, and it is, finally, this *taproot value of the person* that characterizes Prospect's particular educational stance and that gives meaning to the descriptive processes. It is the ethical insistence on the hard work necessary to accord to others—*all others*—the status of person, with all the complexity, capability, range of emotions and desires, and possibilities that we know ourselves to have. Prospect seeks to start from the most spacious understanding of the person in thinking about children and education. In a recent paper, Carini (1995) says it this way:

> What I want to say . . . is that it takes vigilance—hard, recursive work—and it takes educating ourselves in the largest sense of that word to keep alive this awareness of human complexity. It takes an active attunement to the fullness of passion in each person, to the driving desire of each person to make and to do, and to the strong, basic *need* of each of us—and all—to be valued and valuable. (p. 2, emphasis in original)

The Prospect processes, in their formal, respectful, dignified attention to others, have been developed as a method of inquiry for doing this hard work of valuing the person as the center of the educational project.

These processes disrupt the pressure of the utilitarian or the efficient. They jar the conventional ways of doing things. They offer a refreshing return to fundamental values in education. They challenge the corporatization of education.

INQUIRY AND COMMUNITY

Descriptive inquiry also produces a powerful teaching community through collaborative talk as a "made thing." As Cecelia Traugh and colleagues (1986) note, "the art of teaching is best cultivated within a supportive community" and in collegial spaces where teachers can talk about their practices and the children they teach, where they can help each other find patterns and meanings in the daily details of classroom life, and where they can come to assert that knowledge with greater and greater clarity and authority (p. 5). Teachers associated with Prospect, for example, meet at summer institutes and at the annual November fall conference, among other sites, to do descriptive reviews of the children they are teaching; to write up child studies or reviews of practice; and to reimagine their own teaching through collective conversation focused around key words, stories, and memories.

They also read together. It has always been Prospect's practice to juxtapose the close, detailed description of children and their works with the close, detailed reading of the novels, essays, poetry, and books of thinkers such as Toni Morrison, Mike Rose, Isaiah Berlin, Adrienne Rich, Marjorie DeVault, Maurice Merleau-Ponty, and Alfred North Whitehead. At institutes and conferences, even at working board meetings, Prospect's approach to thinking about education "has been characterized by [this] exploration of the reciprocal relationship between philosophical ideas and classroom practice" (Traugh et al., 1986, p. 2):

> This relationship can be described in several different ways: as reciprocal, as one grounding the other, or as running parallel. In this case, our experience affirms a strong relationship between these ideas and teaching. Each gives the other a fuller, deeper meaning. We understand our experience more fully as we come to understand some of these philosophical ideas; the ideas gain substance from the particulars we bring to them; what we do is informed, in part, by the ideas. (p. 109)

Reading and discussing ideas, alongside detailed description of daily classroom life, give teachers the time and space to think about teaching from many perspectives.

It is this kind of juxtaposition, as trope and method, that characterizes collaborative inquiry at Prospect. The descriptive details, stories, observations, and claims about a child or a work authored by a child are set along-side each other, with full respect for tensions, complexities, nuances, gaps, and continuities. The daily details of teaching are set alongside large and spacious ideas about the person and the world. The many perspectives produced in collective reflection on key words are set alongside each other as the chair draws the ideas together and notes clusters of thoughts, continuities, and discontinuities. As phenomenological inquiry, observations, ideas, and reflections provide an enlarged context for understanding children, classrooms, and ourselves as teachers and persons; they also produce an enriched context for teachers to think in together.

ABOUT THE BOOK

In this book we have tried to re-present the spaciousness and open-endedness of descriptive inquiry, along with its formal and disciplined procedures, in order to re-create in written form as best we can the oral context in which most people learn to use the processes in their teaching. There is formal consistency across the reviews, even as those reviews are about very different children in very different school contexts. The "Afterthoughts" at the end of each review draw some of the threads of the review together for further reflection, though surely every reader will find him- or herself wanting to raise other points or ask other questions. The book tries to balance coherence with a roughness around the edges, in the belief that full understanding is not an achievable goal, except at the cost of reducing people and events. The book also juxtaposes accounts of actual descriptive reviews with essays that both *embed* those reviews in a more articulated philosophical context and *extend* them by showing disciplined description at work in other sites and for other purposes. As at a Prospect institute, we want readers to read a descriptive review, have questions, think more as they read an essay, and then head into the next review.

We try here to *teach Prospect* by telling lots of stories, not as examples or instances of larger claims, but as narratives that do what all narratives do—describe, evoke, resonate with other experiences, tap memory, call forth further stories, and produce thought and question and action. By *story*, of course, we refer to the fundamental human act of narrating, not to the specialized act of creating fiction. We combine the discipline of description with the power of storytelling, because

> Stories (and memory) hook us into human-ness. . . . Stories (and memory) pluralize us. Stories stretch our narrow, individual frames and minds, making us big and roomy. What was singular, multiplies. Through stories (and memory) we step across eras and even aeons of time, glimpsing worlds we never knew

but which also remain—through stories. Stories (and memory) are powerfully educative. (Carini, 1997, p.5)

These Prospect stories, then, as they teach the Descriptive Review of the Child, serve as meeting places where acts of learning can take place. The child comes to be understood, albeit partially, as a particular learner and thinker who is making an entry into the natural and cultural world. The presenting teacher recognizes how much she already knows, and learns how to draw that knowledge forward into action in her classroom. She and the other participants share a collective act of learning in giving each other the respectful time and attention the processes require and in rewarding that effort with understanding and renewed spirit. The reader of this book, while not as directly engaged in the processes, witnesses and at a remove participates in these acts of learning through an imaginative involvement in the stories reprised here.

CHAPTER 7

THE DESCRIPTIVE STANCE: PROSPECT TEACHERS WRITING

Ellen Schwartz, with Anne Martin and Karen Woolf

Come into a room at Prospect. People are seated in a circle, pens poised over notebooks, ready to take notes. Oral inquiry begins to take written form, as they map out what they hear in charts, graphs, webs, phrases, and sentences. The presenting teacher arrives with reams of notes. As the review begins, the chair tries to capture people's comments fully enough so that his or her integrative restatement can represent the fullness of the conversation and can be read and understood later by others. The Prospect Archives are full of notes—from descriptive reviews, from conversations about children's works, from meetings and seminars.

At Prospect, writing is infectious. It is also a discipline.

Back in their classrooms, teachers associated with Prospect produce narrative records about their students and often are avid journal keepers. They write up descriptive accounts, based on the observations and stories they have gathered in order to understand their students better. Writing that remains close to the lived life of the classroom and that provides a richly detailed space in which to think about teaching and learning is woven into their daily work. The discipline of writing supports teachers as observers and describers of children. Those who attend summer institutes bring with them the writing projects that they are working on—for peer reading, for support, maybe for publication.

As demonstrated by the "Prospect-Related Publications" in the Appendix as well as by the References at the end of this book, a large body of books, monographs, and articles has grown out of the work of Prospect over the years. Much of it has been written by classroom teachers, often for publications with a nationwide audience, such as the *Harvard Education Review, Language Arts, Pathways, Teaching & Learning, Changing Minds,* and *The Nation.* Monographs have been published by the North Dakota Study Group on Evaluation and the National Center for Restructuring Education, Schools, and Teaching. Teachers in the network have also contributed to books on education and educational research such as *Inside/Outside* (Cochran-Smith & Lytle, 1993), *Teaching Social Studies: Portraits from the Classroom* (Rogers, Roberts, and Weinland, 1988), *Students Teaching, Teachers Learning* (Branscombe, Goswami, and Schwartz, 1992), and *Reading Your Students* (Martin, 1983).

This summer (1998) my colleagues Anne Martin and Karen Woolf and I took some time to read across a large collection of these writings. Each of us had read most of these pieces previously, but, as we discovered, it is a very different experience to read them successively, one essay following the next. Reading them that way, collectively, we were fascinated to discover themes and other characteristics linking these diverse pieces and their many authors. As we talked about these similarities, the idea was born to put together this essay to give others a taste of the distinctiveness of writing by Prospect teachers.

The real task turned out to be selecting a manageable number of themes and characteristics, knowing that any selection entails the risk of eclipsing others no less important. What helped was to notice that it isn't so much topics or subjects that make the writing distinctive, but how these are treated.

Here, I'd like to introduce the body of work that has been published by Prospect-associated classroom teachers by providing examples of that work and by suggesting the dimensions of thought and value that stand out in it.

At the heart of Prospect writing is the commitment to human capacity and to description as a way of forming knowledge. In these essays and books, we find teachers *taking a descriptive stance,* staying close and caring, attending to the complexity and ambiguity of lived experience. We find that the writing often takes the form of story or journal or conversation. We find the desire to describe in respectful and detailed ways, staving off the impulse to generalize or to make large sweeping statements.

Through their writing, teachers develop and share an *intimate knowledge* of students, classrooms, schools, and teaching practice. The effort is to find the language, the right words and images, to bring the child or classroom to light, rather than to score points or to make a clever argument. We hear students' *voices,* individually and in dialogue with each other or with teachers, and we hear teachers using conversation with colleagues to move their own thinking along. These voices bring us, as readers, closer to the experience of teaching and learning, closer to real classrooms. The writing aims at producing a large *thinking space* for the writers and readers—and we can often see the writers' minds at work—while at the same time providing a vehicle for *public statement* about issues of concern. Reflection and question take their place alongside description as valued ways of forming knowledge.

Undergirding all this work is a compelling grounding in the value of human capacity, widely distributed. It is a passionate commitment to this human value that keeps these teachers looking and looking again, seeking to describe, to give language to that capacity, so that others might see it as well.

THE PRESENCE OF VOICES

Students' and teachers' voices are always close to the surface in the Prospect writings, and it is the presence of these voices that keeps us, as readers, close to lived experience. The fullness of the teacher narratives does this in *Speaking Out* (Traugh, et al., 1986). Six Prospect teachers collaborated on this monograph, which weaves together stories from many teachers who talk about classroom life, possibility, hard times, community and collegiality, and teaching as art.

What's distinctive about this project is that these chapters are not based on interviews between a single interviewer and a lone teacher. Rather, groups of teachers engage in conversation, sharing recollections of coming to teaching and stories about classroom life. Excerpts from these conversations are placed alongside each other; the commentary between the excerpts is descriptive and guiding. It responds to the teachers' voices, highlighting ideas that stand out to the commentators, but not seeking to replace them. As the title suggests, it is the voices themselves that have primacy:

> Having a voice is critical and political. We create, share, and change our world with and through language. Recognizing that day-to-day experience is a powerful source of understanding and knowledge, which, when articulated, can be fed back into the quality of work is critical for teachers in gaining a voice. Recognizing knowledge and voicing it is basic to changing the ways teaching is thought about and enacted. (p. 1)

The teachers' stories are what give breath to the book, as they do to the activity of teaching and the lives of teachers.

Anne Martin's (1981) monograph, *The Words in My Pencil: Considering Children's Writing,* is rich in children's language. Martin tells us in the introduction that she is not writing a how-to book. Rather, she is studying her students' actual writing in a "search for better ways to release children's thoughts on paper and . . . for what [the writing itself] can teach us about the children" (p. 2). She explains, for example, how she chose and arranged the writing:

> These pieces of writing were chosen because I responded to them, whether I could understand them or not. I have purposely avoided arranging them by subject or form. This may seem haphazard, but in order to communicate the richness of emerging writing, I want to present it in the random fashion in which it occurs in the classroom, often unanticipated and surprising. (p. 21)

Martin's down-to-earth description of the children and the classroom makes it immediately recognizable. She begins: "The one outstanding characteristic of this class was the children's absolute inability to work as a group or listen, and, by contrast, their amazing ability to produce fantastic work individually" (p. 5). I can picture the group, or at least picture *similar* groups that I have taught, and I can identify with the challenges that will lie ahead for Martin as the teacher of this class. It would be easy in this situation to see it only from one side. But Martin does not situate herself, the children, and her readers in a bleakly one-sided world. The group may struggle with group work, but the superlative language in "their amazing ability to produce fantastic work individually" creates a large window of possibility.

The effect of Martin's approach is a closeness to the life of the classroom and, at the same time, tremendous roominess. Most teachers instinctively know that there's value in the actual: the actual children they teach, the actual work the children do, the actual work they do, the actual life of a classroom and a school. Informal teacher talk is full of anecdote. Unfortunately, the actual often gets reduced to the pragmatic, so, for instance, a common complaint about in-service or course work is, "I didn't get anything I could use tomorrow." The descriptive work of Prospect values the actual without reducing it to the practical. Teachers may indeed get a wealth of practical ideas from descriptive study, but the guiding questions are invariably about enlarging understanding, not merely about adding a new technique to one's repertoire.

UP CLOSE AND ALONGSIDE

Through description, journals, and story, a teacher invites us to stand alongside him or her in the classroom. Placing oneself amidst or alongside is characteristic of Prospect's work, and many of the Prospect publications achieve this as well. Lynne Strieb's (1985) *A (Philadelphia) Teacher's Journal* allows us to have a close-up view of the life and work of a teacher over the course of an entire school year. From the first entry, we are brought right into the classroom: "What should you do when someone is talking to the group at class meeting? We had long discussion about behavior at meeting" (p. 7). As the year unfolds, we see not only what Strieb says and does, but also how she reflects on the children, their work, their conversation, their play, their relationships to one another, to her, to the curriculum, to ideas. The specificity of the journal is what places us, with Strieb, in the midst of the life of her class.

Strieb's (1985) *Journal* is also full of instances where she places herself alongside children. This is not a textbook on how to develop a curriculum out of children's interests or how to teach responsively, but in her writing and in her grounding in the particular, she makes ideas—such as the emergent curriculum—visible and imaginable. For example, the February 16 entry begins: "Belinda came in and said she'd had a terrible dream last night" (p. 46). Strieb goes on to note that other children begin talking about their nightmares. She recognizes the children's need to discuss this and opens the discussion:

> I asked if anyone had ever had a scary dream or nightmare.
>
> It was clear some of the children were uncomfortable talking about their dreams: *When I talk about it, it scares me again.* Belinda said what I was about to say, "My mom read in this book, *Child Behavior*, or something like that, that you should talk about your dreams. It will make you not so scared." "Well, that's just how *I* feel about it, Belinda. But my son Max once had a bad dream about a bear, and he refused to talk about it." I asked the children to raise their hands if they wanted to speak; told them that everyone would not have a turn; and if they did not want to, I would not force them. (p. 46)

This entry lets us see Strieb thinking on her feet: how she creates space for the children to explore their fears (both the dreams and their worries about retelling them), how she respects those who wish to talk and those who don't, and how she brings herself into the group not only as teacher but also as parent and person, with the story about her son. Later the children can choose to draw and write about their dreams, and Strieb joins them in this activity, drawing and writing about her own. The next day she is typing up the dreams and putting them into a binder so that they can become a class book.

These journal entries let us see that an idea like emergent curriculum can be small as well as big—that it is grounded in recognizing students and responding to them, not only in creating full-scale studies (though it can lead there). We are able to see Strieb's maternal response to the children, as well as her teacherly one. We are also shown how much the work of teaching is, for her, based in shared human experience: She's had nightmares, too, and knows the scary feeling. She feels that talking about your dreams can lessen the fear, but lets the children know that her son didn't want to talk about his dream. She gracefully provides children an opportunity to tell or not tell, leaving the choice up to each child.

Similarly, in a series of short articles, Alice Seletsky (1985, 1988, 1989, 1990) captures the quality of teaching as a work-in-progress and the complexities that characterize the classroom. In an article called "Where the Action Is," published in *The Nation*, Seletsky (1985) includes lengthy chunks from her teaching journal. A teacher's journal is a fairly raw record of the life of the class. Written for the teacher alone, written close in time to the events it recounts, it is a first sifting through the many events and encounters that fill a school day. The journal excerpts Seletsky cites bring us right into her classroom, a place where children can't do their homework, confuse odd numbers and primes, get angry when they "mess up" or when others spoil their work, plan a dramatization of *Bridge to Terabithia*, do "gorgeous" illustrations, and meet with Seletsky to edit their writing. The room seems a beehive of activity, all of it recognizable to anyone who teaches.

What stands out in Seletsky's writing is the *value* she places on this ordinary experience:

> There are moments just before the start of school when I wish the children didn't have to show up. The room is ready, with everything perfectly in place. . . . And along come the children, all 30–32 of them, with their own ideas, separate interests, and unique style of thinking and working. The path of learning, mine as well as theirs, grows rocky. There are all kinds of unexpected bumps and ruts. We turn a corner and a whole new vista opens up. (1988, p. 10)

The description that emerges is of a *real* classroom full of *real* children and a *real* teacher. Nothing rarefied here.

A QUESTIONING GAZE

Prospect writings are peppered with questions, always more questions than answers. Questions are raised to move thought along, but not in expectation of answer or solution. This distinguishes Prospect from much teacher education and writing, where questions are posed (in the worst cases, rhetorically) to be answered, where problems are presented to be solved. Prospect's standard is not about solution. It is about understanding. The assumption is that expanding understanding can lead to change: that, for instance, teachers can change things they do in their classrooms based on their growing understanding of a child or a group of children without looking at those children as "problems" to be solved.

Judy Buchanan's (1993) "Listening to Voices" documents the way in which a student's question leads her to a year-long inquiry into his writing. The story begins on the second day of school, when:

> Anwar [pseudonym], a fourth-grader, asked a question during math class that I noted, answered, and filed away to think more about later. *"There's just one thing. What exactly does p. mean?"* I had written an assignment on the board after a math lesson using the abbreviation for page, and Anwar was uncertain as to what to do. The question surprised me. Had I forgotten what most fourth-graders knew after being way from the classroom for a year? (p. 213)

Buchanan decides to focus on Anwar's writing in staff development work she is doing in her school. As the year progresses, she sees change in the way Anwar uses questions. As he develops friendships, he turns more to peers and asks fewer questions of teachers. A richer understanding of Anwar as a learner enables Buchanan to "see connections between Anwar's ability to observe the world around him . . . , his constant questioning, and his ability to reveal his thoughts and voice in his written work" (p. 218). She tells us that "he often seemed to have an urgent question about the texts he was reading" (p. 218). We see him questioning to create context for himself: reading biographies of Jackie Robinson and Willie Mays, then asking if they ever played against each other.

Studying Anwar's questions as part of his work leads Buchanan to questions of her own. She wonders how he approaches each writing assignment, whether he takes risks as a learner, and how much she should insist on revision and editing. These questions turn her back to her classroom, to take another look at Anwar, but also at the way she works with revision and editing with her whole class. In this way, a question that started with one student opens a broader inquiry into her teaching practice.

By year's end, Buchanan is able to see the progress Anwar has made as a writer. She has found new ways to support his learning *and* is "left with more questions to think about" (p. 220). She wonders how Anwar's questions helped him as a student, how she might develop structures that support students' questions, how she might support student dialogue given the fragmented nature of her school day. Her questions have enabled her to make changes in her teaching, changes that have been beneficial to Anwar. At the same time, they have given her a place for further thinking, in the way that questions with neat answers do not.

Betsy Wice, too, brings her interest in questions into a fifth-grade class she works with as a reading teacher. In her essay, "Questions" (1994), she describes how the students keep "I Wonder" or "Research" books, notebooks full of their questions and her responses. She helps individuals pursue their questions, and also notes themes running through the questions. In response to these themes, she arranges for trips, visitors, interviews, and other activities that foster investigation. The standard is not about finding answers to every question (some of which are, indeed, unanswerable) but about honoring students' genuine curiosities and about helping students use their own questions as springboards to inquiry.

This idea is elaborated in a full and thoughtful way in the Friends' Select Middle School Search Curriculum described by Cecelia Traugh (1989) in her paper "Creating Knowledge in a School Setting: A Story." This statement of the standards to which the students are held captures the way in which an interrogative attitude is valued:

> In topic selection, we look for real personal connection and interest (not for an easy or impressive topic). In the information-gathering process, we look for a variety of sources, and a certain adventurousness in finding them, for an on-going and connected quality in the pursuit of them (not a hodgepodge of facts, except early in the process), for a growing focus on what matters or is of interest or importance, for new or deeper questions or concerns. The Search Journal . . . should achieve one or more of these: a record of effort; a place to think things through on paper, a dialogue between student and teacher. The Narrative should show the personal connection to the topic. We look for a lively, interesting, informative, and honest story, one that goes beyond the writing-up of facts to the story of an understanding (and perhaps of new questions). (p. 13)

In these accounts we are able to see how the questioning stance that is so much at the heart of the collegial work of Prospect gets brought into work with students. The approach may vary somewhat, but value is always placed in *real* questions, those which matter to a person. There is trust in the power of questions to open inquiry and of persons to investigate their inquiries. Teaching, framed in this way, has much to do with guiding and participating in the process of inquiry.

THE DISCIPLINE OF WRITING

In the introduction to her *Journal*, Strieb (1985) writes:

> By November 1980, I realized how valuable the journal had become for my practice. The more I wrote, the more I observed in my classroom and the more I wanted to write. As I re-read my journal I got more ideas for teaching. I ex-

panded the journal to include other aspects of teaching—anecdotes, observations of children and their involvement in activities, interactions with parents both in and out of school, my plans, descriptions of the pressures on public school teachers. I also wrote about my continuing education through my own reflections and the questions that emerged, through books, and through association with colleagues in the Philadelphia Teachers' Learning Cooperative and at the Prospect Summer Institutes. (p. 3)

Though the body of writing associated with Prospect is often reflective of collaborative work, it shares with all writing a solitary dimension. Teachers who write write alone. Strieb gives us a glimpse of what the writing makes possible for her: more observation, teaching ideas, reflection, and questioning. Each writer would undoubtedly describe the value to him- or herself differently.

It is easy to get caught up in the busyness of classroom and school life. Keeping up with the workload and balancing the varied demands of the job can seem overwhelming at times. The work of Prospect is based in observing and describing. With so much going on, how can a teacher decide what to select, where to focus at any given point?

Writing provides a vehicle for teachers to stand back and reflect: to work on what is happening in their teaching lives; to see the shape of a month, a few months, or a year; to explore connections between their own work and trends and policies in the world of education.

In my own case, it was a question raised by educational researcher Ted Chittenden at a Prospect Science Symposium that prompted the first telling of a story. Later, at the urging of Prospect colleagues, I wrote it up as "An Over-Repeating Story" (Schwartz, 1987). Introducing the written version, I say: "In the telling, and later in the writing, I began to recognize themes and questions that had persisted through the year. Similarly, connections between those themes and questions and the curriculum came into clearer focus" (p. 12). The writing, done in solitude and spread out over time, gave me a way to look back at what had happened in my classroom and to think about practices I was trying to make sense of as a new teacher. I had watched the children draw connections between the life cycles of insects and the pattern and repetition in folktales, between wasps' nests and crystals. I was interested in the particulars of how this had unfolded in my classroom and also in the children's interest in big ideas about pattern and repetition.

At the same time, integrated units were all the rage in my district, the focus of much in-service training for teachers. I hadn't found that work exciting or helpful, and writing about what had transpired in my class that year gave me a new way to think about "units":

> There's a problem for me in defining curriculum in terms of units, even "inte-
> grated" units; it erodes the ease with which we gain access to the larger ideas
> by focusing our attention (and the children's) on *x* (e.g., insects) as distinct from
> *y* (e.g., crystals). A unit implies one, a thing that stands apart, on its own. An
> integrated unit seems to me a contradiction in terms.
>
> I see integration as a human activity rather than an attribute inherent in
> curricula or materials. (Schwartz, 1987, p. 20)

In that essay, I note that the possibility to see and nurture this sort of
integration is linked to providing time for children to move back and forth
among different kinds of work and for the teacher to see the connections
children are drawing. The spaciousness of time associated with the Prospect
work supports this kind of reflection. The willingness to spread out the work,
to look at it as terrain for exploration, invites further questioning.

TAKING A PUBLIC STANCE

Teachers who value human capacity and intimate knowledge and who take
a questioning stance in their classrooms often find themselves at odds with
the schools and systems in which they work. Andrias, Kanevsky, Strieb, &
Traugh (1992), in *Exploring Values and Standards: Implications for Assessment*, examine implications of Prospect's work for the national discussion
of standards. In Prospect's work, close knowing, grounded in relationship
and necessarily subjective, is valued rather than being discarded as biased.
Standards are assumed to rise out of values, rather than some objective value-
free world.

The national call for standards is rooted in quite different assumptions.
As Traugh writes in the introductory essay to this book, "A basic assumption [of the current discussion] is that only external standards can be public
and shared" (p. 3). In the monograph, teachers describe students in depth.
The knowledge gained from these descriptions is placed next to expectations
held by the students' schools and school systems. What emerges is a portrait
of youngsters and teachers negotiating territory that is often alien to their
values.

Lynne Strieb's (1992) essay in this book, "When A Teacher's Values Clash
With School Values: Documenting Children's Progress," describes the Student Progress Record Book required of teachers in all Priority One schoolwide
project schools in Philadelphia. These schools serve largely poor children.
Like all Philadelphia public school teachers, these teachers were also required
to follow a standardized curriculum. The Kafkaesque situation that results

would be funny were it not that real children were involved. Strieb cites an interview with a teacher:

> Math is my biggest pressure. . . . Often I get contradicting messages. "You're not on strand," the principal says, and I say, "Right, that's because my kids are having trouble understanding this." And the principal says, "That doesn't matter, you have to stay up with the curriculum." Then, two minutes later in the conference he'll say, "You have five kids flunking math. What are you going to do about that?" And I say, "That's why I stay in the strand until the kids know it." And he says, "No, you have to move on with the curriculum." (p. 14)

Strieb examines the records she is required to keep for reading and concludes that "a child learning to read gets lost in all of this. A teacher trying to teach gets lost in all of this, too" (p. 17). She keeps her own narrative records as a way of remembering "what the children do and how they do it and . . . what I do" (p. 17). She will not allow the children entrusted to her care to be reduced to numbers. She is aware that the official record is used "to monitor the progress of the children of parents who are poor and, in many cases, powerless" (p. 17). She knows that describing the children can make them visible, as Gabriel, Victoria, and Nile become visible in this book. An invisible person *is* discounted. By keeping her students visible, Strieb refuses to allow her own arena to be a place where students are rendered powerless. By going public—talking and writing about her students as persons—she takes this one step further.

Between 1986 and 1998 Anne Martin (1986, 1992, 1996, 1998) wrote four articles about kindergarten checklists. In reflecting back on her stance on reporting, she comments:

> For many years now . . . I refused to use the official checklist report forms and surreptitiously substituted narrative reports, figuring that probably nobody in the administration would know or care. This turned out to be more or less true. While my principal eventually found out, he didn't mind because my reports were sometimes helpful to him for parent conferences. So I probably would have continued on my deviant path unobtrusively if the administration had not handed down yet another version of the checklist. At that point, I was overcome with indignation at the implications of assessment by checklists that seemed to me not only trivial and superficial but potentially damaging to people's views of children and their learning. Over eleven years ago, and several more times since then, I felt compelled to speak up publicly to denounce checklist reporting and affirm the greater usefulness of narrative reports based on careful observation in the classroom. (Martin, 1998, p. 5)

Martin could have continued to quietly do her own thing. Through her actions she had created space for herself to report on students in a way that rings true to who they are and informs parents about their children's school lives. She made her voice public out of *indignation*: the indignity to children (even if she manages to exempt her own students) was too great for her to watch in silence.

For all its exploration of interiority, the work of Prospect often moves teachers to take a public stance. One could locate the roots of this publicness in a number of places, but I think that at core they stem from what Margaret Himley, in Chapter 6 of this volume, calls the *taproot value of the person"* (p. 131). The closeness to persons engendered by attentive observation, by the search for descriptive language, and by the withholding of judgment can move a teacher to act, speak, and write in the public arena when policies or actions taken in that arena threaten children and teachers by making them unrecognizable as the persons they are. Teachers in the Prospect network have found over and over again that disciplined description brings students' and teachers' capacities to light and develops language in which to talk about them. Faced with school practices that render students' and teachers' capacities invisible and with language that restricts "thinkable thought" about students, teaching, and learning, many of the teachers in the Prospect network have turned to writing as a way of advocating for their students and for teaching practice that will recognize and foster human capacity, widely distributed.

PART III

USING DESCRIPTIVE INQUIRY IN SCHOOL SETTINGS

We turn now to the third and last descriptive review. This review took place as part of the ongoing work of a group of middle and high school teachers who were interested in questions about adolescents and reading. Nile is a 13-year-old boy attending an alternative high school in New York City. Kiran Chaudhuri, his teacher, is a member of the Prospect board and a participant in summer institutes. She has worked with Cecelia Traugh, who chaired this session, over many years. As a result of their close collaboration, they did not meet for a planning session. In this review, the questions and recommendations stage is a particularly strong and important part of the process. In that dialogue, which is quite extended, the participating teachers grapple with difficult issues—among them, how to include and evaluate what a child learns and knows from contexts other than the classroom and how to distinguish what Kiran calls "studenting" from thinking and learning that is self-directed. Kiran's "Afterthoughts" mirror the range and depth of the dialogue, reflecting how much she learned from the process of the review itself—as the other teachers surely did also.

The essays that follow illustrate how descriptive processes and collaborative oral inquiry can play an important role in the context of schools and programs. In Chapter 9 Cecelia Traugh describes how she works with the whole staff of a school to better understand how a school's values are (and are not) enacted in its practices. She recounts the work she did over a year with the staff of Neighborhood School in New York City, as they traced how the idea/value of heterogeneity played out in all sorts of complex ways in their daily lives. She demonstrates the value of descriptive work in whole-school settings.

In Chapter 10, Margaret Himley, too, demonstrates the value—and the values—of collaborative oral inquiry by recounting the story of a group of writing teachers at Syracuse University striving to understand more fully, more clearly, how questions of "the political" (or power) played out in their classrooms. She argues for the democratic potential of oral inquiry and for the value/s of small changes produced by careful attention and vigilance.

CHAPTER 8

NILE

I AM PROUD OF MY CULTURE BECAUSE

I HAVE THE DEEPEST CULTURE IN THE WORLD I AM WEST INDIAN AMERICAN:

MY PEOPLE WERE BRUTALLY ENSLAVED AND KILLED OVER SOMEONE ELSES WANTS. THOSE WHO WERE FREED FROM THE HANDS OF SLAVERY WERE PROMISED EQUAL OPPORTUNITY. WE GOT THAT AT THE SAME TIME WE ELECTED A BLACK PRESIDENT. WE AS A PEOPLE WERE FORCED TO LIVE THAT AMERICAN NIGHTMARE, AND ALMOST ALWAYS DONE IN BY MY DEVILISH UNCLE SAM. IT'S AN HONOR TO KNOW WE RISED ABOVE THIS.

FROM MY AMERICAN BACKGROUND I GAINED THE ABILITY TO BRING HOSTILITY TO WHEREVER I GO.

FIGURE 8.1. I am Proud of My Culture, by Nile.

 ISBN 0-8077-3931-6 (paper), ISBN 0-8077-3932-4 (cloth).

CONTEXT

Cecelia Traugh

"What can we do when our students can't read?" This was a question some teachers in New York City Writing Project courses were asking more and more frequently. Often asked in a tone that implied the answer "Not much," the question expressed strongly felt frustration. Asked to increase the rigor of the work they do with students and, thus, to raise the test scores of their schools, teachers can respond in anger at students they see as struggling and "behind."

In the fall of 1996, when the director of the New York City Writing Project, Linette Moorman, and I were talking about the question and the issues it raised, we wondered together what the question really meant in terms of adolescents' reading. What did "can't read" mean for high school students? How were the teachers of adolescents who struggled as learners in school working with these students as readers? What does it mean to be a reader, anyway? We both wondered what we, with a small group of teachers, could learn about these questions and others through an inquiry using the Prospect descriptive processes.

Linette gathered the group together. We were professional development people from the Institute for Literacy Studies, which is the home of the New York City Writing Project, as well as teachers from small high schools in the Bronx and Manhattan and a new middle school in the Washington Heights area of Manhattan. We had a range of experience with adolescents: as parents, as new and experienced middle and high school teachers, as a middle school director, and as a person with a master's degree in reading whose current work is with community organizations. The people who joined the group were interested in adolescents, in reading, and in exploring what could be learned about literacy learning through the use of descriptive processes, particularly the Description of Work and the Descriptive Review of the Child. When this review occurred, the group had been meeting monthly for a year. At our meetings, our numbers ranged from four to ten.

In addition to Kiran Chaudhuri (the presenting teacher) and me (the chair of the review), there were seven of us at Nile's review: Paul Allison, a teacher for fifteen years, twelve of them at University Heights Secondary School in the Bronx, an active participant in the New York City Writing Project and Nile's teacher for his Service course; Elaine Avidon, co-director of the Elementary Teachers Network, a program at the Institute for Literacy Studies, and the teacher-consultant working one day a week in the Community Service Academy, a new middle school in Washington Heights; Marty Gensemer-Ramirez, a sixth-grade teacher who has taught for seven years, three at

Community Service Academy; Rick Levine, a founding teacher of Fanny Lou Hamer High School in the Bronx (a school with purposes and practices similar to those of University Heights), who came to that work after 15 years at Kennedy High School in the Bronx; Judith Scott, an educator for 26 years, most recently an assistant principal at The School for the Physical City and director of the Schomberg Satellite Academy in the Bronx; Lena Townsend, an adult educator with a deep interest and expertise in reading, who currently works chiefly with community organizations interested in literacy programs; and Linda Vereline, a middle school teacher, who currently works as a professional developer in middle schools across the city of New York.

The content of our inquiry had been drawn primarily from the work of the classroom teachers of the group. Many of our meetings focused on descriptions of student work, primarily the various forms of writing students had done alongside reading they were doing. This work ranged from double-entry journal entries to formal essays. We looked closely at the assignments we frame for students. One teacher presented a review of the work she was doing with an individual student around reading. In response to questions we began to have about reading difficult texts, we brought in for close description texts we ourselves found difficult to read and understand. And we did a close reading of Toni Morrison's (1997) lecture and acceptance speech upon receiving the Nobel Prize, because of all the important ideas about language she lays out.

As we worked together, the group became interested in thinking about the process of reading as experienced by an individual adolescent. Kiran and Paul volunteered to do a review of Nile, a young man they both taught who could read but wasn't reading, at least not for school. The question they brought to the review centered on how to help him take more interest in the content of the school's curriculum so that he would do the reading and writing work necessary for moving through the program.

When she presented this review in March 1997, Kiran was in her fifth year of teaching. During her tenure at University Heights Secondary School, she had primarily taught the older students in the school. Nile was one of the youngest students she had taught. Kiran's teaching area is Humanities, and during the year of this review the curriculum consisted of studies of how African Americans and Latinos had gained power in the city of New York and of the Harlem Renaissance. The first hour of each day is spent in Family Group, where there is talk about things that are going on in group members' lives and work. For the remainder of the day, each teacher and his or her Family Group are paired with one or two other Family Groups, forming a seminar. So Nile, the subject of this review, had Kiran's colleague, Lee, as his teacher of Math, Science, and Technology, and two other teachers for short periods each week for Service and Health.

Prior to teaching, Kiran had worked with community-based adult literacy programs. She student-taught in a middle school and helped to open a new middle school within University Heights. Kiran is experienced with descriptive process. In 1995–1996, she and I had co-led a year-long project that centered on helping interested teachers from small Bronx high schools learn and practice descriptive process. Given our extensive experience together, we did not do a planning session before the review. Judith Scott and Rick Levine, two of the reading study group's members, had been participants in this project.

DESCRIPTIVE REVIEW OF THE CHILD

Kiran Chaudhuri

Participants

Paul Allison
Elaine Avidon
Kiran Chaudhuri
Marty Gensemer-Ramirez
Rick Levine
Judith Scott
Lena Townsend
Cecelia Traugh
Linda Vereline

Focusing Question

"How can we identify Nile's learning strengths, so that he might come to value formal school learning more?"

Background

Cecelia: We're doing this descriptive review in the context of our beginning to think about high school students and reading, or adolescents and reading. We're trying to explore a variety of ways of getting an understanding, a direct understanding, of what some of those reading issues are with the students we work with. So Kiran and Paul have agreed to bring us a student they share. Kiran is going to present the descriptive review, and Paul will add in. We will all have the chance to ask questions.

The focusing question is about helping Nile see what his learning strengths are in a way that could help him come to value more what formal school learning is and how it can serve him. So, we are listening here now for those pieces that connect for us around what his learning strengths are, and then thinking more particularly about formal, disciplined learning—school learning, reading, writing—those categories of learning.

The way the process will work is that Kiran will do the description, which Paul will supplement. I will review the main threads of the description. Then there will be a time for questions. Keep track here of things that you want to ask Kiran and Paul for more information about. I'll do a brief pulling together of the new content, and then we'll make recommendations and responses to the focus question.

History

Kiran: I'll start with some basic information, to introduce you to Nile, who is 13 years old. He lives with his mother; his sister, who's 19; and his sister's daughter, who's 10 months old. He sees his older brothers, who are 28 and 30, and their wives, about twice a week. He and they talk on the phone on days when they don't see each other. His father lives in Queens, and Nile goes to visit him. He sees his grandmother several times a week. English is the home language.

Physical Presence and Gesture

Nile is a light-skinned person of mixed heritage—West Indian and Jewish—which is important to him. His complexion is even and clear of blemishes. He's large-boned and broad-chested, with an athletic build. He informed me when I asked a couple of days ago that he's 5 feet 7½ inches tall. And he has, I've noticed, grown taller since September. Nile smiles a lot. When he shambles into the middle of Family Group, dragging his bookbag, he'll be smiling. He has brown eyes that dance when he smiles. In repose, he'll often cock his head to one side, his eyes narrowed, focusing on an invisible point in the room. He comes roughly 25 minutes late to Family Group, which is a kind of advisory group where we talk about things going on in people's lives. As the Family Group teacher, I'm responsible for keeping track of the students' progress through school. And he comes in roughly 10 minutes late to both the 10:15 and the 1:00 P.M. seminar meetings. Although he comes late to school, he also stays late after school, playing football out front.

At times he'll initiate side conversations in the middle of a whole-group discussion or when I'm giving directions. Sometimes he's talking to himself with a smile, chuckling, head shaking, eyes downward, which means he may not see others looking at him. He sometimes gets carried away with playful banter back and forth with one or two of his classmates, even when another classmate is trying to be heard. I'll stop and wait. And finally, Rachel [pseudonym] or Ann [pseudonym] or another student will yell something like, "Be quiet," and he'll stop talking for the moment.

Once, play-fighting with a boy at lunch, it got out of hand. I met with Nile, his mother, and our school social worker to discuss his ability to control his behavior and to know his own strength. He agreed to stop play-fighting at school and has pretty much managed to keep this agreement since. His mom and he talked at that meeting about how he needs to draw a line between home and school when it comes to play-fighting. They talked about how they wrestle, and how she notices that he sometimes forgets his own strength with her. He also wrestles his older brothers, who are 28 and 30 years old, and sometimes he wins. He recommended for himself that he play more football. This was his recommendation at the end of the meeting, so as to become better at knowing his own weight and his own strength.

Nile does not always involve himself in the whole group in Humanities. Often he insists on sitting outside the circle at a table by a window at the far corner of the room. The Monday after I talked with his mom about this, he started out sitting outside the circle, but then, as we got into an interesting discussion about the movie we had all just gone to see, *Rosewood*, he moved in and sat right at the table to make his point at the discussion.

Disposition and Temperament

I'll start with the story of Nile's response to the ban on Walkmen we had to institute as a class. At first, he could not agree to comply with the new ban. He insisted on wearing his headphones around his neck. Since we have talked to him about it in private, however, he sometimes puts his Walkman away as he's entering the room—not consistently, but there are moments when he decides to do that. He internalizes rules, given a good reason and his own decision to do so.

Several men on staff have described how Nile jumped into relationship with them with an "I can deck you" brashness. And then, after a while, they would sense something change in their relationship with him. They would find him much more affectionate with them. I saw him go up to Steve, and say, "Steve, go like this. You know, put your arms up, out, away from your body." Steve kids, "I don't know if I should, Nile. What are you going to do to me?" Then Nile butts right into him, so they bounce. And Steve smiles. Nile has won the affection of many people on staff. I often see Deborah, our principal, and Benoni, another teacher, smile when they see him coming. And I've seen him respond to Deborah by making himself welcome in her chair in her office.

He's playful in a competitive way. He likes to compete in chess, football, basketball, track, verbal repartee, and Monday morning quarterbacking on NFL games during Family Group. Paul, can I quote from you? Paul wrote in his January report: "Nile has enjoyed the occasional challenge to race around the track with me. He always won." He is most engaged when he's competing.

He wanted to leave the middle school in September, but his mother and the director of our middle school felt that, at 13, he might be too young to succeed in the high school. By October, he had expressed his desire to be in the high school so strongly, and sometimes disruptively, that they did transfer him.

Nile has strong likes and dislikes which he is open and up-front about. At one point, he insisted on something like, "No, I'm studying the Black Panthers, not the Young Lords *and* the Panthers. The Young Lords were pussies. They just bit off the Panthers."

He refused to accept David Lamb's [1994] book *Do Platanos Go Wit' Collard Greens?* from me. We were kicking off our reading of the book in class by reading aloud the first chapter. This was going to be a whole-class text. Before we started, I asked students to write an initial entry responding to the title and the book jacket. After we read, I asked students to pick one of the prompts on our reading-log prompt sheet to use in responding to the text. At the top of that sheet was our essential question for the cycle: "How have African Americans and Latinos struggled to gain power in New York City?" Nile said he thought the book was stupid and sat away from the circle, by the window, for the duration of the class.

On Fridays, Lee and I use Family Group time for open work time. Lee is my partner teacher. So my Family Group doesn't meet in our little room, but instead comes into our big classroom to use the computers and to do work at the tables. At 10:00 everybody goes to the gym class they've chosen. Sometimes there are hitches. For example, in January, we had one of the four assessment weeks of the year, which involves students presenting portfolios of the work they have completed at what are called "round tables." On the Friday of that week, we thought we didn't have enough personnel free from round tables to run gym. So we canceled gym. When Nile found out that there was no Family Group and no track class, he said, "No, you're not saying this. You can't be saying this. The two things I like in school you're canceling? I'm going home." I was relieved when, soon after, Benoni announced that he was after all available to open up the gym and run basketball. I told Nile, and he went right over.

Speaking about Nile, several teachers have described how he reminds them of a bear cub or a puppy. He's testing and searching to know things by pushing up against what's around him, physically in play fighting and in football, intellectually in taking all of his opponents' pieces in chess, initiating verbal repartee, using the Internet, asking challenging questions.

Connections with Other People

He does this pushing-up against his environment in his connections with other people also. He does it by being up-front about his strong likes and dislikes of people. He'll share "I don't like her" or "I like him" about teachers. He liked Yolanda [pseudonym], who was the one girl in our seminar of 44 kids who was younger than 15. He mentioned that he went out with her for two weeks in October. At one point in October, he disliked Marcus [pseudonym], a 15-year-old boy in the class, so much that he was moved to make fun of him in snide comments in class. When I took him aside, he said it was because Marcus "didn't know how to act." Two months later, Nile joined Marcus's a capella group to prepare an act for the talent show.

He's mildly competitive with his cousin. Nile's mother wanted him transferred into my class. She knew her nephew was already there. At one point, Nile's and his cousin's families went to North Carolina, so they came into school after a few days of not having been there. And when Nile heard his cousin had come in the first day that they got back, he said, "Oh, he came in? He's always trying to prove that he's better than me. I went over to his house to see whether he was going to school yesterday, and he said he wasn't going. And I said I was going. But then I didn't. So he had to come."

Nile became something of a leader in his second year in the middle school as an eighth-grader. He would field questions that classmates had. There was one time when he noticed that all the girls were on one side and all the boys were on the other. And he tried to get the two sides together by sharing this observation. That time and a few other times he joined the girls' side to demonstrate that the class could change the mix if they wanted to.

Paul wrote in his January report: "I've sensed that Nile has been working his way out of the class clown stereotype that he has fallen into. In Passages class, a class designed to support students as they deal with transitions and boundary setting, he can be acting the fool or acting out one minute and the leader the next. He has grown to show me respect, and he respects his peers when they suggest something. One experience that shows this growth was when we did an initiative called 'Turn Over a New Leaf.' During the initiative, Nile was full of good ideas, but the class wouldn't or couldn't listen to him, partly because he wasn't clear and partly because they weren't taking him seriously. In the debrief after this initiative, the other students were able to say to Nile that they wanted him to be more serious in class because he has a lot to offer."

I'm talking about connections with other people here, with Yolanda, with Marcus, with his cousin, with his middle school class, with his Passages class, which Paul teaches. And with Tom [pseudonym] and Rick [pseudonym], both seniors. They often stop by, peeking in, looking to tell Nile that they're staying after school to play football and to make sure that he has his equipment and that he's going to be there.

Strong Interests and Preferences

As far as strong interests and preferences go, football is big for Nile. He plays for the Abyssinian Baptist Church, and he plays in our school's informal scrimmage group out front with those seniors and some other boys. Another interest is the rapper KRS-ONE's songs. He has them memorized, and he sings them. Rhyming is another interest of his. He has two rhyme books that he writes in at home. He does some writing in them at school. He was rather shy about showing them, but he did with one of my student teachers, and then he showed them to me after about a month and a half of being with us in the high school. Yet another interest is the Black Panthers. His interest in the Black Panthers moved me to listen for other interest in the class as a whole regarding the Black Panthers, and to start building curriculum that would flow from that interest. Both KRS-ONE and the Black Panthers have strong expressions of what is just and unjust.

Chess is another interest of his. He was able to teach other students how to play. He gave Lee, who teaches the chess class, suggestions for how a tournament should be set up. There was room for even more leadership: Lee asked him if he would run the class with her. But he was quite involved in playing chess. He entered several tournaments outside of school on weekends, and he came in twice on Monday morning, reporting that he'd won.

Modes of Thinking and Learning

I'll tell you the story of his response to one of my proposals for his learning. I brought in Pedro Pietri's poem "Puerto Rican Obituary," hoping to get the idea out that writing poetry can be a political act. I encouraged Nile to make his final exhibition a "teach-in" on how to write political poetry and to model for us by writing a political rhyme about the Panthers. I thought about showing him Roberto's [pseudonym] rhyme about the Vietnam War, but I was apprehensive that he would perceive this as an affront to his originality. I wanted to help him shape the prompt for himself. At the end of that project I didn't feel successful. I did not feel that I had done that.

In his room at home, according to his mom, Nile reads and writes about whatever he is investigating at the moment. He writes rhymes. He's different from students who think of their education as happening only in connection with the class. He looks things up on the Internet at his branch library. Nile passed all his New York State Regents Competency Tests (RCTs), including math and science, as well as Sequential One mathematics, last year. These are minimum-competency tests for high school graduation. And he did that before he got to high school. In our interactive mathematics program, I worked with him on "Demosthenes' Puzzle," the one where the man has spent a fourth of his life as a child, a fifth of his life in his dotage, and so forth, and you have to figure out how old he is. Nile relished that. However, he did not do enough work in Math, Science, and Technology (MST) this cycle for Lee, his math teacher, to feel that she could assess what he'd learned.

Nile challenged his chess teachers, Lee and another teacher, that he could beat them. They let him know they doubted that. He was surprised and deflated when Lee beat him. "I can't believe she beat me," he said. Nile told Howard (the school psychologist) that it was his dad who taught him chess and that his dad had shown him how to remove his opponent's pieces off the board, and then use the end-game to win.

Nile is precise with language. One example is a connection that he noted on a Post-it when examining the timeline the class had assembled on the Harlem Renaissance. He wrote, "Malcolm X's birthday, 1925. 1920 the Klan grew. It's ironic that the black-hating union was born the same time as the white-hater." Another time he showed his precision with language was when I called a quick conflict resolution for him and Rachel after Family Group. Both stayed and were quite reasonable. He summed up the conflict at the end of our small mediation with just a brief well-worded statement that left us reassured.

Nile wanted information on the Black Panthers. I suggested that he talk to Phil, our colleague who is a long-time activist, and he did. Phil had a pamphlet on the Black Panthers, which he gave Nile. The funny thing was that Nile would keep leaving it behind, for days, so whatever computer he had been working at, the pamphlet would be there.

On one occasion when I got a chance to talk casually with Nile, I asked him why he so often sits outside the circle, observing but not participating. He said he was bored. When I asked what interested him, he said that he likes to write rhymes. He began telling me all about KRS-ONE and about the book he was reading, *The Science of Rap*. I suggested he bring it in to read for independent reading time, and he did do that a couple of times.

Cecelia: Paul, why don't you add in here?

Paul: I'll start backwards. Just yesterday, the school psychologist told me how much he appreciated working with Nile. He quickly said to me, "I know I don't have to deal with all that group stuff he gets involved in, but it's amazing to work with him. He's wonderful to work with." Last week, Nile came down to the principal's office (I happened to be there at the time), and he said something like "They want me to go into therapy" or "They want me to go talk to Howard." And he was upset. We tried to figure out why he was upset, saying, "You know, we see Howard, too. We see Howard." (*laughter*) And he said, "No, no. I'm not upset about that. I love therapy. I'm just upset that they're not coming more directly and telling me that I need this right now." I don't know why I am telling that story, but it feels like there is something about his individual attachments to teachers and other adults in the building that is very important to him.

At the end of the track class and the Passages class that I teach, we always do some writing, some reflecting on the experience. He rarely does it. If he does, it's short and to the point. He doesn't really want to do it.

Something also—I don't know if it's important or not—his family has been in our school almost from the beginning of our school. And he sometimes refers to his cousins, to their memory of me and others in the school at the time they were there. That feels important to him. He has a real connection to the school.

Once in Passages, when we were talking about getting jobs or needing jobs and about the importance of jobs, he described a job that he had. Everybody was surprised that he had one, because he is younger than they are. He described a job that he has where he works putting labels on demo tapes for a recording studio. It's connected with his family again, with his brother-in-law. People were impressed that he was in that. He referred to somebody, some rap star, I think, who had been there, at the office where he did his work. I'm sure there are other things, but. . . .

Integrative Restatement by the Chair

Cecelia: Okay, let me pull this together briefly, and then we'll open it to informational questions.

Kiran began by describing Nile's family, and she described the expanded nature of it: There's a lot of contact with family. Paul added in a piece about the family having been in the school for many years and that that family connection feels important to Nile.

I began to get really interested in this thread of home and school alongside each other. I first picked this up when Kiran was describing the line that needed to be drawn between his play-fighting at home and at school, that line between what's okay behavior-wise at home and school. This became a thread all the way through in terms of the reading and writing his mother says he does at home and what he does, and doesn't do, at school. With the play-fighting, home and school are at first blended, and Nile has to learn to differentiate between them. In terms of using reading and writing to pursue interests, home seems to be the setting where he sees this as possible. He seems to use the school context for other purposes.

Also there's the idea that, in the particular incident of the play-fighting, he made a recommendation to himself. He also had recommendations in that "Turn Over a New Leaf" game. He made a lot of recommendations to other people, to the class, to the group. Kiran said they didn't pay so much attention to them, but he had a lot of things he would recommend. The idea of thinking about what a recommendation is, or a suggestion, is an interesting thing. Not everybody thinks in those terms, but he was recommending things to himself, to other people. And just to add on to that, another thing that Kiran said was about his internalizing rules when he sees a reason for it. I think those may be connected as a mode of thinking.

Kiran made a point in a couple of different places about how he usually starts away from the table, and then moves in to the table. He'll move in if he's really interested, but when asked about why he stays apart from the table, he'll use that word *bored*.

In terms of relationships with adults, Kiran described how he established contact with adult men physically, and that by and large those relationships with adults in the school seemed relatively positive, playful. Paul added that Nile was not upset about talking to the school psychologist; he just wished that the teachers had been more direct, that he felt they could just have said it directly.

Nile has strong preferences, and he plays those out. Kiran described his acting on those strong preferences in a couple of several different ways. One, in a study, he will do this, not that, because that isn't part of this. Like the Black Panthers and the Young Lords: He felt the Young Lords did not meet the quality of the Black Panthers and were not worthy of study. He will act on a preference. I don't know what happened in the whole-group book reading, but what Kiran did describe was that initially he acted on his preference. He refused. That was an action. He refused the book. And then a third way that he acts on his preferences, preferences for people, is he will say openly whom he likes and whom he doesn't.

I got the picture of a youngster who knows a lot of people in the school. I mean, he's young, but he knows seniors to play football with, and he knows teachers. He has talking relationships with many adults around the place, he is sitting in the principal's office, sometimes chatting, and now he has a relationship with the school psychologist.

And then there's quite a list of interests, some of them coming together around the idea of justice.

Then there is this attention-getting behavior. He passes his tests, but he doesn't do the work that he needs to do to pass a class.

RESPONSE: QUESTIONS AND RECOMMENDATIONS

Cecelia: This next round is to ask for more information, and we have two sources here, so the questions can be answered by either Paul or Kiran or both. And these are informational questions, ones you ask because you want more information about this young man.

Rick: I'm not sure whether this question is appropriate or not. What I still don't know is what makes Kiran think he doesn't value formal school learning.

Kiran: Because of his ability to play the role of a student. The "studenting" that he does is minimal. He comes late to class. He isn't willing to investigate something that doesn't immediately strike his interest, although he will linger with something that does, and he will tussle with a math problem. But he's not interested in the wall chart with stars I resorted to doing this this year. But Nile has no need for the chart. He doesn't even look at it.

Paul: He doesn't finish projects. It doesn't seem like he finishes things. This may be going too far, but it's almost like Nile learns from the hidden curriculum schools have. I'm not sure he learns from the up-front curriculum. It's funny. He really plays the school well. He never read *Do Platanos Go Wit' Collard Greens?* [Lamb, 1994], right? He never read the book. There are a lot of things he doesn't follow through on. He doesn't do the work that's expected.

Kiran: He doesn't make himself open to things that he might not other-wise. . . . There's a certain amount of open-mindedness that you need in order to get a formal education.

Paul: There's also a lack of connection with his peers that I would define as a lack of formal learning. Like in discussions in class, he's not there.

Cecelia: That kind of connection, not social connection?

Paul: Yeah, social connections are absolutely there, but not a connection in intellectual conversation.

Linda: When he's in Math, Science, and Technology, what is he doing? I mean, if he's not doing the work, or he's not reading the book, what does he choose to do?

Kiran: If we're having a whole-group discussion in Humanities, and he's at the edge of the room by the window, he'll be observing the whole thing. He sits in a place where he has a vantage point, and he observes and listens. In Math, Science, and Technology [MST], he may attack the problem. But then he diverges into conversation with a classmate that's not intellectual conversation about the problem at all. He is not concerned with completing the problem or taking it further or going deeper or turning anything in.

Paul: In one class, he also throws things at other kids.

Linda: Do people talk to him about—I don't know what to call it— "doing school"? How does he react to the "doing school" speech? Does that conversation go on? I mean, you've spoken about this some by saying that if the chart's up there with the stars, he does not even notice it. But what would be his sense if you said to him "Why are you in school?" What would his answer be? What would he say about why one comes to school? Or why he, in particular, comes to school?

Kiran: He might answer, "'Cause I want to." His mom just read him the riot act. It's the second week in a row that this happened at home. She shared that with me on the phone. And I had a conversation with him about it. One example is yesterday. I said at the end of class, "Nile, I understand that you want to get a list of the work that we've done that we need for you to pass in." And he said, "Ah, yeah." And I said, "It's on the wall chart. So go on, take a look at it. Choose some things you're going to do over the weekend." He said, "Well, I'm going to do MST tonight. I'm going to do something for MST tonight, and tomorrow I'll do something else. I'll do one a day." He has a plan. But there are 17 assignments that he hasn't done, and that's just in MST.

Elaine: In that project that you set up with him that was around his interest—the poetry writing and teaching of the class—I was wondering why you said, Kiran, that it wasn't successful.

Kiran: Well, I wasn't successful in helping him to negotiate the curriculum for himself. I felt like I didn't know how to help him to say, "You mean, I could do that? Okay. I'll do that."

Elaine: What I was asking within that question is, "Where are the places where something that you have suggested *has* worked?"

Kiran: Well, I said the gym is open.

Elaine: Where are the places within formal learning. Are there any places within formal learning?

Kiran: That *is* important, though. I mean, he's an athlete. But, okay, you mean, where are the places in his formal learning where he's taken suggestion?

Elaine: Yeah. Are there any places that you can remember where he's been outside the circle and he's come in? And what's been the role of the teacher in that, if any at all?

Kiran: Okay. Well, with the *Rosewood* discussion, everyone else was in the circle, and I looked at him, raised my eyebrows. Then he at least turned toward the circle, and I allowed him to be there [away from the table, at the back of the classroom]. Then we got into a discussion that he felt he wanted to be part of, and he came to the table. I proceeded, hands off, with an acceptance of his stance and of how he learns. I think that was part of what I was doing that enabled him to come to the table and start talking. But I don't think he's not learning when he's observing the whole thing.

And then he did decide, "I'm going to do a project on the Black Panthers." That was what he wanted to do, and I built the curriculum around his idea, so everyone could learn about them. At another point, he wanted to borrow the film *Palante! Siempre Palante!* [Morales, 1996] to see with his mother. She was in the Young Lords at one point. So if you allow him the space to make his own decision about when he's going to take, when he's going to grab this or grab that, he will.

Paul: The times that I've experienced the most of Nile coming forward are times about identity, like when we talk about the topic of religion, which is very important to him. His beliefs—or the lack of them—are very different from many of the other students. His description of that has been important to him. Also his identity—who he is, what his father is, what his mother is, what his cousins are—that's all sort of important. There are moments when he's really there and connected around that stuff.

Kiran: Several of my students last semester did cover letter sections on basketball and intramural basketball, and on being on the varsity basketball team, and on softball. He knows that they did this. Because he's an athlete, and he talks about being an athlete and how important football is, especially, for his well-being, I wonder what it is that makes him say, "Well, I'm going to do this for a project. I'm going to turn this into something formal, to assess myself on my football."

Judith: You know, I'm looking and I keep thinking, he's 13, and he's a boy. This kid seems to be enormously active. And the things that he's active in are physical, boastful, competitive. They involve space and physical challenge, face-to-face challenge, and they are very spatial. Football is an understanding of where everyone's supposed to be at any time and what the different plays are. When you're playing football, it's "boom." Chess is face-to-face competition, "boom, boom, boom." Rapping and rhyming, it's face-to-face boasting. He's 13, and he's taking on adult men in these areas, which takes an enormous amount of time and energy, and he's doing that. He's working through this.

He's working out what it is it to be a Black man, as if he's saying, "I'm taking Black men on and I'm feeling comfortable doing it. So what's all this other stuff that people are asking me to do?" I mean that very literally. What are you asking him to do? He's 13. What does that mean to him—"Reflect on what you're doing"? The things that we're asking him, what do they mean in his head? And I'm wondering, at 13, if those other kinds of questions make sense yet? You know, like the questions about *Rosewood*, the questions that happen in high school Family Groups. If they make sense to him yet, in a very bottom-line kind of way.

I know when I was teaching first-semester ninth-graders, what I was discussing in the senior class just didn't make sense to them in a lot of ways. He's taking on the world. How does this other stuff translate to him? Does he see what it is and why it is?

Cecelia: These are on the edge of being recommendations. You have a question, Marty?

Marty: I was just wondering more about the move from middle school to high school. It takes off from what you were saying, Judith. I don't know what he was doing before, but what was it that actually convinced people that moving him was the right thing to do for him?

Kiran: I don't know.

Marty: This is not one school, right?

Paul: It is one.

Marty: Oh, it is one school.

Kiran: What I do know is that he had completed all of what it takes to get into the high school and that the middle school didn't know how to serve him. They could have changed their curriculum and their assessment to be more challenging for him, but he was very sure. He *knew* that he was ready.

Linda: Do you know if he was doing his work before?

Paul: We don't know the details. He was doing well. I don't know if we'd say that's changed a lot now. I don't know. I guess we would. Has he changed? Maybe. Maybe not.

Kiran: I've heard people say that he's changed a lot. But if there was a feeling in the middle school that we can't quite serve him, we don't know how to work with him, and if there's a feeling on my part that there's something I don't get about working with a 13-year-old, then right now our school is having kids who are making the transition fall through the cracks.

Cecelia: That's interesting. Do you have a question, Lena?

Lena: I have a few. I'm not sure how they're related to each other though. One is, Kiran, you said that when he's out of school, that he reads and writes. He uses the Internet at the library. He does all those kinds of things. Then what does he read and write about? And what is he using the Internet for? Is he doing his own informal projects on things he's interested in? What's going on there? Do you know?

Kiran: I need to find out more. I know he used the Internet when he looked up the Young Lords. That was before he decided that he wasn't interested in them. There was a shift in his thinking about them. So he did learn about them. He did take in a lot of information.

Lena: And in terms of learning about the Black Panthers, where did he go beyond the pamphlet that someone gave him? How did he move beyond? What is he doing?

Kiran: Nothing that I know of. So that's on me to help him pursue that interest, even as we move into working on the Harlem Renaissance. And there are a lot of ties. In fact, for Nile, I could imagine him tying KRS-ONE and the Black Panthers and certain people or events in the Harlem Renaissance that interested him all together. He could do a summing up, a connections piece. He's really good at making connections. He's very to-the-point.

Lena: And academically, it sounds like you're not saying that he is having difficulty. I imagined when you first started talking about him that this was going to be someone who was having difficulties with literacy and reading, since this is a group discussing that and we have talked previously about people who were having difficulty. So I thought that this was going to be someone who was having difficulty reading, but it doesn't sound like that's the case. It sounds like even though he doesn't do the projects, the school kinds of things, he *can* do them. He has the potential to be able to do them. Is that true?

Kiran: Yeah. There's something hidden about Nile, for me, at least. It's difficult to find out what he's reading—

Lena: —but you do see him read something? He does read?

Kiran: He responds to anything he reads. He forms a response to anything he reads, and to most math problems he encounters.

Elaine: I'm just curious about his social relationships, not with the older kids but among peers in the high school.

Paul: Peers in the high school or middle school?

Elaine: High school.

Paul: He has them in both places.

Elaine: Yeah, but I think my interest is in where he's located now, with kids who are in the same space, whom he sees regularly.

Kiran: Well, Marcus is 15, two years older than him. And he joined Marcus's singing group, but then he became irritated with him and left it. He likes Yolanda, the one girl who's closer to his age and who he says he "went out" with for two weeks.

Paul: I see him connecting more with Janet [pseudonym], her sister, who's two years older than Yolanda.

Kiran: That's true.

Paul: So my impression is that he does much better with older students, in connecting socially. With students his age, it doesn't work out so well. I'm not sure why.

Elaine: That time when he made those recommendations and the kids didn't take him seriously, and then afterwards you did some kind of process talk around that, and they said to him that he should be more serious—do you have any sense of his response to that? What happened around that for him?

Paul: I think he blew it off and said it was my fault that they hadn't listened to him because of how I had posed the directions. It might have been.

Kiran: I have a question.

Cecelia: Okay.

Kiran: What does a person who's entering high school and who's 13 need to learn? And why does it feel like I would have to have separate and different expectations for him, for the 13-year-olds, compared to everybody who's 14 and above? And how can I make my curriculum and my expectations so that it doesn't feel separate, so that my projects are more multilevel, so that the expectations are more seamless?

Judith: My question is like that.

Kiran: How do we make the curriculum more inclusive of 13-year-olds?

Judith: Because it's not only about curriculum but about engagement. The engagement that I see with Nile is mainly physical engagement. It's social with just a couple of kids. Does he have serious discussions with these kids, and, more importantly, do they have serious discussions with him? Are there times where they sit down and share ideas?

Kiran: He was really intrigued by Roberto's take on Islam and was one of the few students who wasn't irritated by Roberto's talking at length. Nile didn't necessarily need to get a word in edgewise. He wanted to hear more, and more and more and more. So he does have intellectual discussions. That was in Family Group.

Lena: It sounds like his family is playful. There's the physical piece, but is it also your sense that he has discussions, intellectual discussions, with them around issues a lot?

Kiran: Yes. I have the sense that that happens.

Linda: He's a year younger than everybody else?

Kiran: He's fully a year younger than everyone else in the class and in the high school except for Yolanda and his cousin. They're each 13. And also he's younger than any other member of his family, and that includes his extended family.

Rick: Something just escaped me. What position does he play when he plays football?

Kiran: I don't know.

Rick: Do you know?

Paul: No.

Cecelia: Why? Add in why you ask, Rick.

Paul: I think he might play the quarterback. But I don't know. I'm guessing.

Elaine: That may be the only position we know. (*laughter*)

Paul: That they can't go out and play without him is important.

Kiran: Yeah, that's true. That these 18-year-olds are coming to the door and asking for him.

Rick: It has a lot to do with what parts of this are physical, what parts of this are intellectual, and what kinds of physical skills are being relied on, what kinds of intellectual skills are being relied on.

Kiran: He talks about plays, about the plays they use.

Rick: That's one of the reasons why I asked you what makes you think he doesn't value formal learning. That was one of the things that occurred to me. But then it suddenly dawned on me. I'm trying to get a clearer sense of his physicality because we keep talking about him wrestling, and he's 5 feet 7 inches. That's not small for a 13-year-old, but it's not immense. I was just trying to get a clearer idea of some of that stuff.

Integrative Restatement by the Chair

Through the questions we learned more about what Kiran and Paul mean by "formal learning" and why they believe Nile doesn't value it. One set of standards for formal learning has to do with the role of a student—for example, doing assigned work, staying on-task during class, learning to use teacher suggestions to shape work, and completing projects. Nile does not usually meet these standards. And we learn that a reward system does not work with him and that an effort to bring his mother into the homework picture produced a plan to get back work done. Another set of standards *re* formal learning is more intellectual in content—being open to new things, being intellectually present and connected to discussions, making intellectual connections with peers, shaping projects around his own interests (what Kiran calls "negotiating the curriculum for himself"). Nile does not seem to be meeting this set of standards for formal learning in school. However, Kiran is pretty sure he is engaged in intellectual discussion at home.

We learned a couple of more interests: issues of religion and identity.

We learned more about his modes of thinking and learning: He observes and listens, often from the side; he makes connections; his most active experiencing happens with football, chess, and his ready responses to some texts and math problems. Kiran sees that she needs to know more about what he reads at home and about his football playing.

A couple of schoolwide issues began to emerge. One centers on how the transition from middle school to high school happens; how much the high school teachers know about the middle school program; how much knowledge of students gets thoughtfully passed on to the high school. Another centers on the possible need for the high school to think through the educational and developmental needs of its younger students and their programmatic implications.

Finally, I think Kiran has begun to reframe her focus question to something like this: "What does Nile help me understand about how I can actively engage him and others in the intellectual life of the school?"

Responses and Recommendations

Cecelia: Are we ready to move into recommendations? Or suggestions? Or responses? They don't have to be straight recommendations, like "Do this" or "Do that." They can be things to think about. Kiran has started, actually, asking questions of herself. We can ask questions for her to think about, for Paul to think about, for the school to think about. There are a range of possibilities for what we can say. Okay, Judith, do you want to start us off? Are you ready, or do you have another question?

Judith: I just see a lot of math, chess, spatial stuff, real thinking. I wonder if he plays video games. That would fit right in. There's a lot of that going on at a lot of levels. I don't know. Maybe there's a recommendation. I don't think schools do nearly enough to draw formal learning from the very high-quality learning that young boys are doing a lot of. Chess is high-level math; it's Global Studies. Football is physics. It's everything. And we don't see it. He is happy engaging men in this, and it's important to him. They see him as important. He's doing the male competitive thing in this group, and alone, and a lot of that is hidden. So I think he's doing a lot of very formal learning. I know it's happening in football. But I'm not "the teacher" who can bring that into the classroom and say, "See that?" I can see a lot of Math, Science, and Technology problems coming from football, chess, and all this stuff.

   The other thing I want to bring up is women. Everything is about the Panthers—

Kiran: —and KRS-ONE.

Judith: —and that the mother was in Young Lords, and then you said that his father is Jewish, and I wonder if that's part of what's hidden. I mean, half of him is his Jewish father, right? I haven't seen that reflected in anything. There's a lot of Black male stuff happening.

Lena: When you bring up the issues about his Black maleness and Rick's question about why Kiran thinks he doesn't value formal learning, I thought of all that I've I read as an African American person about how African American people don't value formal learning, which never rang true with me. I kept saying, "That's not true." Then I read another thing that did ring true that said African American people often don't value school learning. I wonder if there's a connection. I wonder if it's *school learning* that he's having difficulty with, that he's not valuing. I don't think it's formal learning or learning. I think it may be school.

But then there's his interest in the Black Panthers, and Kiran said his mother was a Young Lord. It's hard to imagine that this is a family where political issues are not discussed a lot. Or that even if they're not discussed a lot, that those values come through somehow. I mean if your mother was a Young Lord, I can't imagine that she's going to suddenly, completely change on social justice and social issues. And then Kiran said that social justice is important to him. So I'm not sure. I'm not totally sure of the links, but there are links here.

It sounds in some ways like he's advanced. He can talk about issues that maybe kids his age can't always talk about. And then his being the youngest child in a family of people much older than himself. Being the youngest in my extended family for many years, I know personally that you'd have to hear about things. It's different, I think. I'm not sure because I didn't grow up that way. I am an only child. But it's different, I think, than being in a family with young people. And so the depth and maturity, I think, that people get being in a family like that is very different. It might be that he has some difficulties—I don't want to say difficulties—but that he just relates and thinks in a different way than young people. It sounds like he does relate to younger people, but it sounds like he also has a lot of older people, and that he seems to feel comfortable with them. So when you put all of that together and at the same time know that he's 13, it sounds like there are intellectual things that are way out here.

Cecelia: One of the things that I used to get so irritated with our upper school about was that they treated adolescents—13, 14, 15, 16, 17 year olds, in that range, that whole range—who are very intelligent, but they treated them as if they were 25 in terms of their academic abilities. They taught them like they were college students. And these kids could do it. But it was just like that—"doing." It did not always result in deep understanding. It was the weirdest thing. You really are dealing with children here. Their minds are in the process of developing, and they're all over the place developing, but we're forming a program here for a variety of reasons, in this particular school, that is a college-level program, that is abstract. Okay, that is my gripe. I could go on about that. I won't. I'll stop there.

But it has implications for this youngster, I think. Thirteen is a very particular time mentally, and people are in different places at 13 in terms of intellectual development. I just think that needs to be taken into account when on the surface there's so much stuff here that's puzzling in a certain way. He passes all these tests. If you look at the tests, you see that they ask for a certain kind of knowledge, and he is intelligent, so he can do it. And he hasn't had trouble with a lot of the basic stuff, and so he does that stuff. But that doesn't necessarily mean that he's ready with a lot of abstract pieces. And while he has strong interests, it doesn't mean that he knows how to shape his study. That's a very particular thing. He may have this driving interest, but not know how to put any form around it to move right along with it, even if he wanted to. He just can't. He doesn't know how.

There's a lot to play with there. This really relates to the question you've already asked, Kiran: What does a 13-year-old entering this particular school, what should that look like? But I think that's both the high school's and the middle school's question. What is the active side of learning?

I have a recommendation to the school: Lighten up on the need to have all this formalized learning. This kid reads. He probably could write more. But that's what formal learning is about. He reads, he writes, he does mathematics. So what more do you want from formal learning? I think lightening up on that would be helpful. I think that paradoxically you may find students like Nile valuing it more.

Rick: There are two things that emerged out of this for me. One of them had to do with seeing the kid as having a great deal of independence and autonomy. We get to complain about kids being late. But he's setting his own hours. We get to complain about kids not doing the work that we assigned. But he's assigning himself his own work.

Kiran: And his own recommendations.

Rick: Yeah. And for that matter, we get to decide what's appropriate and inappropriate behavior. And he's setting his own standards. All of those things emerged very, very clearly from this.

The question about the learning came up for me because if he's playing in a league with the Abyssinian Baptist Church, there are play books. KRS-ONE is explicitly didactic. He's not about a lot of the stuff that some of these other people are, so he's memorizing all this pedagogy. He's writing his own lines on his own time. He's playing chess. He's got this project that he set for himself about the Black Panther party. To me, that's all about learning.

And then the final thing has to do with authenticity. We're constantly fighting with our kids to not just go through the motions of doing the work. They're supposed to be doing work that means something to them and making meaning of the work. And here's a kid who's obviously doing that. That's not something that you have to bring up with him obviously. So the first thing is the usual thing, which is to look at all the great stuff that there is already about this kid, that really you need to be getting other kids to do what he does!

The other part of it I'm a little less certain about because it has to do with what seems to me to be a need for challenge. And I heard that in a couple of ways. I heard that first about a kid who sits outside the group and then decides to come over when he decides the discussion is worthy of his attention or worthy of his participation. Obviously, he's listening all the time. He's just choosing not to participate except in a certain moment. And his feeling that people are playing him, sort of soft-soaping him, into going to see the psychologist, instead of saying you need to go, there's something about challenge. He's asking, "How are you talking to me?"

And then this physical stuff with the male teachers. I'm feeling like if teachers are going into the gym, if teachers are running with him and racing with him, they need to win sometimes. You know?

Cecelia: This is a recommendation? (*laughter*)

Rick: Yes, it is, it is a recommendation. The boy needs to be challenged. He was taken aback when Lee beat him at chess. Somebody needs to go onto the mat with him and wrestle him to the mat and pin him. And people need to do that with him academically as well. It struck me when Judith said it about all this heady stuff he's doing. But Kiran had already talked about his affection for competition, for face-to-face stuff. If the intellectual work that he is doing is inadequate, somebody needs to go straight in his face and tell him so. You think you're interested in the Black Panther party and you're running around with this pamphlet, and that's work? What do you know about this? These people were at war with one another. Have you seen the different sides to that? And if it's about competition, he needs to lose sometimes. Because he is 13 years old. And he is 5 feet 7 inches. And he needs to know that people are bigger than him and stronger than him and know more than him and all of this other stuff. And that each of these things has its own quality. That's the last part of it.

We talk a lot about writing in math, and we will say that a student who hasn't done a written reflection on the math hasn't done the work. But the math is the work. The math is the work in its own right. And football is its own project. And if he can get a first down, he doesn't necessarily need to write an explanation of how he has done that. That's the work. But then the same thing is true of all of these other things. And so the work itself has to be challenged.

Linda: I have a lot of thoughts. First of all, he's an incredibly compelling 13-year-old—the breadth of his interest, everything about him. I'm struck by the fact that he internalizes rules with reason. He may not like rules, but he listens to reason and will move from that. I'm interested in how he got himself out of the middle school, by making everybody miserable enough, I think, that they took his advice. It's wonderful that Nile is directed; he can take action and get action.

But I'm concerned that that's the sole reason that he got from middle school to high school. It's not clear what that articulation was across the middle school and the high school. And I wonder, in high school, how we honor our ninth-graders. How do we know this ninth-grader, and how do we honor that ninth-grader? I'm generalizing, but the talk I hear, generally, is "I don't want the ninth-graders. They're too immature." So what does it mean to know a ninth-grader?

In the description Kiran mentioned that a number of her colleagues noted Nile's playfulness, his being like a puppy. That reminded me of a teacher I had a long conversation with when I was visiting 850 Grand Street, the site of an alternative high school in Brooklyn. He had been teaching adults and came to teach kids. He was saying how his big learning was that high school students were like puppies, that he needed to play with them sometimes. Without that playfulness, that back and forth, formal learning suffered. Play is a real part of who one is at 13. And as the adult with a 13-year-old, you need to play back. I know you may worry if the play throws stuff all over the place. But it's part of the dance.

I don't think he needs to do school right now. He got what he wanted. He got into the high school. He passed his RCTs. In a couple of more years, when it becomes clear to him that he needs to do those tasks that you set up for him to get out of high school, he won't have any problem. 'Cause right now what I hear is a kid who, when that conversation is compelling enough, shows he's been there all along. He's sitting outside the circle, but he's taking it in, and he joins in when the issue's strong enough, when the problem's intriguing enough and posing enough challenge.

So I guess it comes back to what I was trying to say earlier, which is: What is his school learning for a ninth-grader? And how is it relevant to this ninth-grader or all ninth-graders? You know, it's also what you were saying earlier, Kiran, about how to look at that curriculum and see what it does. How is it seamless? I'm trying to think of some of the other language you used about what it might look like. But I think he's very much where he is, and he'll do what he needs to do, either when it's made known to him or when he sees it as evident.

I do think that if he's really very much the youngest and has operated in his family with brothers who are 28 and 30, then that's a comfortable place for him in some ways. I'm not so sure what that means to operate as the youngest always. There seems to be something in that that's locked into it. He's indulged in some ways, I'm sure, both within his family and within school. And indulged because of his strength, because he's intelligent, because he's direct. I would play to his directness. I would favor being as direct with him as possible, which would go back to what Cecelia said, about having to be direct in the sense of shaping tasks. I mean, be direct, just tell him directly what he needs to know.

Elaine: I was struck by the therapy thing, where he wanted to be told directly. I admired his knowing that he didn't want to be played as child or student or something. You know, just say it to me. Be upfront. Treat me as a human being. Treat me respectfully. I was going in a real different direction from you, Rick. I was really struck by what you said about elders needing to win, but I was thinking about how space or the potential for failure here is so possible. It wasn't school or formal learning for me. For me, it was structures—the structures of the place don't work for him. So he sets up all these structures that really work for him, and that's his strength: what he's doing at home, the book he was reading. There's so much that's impressive. Yet there's this whole compliance thing about school that he seems to be grappling with. So it made me think, you have to pick carefully where you want to show him that you can beat him, and I don't know quite what those places are. You know him better. But it seems like you guys have to make some choices. Like I was thinking about, what does the failing of Math, Science, and Technology do? He didn't pass it this time. He's got to complete the 17 things. He's got a system for completing them. I don't know how those things play out in this school. But I think this is a person who's going to make his own choices. And he respects straightforwardness, and he can be straightforward, so set up something with straightforwardness that recognizes who he is and what he's doing. I want to grade him for what he's doing at home. If somebody sets up a course of study on their own, how do we create structures in our institutions to make room for that course of study? How do we also challenge him? How do we also bring him in?

I'm also curious about him as the youngest and how hard that can be as he moves from the middle school where he was not the youngest into this situation, where he is. How much of this year you've described is a transition time in that we may not really see him until next September? He's figuring it out. He's finding himself out. He's testing the limits. And, again, clarity is real important in all of this.

Choose your battles with him. And when you said that faculty like him, it was like, yeah, there is something so wonderful about this young person who "bumps."

Judith: I have taught many ninth-grade classes. Here are some recommendations from that experience. We did a lot of physical stuff. We beat out the rhythm of words, for example. We would sing the 1812 Overture. And we would cook African food. It was very much that. I even had to make an arrangement with one of the kids that he would have one minute, just his time, to beat a rhythm on his desk. And he was okay for the rest of the time. So the ninth-graders would come to class, and I just let them be ninth-graders.

But I realized that the other kids in the school . . . because they were so close to being ninth-graders and they couldn't be that anymore. You could not be yourself unless there were other ninth-graders around, and they wouldn't do it unless there were. So in a way they weren't themselves unless the door was closed. So the recommendation: He needs, somehow, that kind of fun, crazy, all-out, with other kids—so that he can feel comfortable doing that with them, because I don't know who he'd feel comfortable being a kid with. I don't know. Where is he comfortable being a kid and letting that happen? That's one thing.

And the other thing goes back to structures. I don't think he hates them. I think he loves them. You cannot play football or chess or any of those things unless you know these are the rules. And these are all the different ways you can go around and block them. It's like the kids will sit hours and play Nintendo and video games because the rules are right here. These are the rules. He loves the rules. And I think that for ninth-graders, the other part is highly structured in the sense of, "what are the rules?" You know? They'll yell and scream and this and that, but. . . . I did projects with ninth-graders, but much more so than with any other kids, I would say, "These are the rules." And we called them "the rules." This is what it is. "Oh, is it this?" they would ask. "Yes, it's this," I would respond.

And the Abyssinian Baptist Church and the places where there's KRS-ONE, all this is very structured. You know how you're supposed to be when you walk into that world. And rhymes are incredibly structured. And still, you know, as a 13-year-old boy, he needs grown people guiding him. And then, other things will happen, it's not going to be for too long, you know. And with the other play around, I think that more independence will happen.

Then another recommendation is to think that, as time goes on, he's going to be the only man in the house with his mother, sister, and that little girl. He will be 14, 15, 16, and he's supposed to be the man with all these women around. That's going to be something to keep aware of.

Lena: Also, going back to what you were saying about how he needs to know that there are other people who know more than he does, and that kind of thing—since he's comfortable with older people, I'm wondering if there are older students in the school who might be interested in some of the things he's interested in. You can kind of pair them up. Like any others who are involved in the Black Panther or whatever that he might get paired up with in some way.

Elaine: I also want to say that to me he needs that space to sit outside the circle still. So all this talk of structures and rules, it's not about not also allowing him to make choices in there and have that space. And that's another tension in what we're talking about.

Summary of the Recommendations

Cecelia: I'm going to just pull this together very quickly. One large thread that we're noting here is that this is a 13-year-old ninth grade student. And we know many of the recommendations that we're asking you to think about, Kiran, or suggesting that you think about, have to do with that—with what kind of activity, what kind of outside structures would support him as a young adolescent, as a young person. A couple of interesting things around the structures: the fact that he sets up his own, that he works within his own, that he grapples with the school's. Also he likes structure, he likes rules, and many of the activities that are of real interest to him are rule activities (for example, chess, football, and so forth).

The directness that many of us came back to came up in the story that Paul told about Nile's wishing that folks had been a little more direct with him. Many of us came back to that in terms of . . . well, the language that Rick put around it was "challenge," something that's also related to this business of the things that are face-to-face and telling him the way it is, with the caveat of maybe not saying everything.

A large idea also was to lighten up on the formalized learning business because this kid is learning and because formal learning is just one way of learning about the world. He is learning about the world. And as Linda was saying, perhaps this is a time of transition when he doesn't need to do school. And there's evidence for him being able to do school, middle school, and maybe this is a transitional period where he's soaking particular things up. I also want to underline a point Rick made because it's a really hard thing for us to keep in mind: The way for us to think about him as a football player, or for him to think about himself as a football player, is to watch himself play football, perhaps to use video. But the football, in and of itself, is the activity. We need to understand what's inside football. He doesn't need to write about it. The same way with the chess. There are lots of things that students do, that we make secondary activities. Writing about math is writing about math. It is not necessarily mathematics. So we need to know more about what the actual stuff is on the inside of the things he is doing. And that's in order for him to see what the learning is inside. And we might call it formal learning. We might not. But we would probably call it learning.

And I'm interested in adolescents' interests in identity issues. Multiracial kids have complex threads to think about. That question for Nile is: Who is he going to be? Judith raised this issue—that he's either figuring out what it is to be a man—yes, that is what adolescents do—but also that whole issue of being Jewish, the religious aspects of that, the cultural aspects of that, alongside the West Indian side of him. What's all that? How will it all work itself out? What sense is he going to make of that? What's it going to be for him? It's very interesting and important.

AFTERTHOUGHTS

Kiran Chaudhuri

For me, the Prospect processes are ground I can step back on in order to regain my footing, reimagine my practice and my life, and be affirmed in my values. They are the place from which I can step out into the world with conviction.

I went to my first review when I was in my second year of teaching, sent there as a scout by my principal at University Heights Secondary School, where I was teaching 16-, 17-, 18-, and 19-year-olds. When I got there, I felt as if I'd found a home away from home. I saw how participants were intentional about valuing one another's ways of thinking. I drank in the thoughtful, layered dialogue, and reflected on the day's crush of minute-by-minute decisions. I experienced how the process itself kept one safe from reading too much into a work, remained always respectful of the child. What was astonishing was that neither the age of the child being reviewed—she was 4 years old—nor the community of early childhood educators caused me to feel that I was out of place or that the review was irrelevant to my practice.

The process confirmed for me how categorizing and interpreting shut down my understanding of students, while observing and describing open it up.

Describing adolescents—and children—and their work has disciplined me to be aware of when I am tending toward judgment, when I am seeing only what I expect to see.

My perception of Nile had been showing signs of becoming habituated in this way, and I knew I needed to do something about it. I had been struggling to figure out how to work *with* him, appealing to his delight in rhyming, his identification with the militant action of the Black Panthers, and his enjoyment of therapy, but I was not having much luck. If only I could see that Nile was doing some work, I felt, I would be able to continue to adjust my practice to meet his needs. I was exasperated.

Reviewing Nile opened up my sense of possibility for him. It allowed me to think about how he is grappling with seeming contradictions. Nile is a boy, yet he's competing intellectually and physically with men. Nile is growing taller and more powerfully built every day, yet it's not only a time of physical change for him. It's also a time of a particular kind of intellectual growth. He succeeded in getting the adults in the school to acquiesce to his insistence that he was ready for high school, yet upon getting his way, he felt no need to prove their doubts about his readiness wrong. He rebels against rules, but he loves highly structured pursuits governed by rules, such as football, chess, rhyming, track, and basketball. He passed all his New York State Regents Competency Tests, but he may not yet have developed a lot of complex problem-solving skills. While he has strong interests and is good at making connections, this doesn't mean that he knows how to shape his study, how to give it form. Nile is comfortable with adults and older teenagers, perhaps even more so than with younger people; yet it may be that he does not find space to be his 13-year old self in a classroom 16-, 17-, 18-, 19-, 20-, and 21-year-olds. He is aware of his mixed cultural and racial heritage, but he writes and speaks primarily of his identity as a "West Indian American." He looks for autonomy, but this doesn't mean he doesn't still need and want supervision and guidance.

Nile has taken up our school's invitation to make of it a family. He has been familiar with it since his cousins were attending and has attended himself since the age of 11. He has won hearts throughout the building, making his rounds to connect with people who are important to him. At 9:00 A.M. he is checking in with his buddies in the cafeteria, while the rest of our Family Group is holding its morning meeting upstairs. After the 10:00 break is over, I find him in the hallway with Marcus and Tom rehearsing rhymes a capella for the talent show. At 1:00, he stops by the principal's office to visit the head of the "Family," Deborah, and spin around in her swivel chair until

she throws him out to go to class. At the end of the school day, he goes outside to play football with the seniors who came into the classroom earlier
looking for him. On a field trip, he sits affectionately close to four classmates
on the subway, hailing strangers, "Do you see how tight we are? We're tight!"
As Paul said in the review, "social connections are absolutely there" for Nile.
So is interdependent learning in the form of chess, rhyming, rehearsing, observing the principal in her meetings, and playing football. Nile is giving
himself over to doing things that shape and discipline his creativity. It's just
that he misses chances in the process to connect and contribute to discussions about the in-class learning, and when he is there to work interdepen-
dently with classmates, the social element of their interaction dominates. Had
the review focused only on what Nile was doing in the classroom, I might
have concluded he was learning nothing.

We have structured curriculum and assessment at University Heights
around habits of learning, such as taking responsibility for oneself and one's
community, thinking critically, and making ethical decisions. This means that
students need to produce evidence of having acquired these habits. It was
my emphasis on their production of specific kinds of evidence for assessment
that fixed my sights on what was not there in Nile's notebook and activity,
as opposed to what was.

Does an adolescent have to be generating and reflecting on products in
order to be learning? If so, what kind of products?

Does an adolescent have to conform to classroom expectations in order
to be learning? Does an adolescent have to experience what it is to pull his
weight in a class inquiry in order to be responsible for his own learning?

How can I adjust my practice so that it is a moral act, allowing and shaping Nile's perspective, rather than bulldozing over it?

The review allowed me to think about how to make my classroom a play
space for Nile, so that he can engage in his poetic, rhythmic, playful, exuberant ways of thinking and learning in our midst, and at the same time learn
to respect the needs of the group. I began to feel better about the raucous
back-and-forth that took place in whatever small group Nile would join.
Perhaps I was already allowing him the space to do what he needed to do.

The recommendations regarding how we have structured our school rang
true for me. I found especially thought-provoking Judith's description of how,
in a way, her ninth-graders weren't themselves unless there were other ninth-
graders around and the door was closed. At the end of the year, there was a
movement afoot in our school to narrow our multiage groupings, splitting
off 13- to 16-year-old newcomers from 15- to 19-year-old returning students,
and instituting a senior institute for seniors and others 19 and older. Although
suspicious of its resemblance to many schools' current retreat to homoge-

neous age groupings, I ultimately supported it because it seemed to serve needs like Nile's. It would give him a chance to be in a new position—no longer the youngest—and to try out a different perspective.

I could see, too, how Nile had missed out because he had been insufficiently intellectually challenged to continue in the middle school: He might have taken to the role of elder and begun to mentor other students. We needed to set up a structure to help us think about what a student making the transition from middle school to high school needs and how best to provide it.

The descriptive review of Nile brought home for me how the processes allow us to build on our differences in the group. It pushed us to listen to one another, to wait our turn to speak, and to respect and value and work through differences in perspective and language. I noted how the process harnessed our cultural, racial, gender, and generational diversity. I was especially struck by how Lena, an African American knowledgeable about African Americans' patterns of learning, could see so clearly that it is school learning that Nile is having difficulty with, not learning in general. Judith, who is also African American and whose children are of mixed heritage, pointed out how, in his rhyming, verbal repartee, football, and chess, he is approaching things in a way that researchers have noted is common to Black men.

These recommendations brought to mind some things that I hadn't included in the review. Being of mixed heritage myself, I had recognized how Nile emphasizes his West Indian and African American roots but seldom speaks about his Jewish side. Growing up, I lived the aspect of my dual ethnicity that was dominant in my community. It was the aspect I had more exposure to and more understanding of, and it helped me to fit in at school. On two occasions in class, when we were all discussing our origins, I had looked at Nile, raising my eyebrows, and he had understood I was inviting him to talk about being biracial. He shook his head one time, and said, "No, don't go there" the other. The recommendations brought these moments to mind, and threw into relief how Nile may be negotiating a historical context of anti-Semitism in the community in which our school is located. He is more likely to discuss his dad's Jewish heritage in, say, Passages class, which is smaller and all about social and emotional learning and speaking from personal experience. Considering Nile's response to this kind of prejudice led me to convince my Humanities colleagues that we should devote one of our semesters to an investigation of stereotyping and scapegoating during the Weimar Republic and the Holocaust.

I also learned in the review that Nile respects straightforwardness. In fact, his own straightforwardness is one of his strengths. I was told I should be as direct with him as possible. I got more insight into what this meant through something that happened after the review, when I took my Family Group to Central Park to do the Challenge Course. I saw Nile trying to take the lead and saw, once again, that he had one kind of maturity but not another—and realized he needed to be made aware of that. Elaine had asked just that in her recommendations: "How do we challenge him?" He had the confidence in this situation, but neither the knowledge nor the authority. I wondered how to get across to him the fact that he doesn't have the whole picture yet. I was fascinated as the facilitator straightforwardly told Nile that he was trying to take the lead when that was neither necessary nor appropriate, since he (the facilitator) had it under control and Nile's job was to participate. Eventually, Nile got it, stepped aside good-naturedly, and allowed the facilitator to lead. By the end of the morning, Nile was doing the stomach-to-stomach bump with him, in jubilation over a basketball win. I saw what it is that I have to practice.

All this helped me to see that Nile needs clarity, firmness, and room to play. Rick spoke to this in the review when he talked about how our focus as teachers on things like kids' lateness and completion of tasks makes us miss the point: Nile is assigning himself work, giving himself recommendations, and setting standards for himself. That capacity to be on to something, to find work that means something, is of incredible value. The value of ability to do what is required by school needs to be placed next to it, not on top of it.

Cecelia's recommendation to me and to my school to "lighten up on all the formal learning," and Judith's story of how she would just let her ninth-graders be ninth-graders, both helped me to recognize that I was thinking about school in a particular way, and that I could change that. Judith noted that "with the other play around, I think that more independence will happen." Linda told the story of how her colleague noticed that, "without that playfulness, that back and forth, formal learning suffered." These recommendations gave me a sense of the rewards of undertaking this big shift in my thinking away from product and toward process. Cecelia's framing of her recommendation for my school as well as for me was important, because it enabled me to see how my vision has been formed in context, and how I hone my values with my school colleagues. I started thinking about ways to bring this newfound, fledgling vision back to them so we could consider its implications for our school.

CHAPTER 9

WHOLE-SCHOOL INQUIRY: VALUES AND PRACTICE

Cecelia Traugh

*Camus said that certain cities—he had in mind Oran on the Algerian coast—
exorcised the landscape. We have a way of life that ostracizes the land. . . .*

*How, then, do we come to know the land, to discover what more may be
there than merchantable timber, grazable prairies, recoverable ores, damable
water, netable fish?*

*It is by looking upon the land not as its possessor but as its compan-
ion. . . . We would have to memorize and remember the land, walk it, eat
from its soils and from the animals that ate its plants. We would have to
know its winds, inhale its airs, observe the sequence of its flowers in the
spring and the range of its birds.*

—Barry Lopez (1992, pp. 31–34)

A long-lived inquiry produces a discriminating language.

—Barry Lopez (1986, p. 278)

My work is in schools. I frame this work as whole-school inquiry. For all five
of the small schools I currently work with, the full staff of each place, including the school's director, are engaged in inquiries largely about their ongoing
struggle to be accountable to the values that underlie their practices and structures. In order for this to happen, school staffs commit themselves to changing the nature of their work together by going beyond day-to-day problem
solving and moving to a focus on this guiding question: In what ways is the
school working to make its actions live up to what its staff say they believe?

Several aspects of this knowledge-making, action-producing inquiry
process stand out. I see school staffs exercise the power of making the work
of the school public and discussable—the work as it is done by individuals

and by the body of the staff. I see staffs developing language that they have thought about carefully and that they use confidently to think about their work and articulate their beliefs and practices to themselves and others— parents and other teachers in the school. I see how the inquiry can help a staff lift their heads out of the ongoing stream, get their bearings, and chart a course, thus working against the feeling of being directionless that often results from immersion in the full dailyness of school.

I also know from my experience that while a school's staff can never fully succeed with a group of children in the way they envision, it is possible to work toward that vision. Even a group of teachers who think there are few ways to deal with the hard issues children can present can learn to work on those things if they imagine a different possibility. It does not mean success is sure; it is about a commitment to trying. I chart the course of inquiry by urging that problems be framed as questions and by working to prevent a narrowing view of human possibility from becoming "fact."

The inquiry structures (see the Appendix to this chapter) I bring to these schools provide a space in which teachers can explore the idea that their work has value, individually and collectively, and that it can grow powerfully and deeply; a space which gives importance and meaning to the work of putting values into action and downplays the insistent press for lists of things to do when one returns to the classroom; a space in which thinking, feeling, memory, and experience are of utmost value as starting places from which education can grow.

I believe that working with a group of teachers should not be imperialist, that is, imposed from above. I think about that work in the way Lopez (1986, 1992) talks about knowing the land—as happening over a long period of time, as always incomplete, as happening in relationship. It is about being in dialogue with the place as the place it is and with that particular group of people—who they are and what their idiosyncratic riches are.

THE NEIGHBORHOOD SCHOOL: EXPLORING HETEROGENEITY

I turn now to the story of one of the whole-school inquiries I have been doing over the past five years. The Neighborhood School is a small school of choice on the Lower East Side of Manhattan, and my work there was funded by the Center for Collaborative Education as part of the New York Networks for School Renewal. I tell here the story of one year of work (1997–1998) because what we worked on is so important—the value of heterogeneity and its place in the life of the school.

I was invited to the school in 1995 to help them learn more about descriptive process, particularly the Descriptive Review of the Child and the

Description of Children's Work. We also began to do recollections and storytelling along the way that first year. As my work with the group evolved more and more into working with questions and issues the staff wanted help in discussing together, the staff continued to conduct descriptive reviews on their own. The fact that they do them on their own is important, since it enables increased depth in the work we do together.

At first, I thought that I was working with a group of people who liked to float on the surface of issues and didn't want to get underneath them. But I was mistaken; they have turned out to be a very thoughtful group, willing to go into depth with issues. My initial impression could have been related to an issue we identified for ourselves after our first sessions—that of not speaking, feeling silenced in the group because of the pace of talk, because of the topics, because of personal habit.

Like all school staffs who try to be thoughtful about their work, the Neighborhood School staff faces many serious issues each year. They had decided in the spring of 1997 to work on the topic of heterogeneity, an issue that had surfaced because of a division between the early childhood teachers and the teachers of the older children. This was only the second year the school had had a sixth grade. There were two teachers of grades 5–6. One was Mark, who was relatively new to teaching and in his second year at the Neighborhood School. The other was Sofia, who had been in the school for a while.

The controversy arose over a couple of key issues. (1) The upper-grade teachers ability-grouped for math. (2) The male grade 5–6 teacher had formed a basketball team by selecting the best players rather than including all who wanted to play. The second issue incensed the lower-grade teachers. The staff as a body thought that heterogeneity was one of their core values and they wanted to know what had happened to it.

We began our inquiry into heterogeneity in October. The basic focusing question was: "What does the staff believe the school stands for around issues of difference and heterogeneity?" I asked each person to describe the school's beliefs in relation to those ideas and the evidence the person had for his or her beliefs about the school. I asked people to do this privately, before our meeting, without checking in with each other. This last was tricky. I wanted them to think about this ahead of time on their own. I didn't want an amalgam of what people thought they ought to say. This guideline came out of my understanding of the group. I didn't want them to check in to see what the group story was, what the "line" was.

At our meeting, the teachers found out a number of things from this sharing, which I later gathered together in notes. I said, "Although a few staff members found it difficult to know what the whole school stood for, I think I heard many staff members say that the school is committed to being a diverse place." There was evidence for this belief in the language of the school, in practices, in commitments. And then I listed the inconsistencies they saw between value and practice: They named the math grouping in the upper grades, the basketball team, and the fact that there are only two men on the staff. Otherwise, they saw themselves as a diverse staff. The school's student population is quite mixed racially and culturally.

They also named purposes and values and standards they saw as parts of the large idea of heterogeneity. For example, they used words like *stars* and *handfuls* when placing children in classes. These words imply standards, but it was not clear that there was a shared meaning of these words among staff members or that there was shared comfort. *Balance* in terms of classroom membership was an idea expressed by many, and this too implied a standard. Tolerance of others and diversity of ideas were values spoken about in the school.

We also learned about important tensions within the idea of heterogeneity. Celebration of difference can be in tension with being in community; an individual's preferred practice can be in tension with shared practices. This second was a very major issue because the director has emphasized the need to make the practice shared so that parents can recognize it from classroom to classroom. Within that context a question becomes: What happens if a teacher wants to diverge from that? A third issue was the idea that meeting kids where they are can be in tension with teachers' expectations and standards.

When I wrote up my notes later, I saw that an additional idea had surfaced for me. In the narrative notes, I suggested that "standards tend to standardization" and that this was a tension we needed to work with in order to live up to a commitment to heterogeneity, and that the school's commitment to diversity was one that everyone in the school needed to continue to learn how to enact. It is not a commitment that can be easily or fully achieved; it needs constant vigilance.

It was a very rich beginning.

In November, we talked about how people used groups in their classrooms. We began with a reflection on *difference* and then described the purposes teachers want groups to serve; the ways they divided children into groups; how they saw group work as supporting or not supporting learning, the classroom community, children's feelings about themselves and others, and their feelings of success as a teacher; and any questions they had about group work. This was also a generative session around purposes, standards, and questions. The questions teachers raised were: How can I know what a child knows if she or he works in a group? When does a teacher interfere in the workings of a group? How can a teacher best help children be responsible for their work and be active contributors to a group? The tension between individual and group was very strong in their thinking.

Again, as I wrote the notes later, I had a few further thoughts, which I framed as questions. One cluster had to do with the choice to use groups instead of having children work individually: How much work done in a small-group context is work that could be better done individually? How much work done in small groups ends up being bigger than the group, bigger than the sum of its parts? In the second cluster my mind went to the assertion that children had trouble working with other children of different abilities: What in the classroom environment supports certain children's not wanting to work with other children of different ability? How do children learn to perceive differences of skill and what connections do these perceptions have to winning and losing—academically, socially, or in a game? What lessons do we adults give children about differences of skill? And, finally, a question I had about a possibility: How can shared interests be a way through problems posed by skill/ability differences?

The second question, what supports children not wanting to work with other children of different ability, came from the group as seemingly given. I interpreted this thought as coming from teachers' own ambiguity and ambivalence about working with kids of different ability or about kids having to do that. The teachers named the issue; I turned it back to the group as a question. Alongside raising the question, I tried to identify ways through the issue. For example, one teacher talked about how kids did come together around a shared interest even though one could read and one couldn't. The shared interest carried them beyond the difference.

In December we took a brief detour. Teachers new to the school in 1997–1998 had not been there when the staff made a commitment to doing descriptive reviews. They wanted to rethink the decision to use time in this way. I framed the discussion around the idea of commitment and what commitments the school and its staff had made and needed to continue to make to keep the valuing of difference of all kinds alive and growing. To get beneath the surface of this question, we began with a reflection on the word *commitment* and then discussed "Building from Children's Strengths" by Patricia F. Carini (1986).

In January I brought the notes from the May 1996 meeting about uniformity as a factor in decision making in the school: How uniform are things supposed to be? The staff had tended toward uniformity of practice to avoid creating *stars* within the staff, to create more coherence of curriculum within the school, and to help clarify standards for teaching in the school. However, these desires were in conflict with their valuing of independent decision making. With the notes, I asked a new question: What does this "old" concern about uniformity mean in the context of valuing heterogeneity and of the question about what they had committed themselves to? One of the things the staff noticed from the notes was how far they had come, how much richer their talk had become over the past several years. For me, this was an unexpected benefit of reviewing the notes.

Then we turned to the questions of the roles, if any, they saw descriptive process as playing for themselves and for the school and whether they should continue their commitment. The only worry new or experienced staff expressed was about having time to prepare. So with this in mind, we worked out exactly what they were committing to: Each teacher would do a descriptive review of something important—a child or a piece of practice—every two years. This decision resolved the issue. They were a staff that appreciated clarity, a quality that indicated their ability to join together and take action. The tensions inherent in valuing uniformity, standards, independence, and heterogeneity and the ongoing negotiating and balancing needed to keep things in motion became more apparent through this passage in the work.

It was now February. And the first descriptive review after the agreement was one by Mark and Sofia, who together would review their math groupings. As part of the preparation for this review, I spent a brief time in Mark's classroom. I saw the children working in groups. The three of us met over lunch, and I had them describe to me the big picture of their work in math. I later wrote up some notes about our conversation, which I gave to them. We met next over winter break to work out the review in more detail. As they described what they had done during the first semester and what they had learned from it, I realized they had some assumptions about the children in their two groups that were beneath the surface but not so deep that they couldn't be brought forward. They were just under the skin of the description. So I said, "It sounds to me that you were assuming this." And Sofia said, "Yes. I am assuming that, and I am also assuming this and this and this." They went on to list the assumptions that they could identify themselves holding about the children in both the lower- and higher-performing groups and about math learning that were shaping the program.

The guiding question we came up with for preparing the review was: "Students are not all in the same place in their math learning. They learn math differently, have different mathematical interests, skills, and abilities. How can we work so that all students can enjoy and learn math?" This was the teachers' question. The question we asked the group to respond to at the end of the review was: "What do you hear in this review by way of implication and question for your own work and for the school?" We had an hour and a half for our meetings, so the focus question needed to be smaller and more possible to respond to than the guiding questions.

I won't summarize here the full content of this review, but because it was such an important part of the year's work, I will give the headings we developed along with a bit of commentary. I asked both Mark and Sofia to share *their experiences with tracking or ability grouping* that were interesting and worth remembering. Sofia was always in a top-tracked class, but her sister was not. Her mother, coming from India, knew that this daughter was not getting the education she should be, and eventually pulled her from public school. Mark described himself as being bumped back to a middle track in high school because he hadn't worked very hard. Then his family moved to Africa, and he attended a "high-powered" school where he did well. Next, they described how they had planned their fall math program and followed this with *what they learned about their students as mathematicians over the first month of the year.* The classes include both fifth- and sixth-grade students, and the teachers had agreed to start the year with their classes intact and spend a month watching. One of the things they learned about the group was that they had high achievers and low achievers, particularly when considering skill with and speed of computation. To make the groups, they agreed to do one unit with Mark working with the higher-performing children and Sofia working with the lower-performing children. Then, for the next unit, they switched groups.

Mark and Sofia's presentation closed with a *description of the assumptions they had made about the students in each group, the structures of class time, what they had learned from working with each group, and their decision to return to working with their whole classes.* Sofia said she did not know anything about more than half her students as math learners. She needed to talk to parents and to write reports, and she didn't have enough first-hand understandings. This was a major issue. In addition, they had also begun to hear some of their higher-performing students say that they didn't want to work with students from the other group. Mark and Sofia were getting the feeling that they were creating an elite group, and this went against what they believed.

The response from the staff to the review was remarkable. It is important to remember that this was one of the issues that brought the group to focus on heterogeneity in the first place. In response to the review, people said, "Now that I know how carefully you have thought about this, I see the decision to group was not made casually. This gives me more confidence about what is going on in the fifth and sixth grade." The early childhood people had been able to get inside and appreciate the work and the struggles of these two teachers of older children.

The review was an impressive piece of work. The teachers felt terrific about what they had accomplished and learned.

The next piece we did came out of our earlier reading of "Building from Children's Strengths" (Carini, 1986). Laurie was struck by the descriptions of children in the article, and she wanted to look at her own descriptions of children. She wondered if she were describing in a way that captured those important things about a child that have large implications. She made a presentation in which she described her purposes for reports, the confusions she had in writing them, the issues of evidence for knowing children, and her hopes for the report writing she does. We followed this with describing one report. My role was to push the group not just to tell Laurie that it was a wonderful report, but to describe it. This review contributed to our inquiry by highlighting the difficult work of observation and description, of trying to convey the particularity of the person. Part of working with heterogeneity is about knowing children well enough.

By April, we had expanded our collection of issues from the two, heterogeneity and difference, to also include grouping and struggle. To plan this session, I had reviewed the notes from our work and found that the question of how children learn to perceive differences of skill and ability had surfaced as a theme through our descriptions of group work (November) and Mark and Sofia's review of grouping for math (February). I said to the group that I knew there were many factors in children's learning in this area. However, the environments offered by the school and the classroom are also important, and they are the environments we have some power in shaping. We focused on the whole school. I asked people to come prepared with descriptions of what in the classroom environment supports children's willingness to work with children of differing abilities and what supports their unwillingness, and to think over the past year and describe the lessons they had seen themselves and/or that the school was offering children about differences of skill (for example, language, responses to children's questions, classroom structures).

This proved to be a difficult and sensitive topic, but the group was game and they did it. A point about the way I conduct whole-school inquiry comes up here. Because each piece of work grows out the work of the group, by and large the questions are very particular to the group—and they usually are not ones I have worked with before. So I can't always anticipate where they are going to go. That means in summarizing I am working entirely spontaneously. Also, we are working within a time frame of an hour and a half. The summary I do during the session is sometimes only cursory. The extended summary is done in the notes. The reason I bring this point up here is that this framing brought forward content that was very close to the bone, and I had not realized the degree to which people would feel this. I realized we were into deep issues the minute people started talking.

Some very important material came out. One point that people made was that when we ask students to make their work public, we open them up to judgment. If students read their own writing to each other, they are made open to judgment. This was an important recognition on people's parts.

In my summary I put this difficulty alongside one of the important purposes of my work with the school, which is learning how to take a questioning/inquiry stance toward the work and art of teaching. This means, I think, that when we look at a value-laden issue—such as how we create an environment that supports children's willingness to work with children of different abilities and what we may do that can get in the way of that end—it is important to keep that stance in mind.

I showed how they had identified practices that were intended to make it possible for children to have equal places in the classroom, that is, attempts to be pro-active and to create intentionally a supportive classroom tone and atmosphere. The list of practices was quite long, and one of the staff's practices stood out as central in creating context and tone, that is, the practice of holding class conversations. I noted the kinds of topics class groups discuss—for example, what reading levels are and what they mean; the factors that affect work, such as familiarity with materials, a point particularly important in multiage classrooms; the different strategies children use to read, to solve math problems, and so forth.

The group's descriptions of practices pointed to an idea we could return to. Efforts to make children's work public and to make reading materials accessible can have the unintended result of children making negative comparisons, of seeing "levels." Some of the other practices teachers identified were wanting children to read books that are "just right" for them and therefore color-coding the books by difficulty level, not by topic; sharing writing; displaying work; and asking children to demonstrate their physical education skills. The question raised by all this was: How can the positive gains of sharing work and making reading materials accessible be maximized and the negative possibilities be minimized? How can children learn to respond in ways appropriate to the "public space" of a classroom community?

This work was rich with idea and implication. Teachers indicated a need to think/learn more about how to respond to children and their work. They named value conflicts, such as how grouping for ability short-changed the less skilled children, but putting children into mixed-ability groups opened a teacher up to complaints from some children; how valuing efficiency conflicted with valuing children who think and/or speak slowly and thus hold up the group. (For the teacher to name this last point when she knew others might have thought it was not "right" was important. Compared to how quiet about those things these teachers were when we first started, I think this was movement in a good direction.) Teachers described children's responses to what they perceive as differences in ability; for example, some children talk about abilities—brag about their own, put others' down, show impatience when they are partnered with a child they don't prefer, know how to find help in skilled peers. Teachers described themselves as responding to these and other day-to-day events in several ways. They worked to preempt, they confronted, they ignored.

The thread running through the entire conversation was the role of comparing in learning. Children and adults compare themselves with others as a way to learn about themselves. This can have a strong competitive edge as well as judgmental quality. The last point raised these questions: How can we help children learn about themselves and their work in ways other than by drawing comparisons? How can we help children notice differences without those differences becoming a way to judge? How can children's strengths be appreciated more collegially and less competitively?

I suggested several ideas as possible directions for further work. We could remember ourselves as children and adolescents working with peers of differing strengths. The group could describe practice around establishing classroom tone. We could think more about the cluster of comparing, judging, and describing. It struck me that making description basic to how everyone—child and adult—responds to work would lessen the urge to compare judgmentally. This would amount to teaching children how to describe what they see and hear in others' work.

In May we reviewed what we had done over the year. I provided a chronology and asked them to think about these questions: What idea[s] and/or questions about heterogeneity/difference/grouping have seemed particularly important and/or puzzling to you over the course of the year? Is there a specific school or classroom event or specific piece of work with a child that highlights or illustrates the ideas and/or questions that are important to you? What issues does this example raise for you? What are you thinking about as your question/idea at this point?

I was struck by several responses. Mark's was the first response. The difference that was most striking to him was that of income. He said that in the sixth grade, the children from middle-income families are going on to a district in which there are many interesting middle school options and in which the students are largely middle class. The children from low-income families stay in their home district, which has few educational choices available. He described himself as pretending that all the parents had the same agenda he has, but he realizes that they do not. It was disheartening for him to see that the mix of income levels seemed to end at fifth and sixth grades for his students. The middle-income children are going on to be with kids just like themselves. He felt he was a participant in this, and he wondered what more he could do to get all the parents involved in the search for a junior high. He said he believed he was not serving that population well enough. Mark's statement was our opening. He was ready to speak and knew what he was going to say, although he had no notes. His saying that he was a "participant" in the problem he named faced them with their own complicity.

Sofia said that their math presentation stood out to her. It had given her an opportunity to think about her practice in ways she never had before. It had put her in a place she never had been—the position of the less skilled student. She said that she would never again group in the way she had.

One of the stories was told by a teacher who was struggling with an issue that centered on an African American girl in the class. The teacher told of having to respond to some children's aversion to the child's seeming physical messiness. She questioned whether she knew how to be helpful to the child and her father because, in addition to the potential racism of the situation, she knew the family struggled financially. There were risks in describing her complex concern, I believe, but she shared it fully. This struck me, because this teacher had been reluctant to express her own concerns. The full description was good in terms of what we were trying to do. The large questions she was asking were: What is it like to be the only Black girl in a class where there are other children of color but no other Black children? And what if poverty is also a factor? These are important questions to raise, ones that need returning to. In particular, I recommended that the staff do a Descriptive Review of the Child so that as full an understanding as possible could be developed.

Throughout the entire session, economic and class differences surfaced. A big issue was how the school works with parents and how teachers cope with being participant in these issues: Do we recognize this and try to make a difference or do we choose to ignore it?

Finally, in this review of the year, the teachers made several comments about the effects of the inquiry itself on the group's thinking. In the summary, I framed their ideas in the form of what is important. It is important to have new questions. While it is uncomfortable, it can enable us to see more and in the end act in ways that are more effective for children. It is important to have one's thinking pushed. It is important to avoid the easy or lazy route. It is important to recognize that there is more and more to learn about the art of teaching.

THE MEANING AND DIFFICULTIES OF THIS WORK

Wherever professional development is going on, people look for change. I see the interest focusing largely on whether or not change happens, what accounts for it or causes it, whether or not it can be predicted and replicated. What is not so much looked at is the nature of the change that occurs. I think that is an interesting question to think about in the context of my work with teachers in schools. Change does happen through this work. What are its qualities?

My beginning place for thinking about this is remembering that I am working with people who have histories and stories. With this grounding, in order to think about any change that may have happened, I must tell the story of the work, for it is through the story that I can lay out two of the requirements for human change—time and context. Change of the kind I believe happens through this inquiry work occurs over time and is grounded in the people involved, the location, the times in which we work, and so forth.

The teachers at the Neighborhood School and I knew that there had been a shift from their habit of silencing themselves. They remembered how they were. We could find the shift documented in the notes. The importance of this change was obvious. It meant a changing set of relationships between and among staff members. It meant that more individuals were willing to share doubts, difficulties, things close to the heart. They were more willing to take risks. It meant that individuals and the group could push themselves to go beneath the surface of issues and get closer to the heart of the matter. This meant that when the staff took action, their move would be more grounded and sure and better understood. I did not predict that this set of changes would take place when we began. People moved in small and larger ways over a period of years. Silence and keeping one's opinion to oneself is a part of the life of many schools, but the Neighborhood School staff's recognition of it as an issue for them was particular to them.

"A long-lived inquiry produces a discriminating language." Lopez's idea resonates with me when I think about the change that descriptive inquiry produces. As we reflect on words that carry within them ideas basic to issues we face, as we pay close attention to the language we use to frame issues and to talk about our work and the children we teach, we take increased care about the language we use. This increased care allows us to begin to talk differently. And language leads thinking. If we are talking differently, we are thinking differently.

Inquiry done in the way I have described does not "fix" a school, a teacher, or a child. I think it does work to widen people's possibilities for thought and action, to expand options available, to provide new resources to draw upon. I think it does change an individual's or group's collective stance and ways of viewing things, when, for example, they begin to see things in more connected ways and as more complicated. It mattered to Sofia and to her colleagues that, through doing her review, she was able to put herself into the place of some of her math students. This shift of stance enabled her in that moment to witness herself from a new angle, to see others from a different place, and to begin to imagine possibilities other than the ones she had originally pursued. I saw the value she placed on a nonelitist approach to learning brought to the fore and its importance underscored. I saw her struggle more with the value she placed on efficiency. Will she, or anyone making a shift of this kind, always act on her new consciousness? Probably not. But it will be there as a more insistent urging. My hope is that she and Mark will create opportunities to work in math in ways that continue to strengthen their new insights.

The inquiry work I do interrupts the familiar and previously unquestioned and creates tension as it does so. I know I interrupt through the questions I raise, through the pathways I provide into issues, and through the reframing of issues in ways that expand ways of seeing. I bring a value stance that allows another view to be placed into contention with what exists. These tensions are part of the fabric of this work, they are what I work with, and I do not want to side-step them. Through the range of contexts within which I do this inquiry work—schools, professional development groups, colleagues interested in adolescence—I have learned that inquiry of the kind I describe here interrupts some of the forces that block us from seeing: disdain for children; a problem-solving emphasis; a content emphasis; evaluation via testing; experiences of being overlooked and unrecognized; familiar practice; expert knowledge. Because inquiry aims to create this tension, it necessarily moves the inquirers into untracked territory. For this reason, it can be viewed as daring and even dangerous.

Inquiry can make visible what is suppressed or unavailable or devalued. As it makes what was previously covered more visible, inquiry insists on complexity. Teaching is complex work, but our urge to simplify and abstract it—and ourselves with it—is great. Complexity is very different from abstraction, which can be an expected outcome of research. To have complexity be part of the expectation of the inquiry—that is, to know that we will come away from each session of the inquiry with more complicated material and many more questions than we went in with—can be both frustrating and liberating. "Where are the answers I need in order to know what to do?" can be a response to the "roughening up" of the issues, the new bends in what was hoped would be a straight path.

However, there is no way around it. Once we start looking closely at a child, a piece of work, an issue, it will become more complex in our eyes, a result of opening things up and making the previously invisible, visible. Seeing the multifaceted nature of things makes it more difficult to dismiss a child or another point of view. We can be caught by all the possibilities and stop ourselves from saying, "I did everything I could."

Complexity is cognitive but not only that. At its heart, complexity is about values and ethical questions. To open up these issues with a school's staff without imposing an agenda or being moralistic requires us to turn to public, collective description of the kind generated by the descriptive processes. To get at the actuality of heterogeneity, we in the Neighborhood School inquiry needed everyone to speak, sharing strengths and imperfections. We needed to hear and try to appreciate each other. We needed the different intellectual and value positions we worked to articulate.

The demands of doing descriptive inquiry are high. What makes it humanly possible to do over the long term is trust. Much that happens occurs because I trust and help the group's members come to trust ideas and their capacity to percolate into work. For me, ideas and values are closely related to our imaginative powers. This relationship makes ideas and values alive and active and able to permeate language and generate vision and possibility. My push to go to the idea of things has its source in this trust.

Trust in process and ways of working is also basic. The group knows there are things to count on in what might otherwise feel a bit risky. They know the boundaries of the conversation and how the session will work. They know they will all have a turn to speak and have been given the opportunity to prepare their thoughts ahead of time. They know everyone in the group is working to be descriptive and not judging or pushing an agenda. They know the pace will be unhurried. They know I will protect the process.

There is also trust built of the inquiry relationships among us. Groups of teachers come to appreciate that they can know and trust the values and commitments I bring to my participation in the group, that I will provide a kind of memory for the group which will help them keep track of the body of thought they are developing, and that I work to know them as individuals and as a group and that the work we will do will be particular to them and their interests. Individuals learn that they have something to contribute to the group and that they know enough and can find the language to speak thoughtfully about aspects of their work. The staff as a body comes to trust that they can work together productively. They can listen to each other and be heard in turn. They can differ and still work together. They can make knowledge about their work, deepen commitments, even change a collective stance. They can chart a course of action based on their shared understandings.

Over the life of our inquiry work, we do become "companions."

APPENDIX: METHOD FOR WHOLE-SCHOOL INQUIRY

Teacher inquiry is largely thought of in terms of individuals who are actively engaged in closely looking at their classroom practice and pursuing interests important to them. Inquiry as a *group* process usually means teachers coming together from a range of schools to pursue their shared interest in children, in teaching and learning, and in some kind of inquiry into those topics. Rarely does a school faculty work together as an inquiring body, as an inquiry community.

At the heart of a school as an inquiry community is the development of an inquiry stance as a shared value among its members. The basis of this value is the belief that human beings are active makers and creators. Some schools acknowledge that their programs for children should work to support this vision through active exploration and inquiry. However, fewer schools find the means to allow the adults in them to be active creators of knowledge about teaching, learning, children, and school culture. Developing an inquiry stance with a school means that additional aspects of teachers' humanity are acknowledged and brought into the life of the school.

Through my years of working with the staff, I have developed some ways of conducting inquiry. The ultimate source of my thinking about this is Prospect Center's Summer Institute II, a descriptive inquiry group which has been ongoing for many years. The stance there is not about goals or final answers; rather, it supports decision making within the frame of revisiting and reworking. It is not about confrontation or argument; it aims to support making difference generative by putting the range of ideas and values of group members alongside each other and seeing what new possibilities emerge.

Framing Questions and Issues

Each inquiry session has a focusing issue or question that has a variety of purposes. One large purpose is to help inquiry participants start and stay with the "event," be it child, a piece of work, or an issue. The frame put around an inquiry session aims to keep the event at the center, to see it in the multiple ways group members offer, and so to give it the context of many points of view. The framing also aims to help group members enter into the discussion, serves as a lens for looking at/thinking about the issues raised by the conversation, and provides a thread for relating the various contributions to the conversation. I have several standards for framing questions or issues. I intend the frame to help people contribute to the shared work of the group and so help make the conversation generative. Paradoxically, this happens best with a frame that both puts some boundaries around the topic and opens up possibilities for thought. A solid frame helps people draw on their personal experience and memory and helps them begin to make sense of that personal material intellectually by putting it alongside what is offered by other members of the group. Basic to it all is the effort to make the framing respectful of all people.

An example. One of the things that school staffs engaged in this inquiry work discover is that with appropriate framing they can talk about things that are difficult for them to talk about in other contexts. At the Neighborhood School, teachers felt that they were hearing and observing a wave of inappropriately explicit sexual behavior and/or talk among the children. Although this is not an uncommon issue to arise in an elementary school and is important to children's social learning, it is rarely discussed. The intensity of the value issues embedded in this topic makes it difficult for any staff to discuss. To frame the issue, I had each person describe a specific example of what they saw as problematic sexually explicit behavior or language among children, the context of the event, the frequency of the behavior, and why she or he found that example a problem. I said that they could only share examples that had been personally witnessed or heard. Second-hand information was out of bounds. This frame allowed each teacher to share his or her concerns, but only in the frame of actual observations. It allowed each person to put observations and their meaning in personal value terms on the table publicly. We learned much about the actual extent of the problem (it was, in fact, limited) through the group's sharing and much about the various value and educational positions staff members held. We followed this meeting up with a session that tried to set school priorities for action, for example, a descriptive of review of a child whose behavior was troubling, areas about which the staff needed more knowledge, and so forth.

In this example, the framing asked people to think about and prepare ahead of time a recollected observation of a specific kind of event. Other issues call for different kinds of material. A group can describe ways in which they, as individual teachers, implement a specific practice, such as forming groups. They can share recollections from their own childhoods. One teacher can do a Descriptive Review of a Child or of a Teaching Activity. We can meet in a teacher's classroom and describe what we observe about the room around a focusing question. We can describe children's or teacher's written and/or visual work. The question shapes the kind of descriptive material I ask the group to prepare.

Process

I send to each person in the school a copy of the plan for the session at least a week before the scheduled date. Most of the time, some preparation of thinking and notes is needed. The plan always includes the focusing question(s), the way the group will work, and my role in the session. When the plan requires a descriptive story from group members, we go around the circle/table hearing each person speak in turn with no interruptions. I ask people to make notes of their questions and other thoughts and to share them when we have completed the round. Going in turn and not breaking into the flow of a person's story or the group's collecting gives everyone an opportunity to speak or to remain silent by passing and allows the full array of the group's thinking to be laid out before particular threads or lines of thought are pursued. My role is to gather up the threads of the individual descriptions, delineating patterns where I find them, pointing out any questions that are forming, highlighting overlapping points of view and areas of difference. I try to keep these summaries brief during the meeting so that there is time for group members to respond to what they have heard in what their colleagues had to say. I write a fuller summary in the narrative notes.

Narrative Notes

I write the narrative notes after each session of the inquiry and send them to the school staff prior to our next session. I intend these notes to provide a record of the work the group has done together. They are a public record shared with and held by the group. I include within each set of notes a statement of the focusing issues and the process we used; a description of the gist of each person's contribution to the work (which a person can correct if I make an error or mis-hear); my summary of the themes, ideas, and divergences; and any afterthoughts the group may have had at the meeting or I had when writing the notes.

As participants in the school and other inquiry groups I lead have told me, the notes convey an important message to a group engaged in an inquiry: "Your thinking matters." I see this as true both for individuals and for the group collectively. As a text that has its source in the group itself, the notes can validate that group, the individuals in it, and the group's shared work.

In the notes I try to capture the thinking and the making of meaning that goes on in the group. As a collection, I see them as a written version of the body of thought that has developed over time through the group's work. As a record of the work of the group, I view the notes as a way of feeding a group's thinking back to itself. In this way, the notes become a resource, a text, to which the group can return to review their work and thinking.

Annotated Chronology of the Work

Because the whole-school inquiries extend over a long period of time—at least one year and most often several years—I find it helpful to pull the work together in the form of a chronological history: We began here, we moved there, we are now at this place, we can see going here or here or here. I use this annotated listing of the content of the group's sessions as the base for the end-of-year meeting we hold for the purpose of pulling our work together and thinking about implications for next year. The annotation serves as a guide to the contents of the full set of notes that have been amassed through the year. I frame the gathering-up work in ways that help individuals identify ideas and questions that run through the work the group has done together and are important to them personally. Once those points are shared with the group, we move to how those ideas/questions sit next to the issues that face teachers in their classrooms or that they see as facing the school as a whole.

CHAPTER 10

THE VALUE/S OF ORAL INQUIRY, OR "YOU JUST HAD TO BE THERE!"

Margaret Himley

I've always been drawn to collective talk: my pleasure as an undergraduate in English classrooms, analyzing John Donne poems with others; my many trips out to the Prospect Center starting in 1981; my many, many years of collaborative curricular work in the Writing Program at Syracuse University; the Political Moments in the Classroom project in the Writing Program (which I'll talk about more later); the rewards of therapy (which I promise I won't talk more about later); my work as a writing teacher at the Learning Place, a neighborhood literacy center on the west side of Syracuse, New York, and my participation in the recent race dialogue circles. These have proven to be powerful dialogic sites that have reconfigured how I think about the world—and how I act in it.

The thing is, something significant happens when people commit to a sustained conversation around a shared topic of inquiry. That "something" exceeds the actual words spoken, and it can't readily be replicated or summarized later for those who weren't there. This is true of teachers' groups and workshops and race dialogue circles and classrooms and so on.

That "something" draws upon what throughout this book we have called human capacity, widely distributed; that is, it draws upon the meaning-making desires and abilities of *all of us* to make sense of the world we live in when we think and talk about the persons, events, institutions, and realities that comprise our lives. Cutting across gender, race, class, education, and age lines, this human capacity is a resource to be counted on. When the talk is collective and sustained and respectful, its power is enhanced by the differences among people and by the recognition of multiple perspectives in deciding how to act in the world. Typically not written down or disseminated beyond the local context, this is *working knowledge*. Even as the world is, as phenomenologists say, put "out of play," this work is *always* undertaken in light of our desire to return to that world and to act in it in *wiser* ways.

ORAL INQUIRY

For the purposes of this discussion, I'm defining all of those practices for producing understanding that depend upon mediated face-to-face interaction, continuity and commitment over time, a shared focus of inquiry, and at least a degree of trust and honesty and mutuality as oral inquiry. I'm interested not only in the *value* of oral inquiry because of the understanding and wisdom it produces, but also in its *value/s* because of its insistence upon living out the belief in human capacity, widely distributed, that is necessary for genuine deliberation and democratic action.

Oral inquiry is, of course, a methodology in the current teacher-research paradigm in education. Marilyn Cochran-Smith and Susan L. Lytle (1993), in *Inside/Outside: Teacher Research and Knowledge*, define oral inquiry by distinguishing it from other forms of teacher talk:

> Oral inquiry processes often follow specific theoretically grounded procedures and routines, require careful preparation and collection of data, and rely on careful documentation that enables teachers to revisit and reexamine their joint analyses. For teachers, oral inquiries provide access to a variety of perspectives for problem posing and solving. They also reveal the ways in which teachers relate particular cases to theories of practice. (p. 30)

Cochran-Smith and Lytle consider the processes developed by Prospect, which have been carefully thought out and formalized over many years, as important instances of oral inquiry and include in their book an essay by Rhoda Drucker Kanevsky (1993), called "Descriptive Review of a Child: A Way of Knowing About Teaching and Learning." They argue that Prospect's descriptive processes serve classroom teachers well, because the many rounds of description, the summaries of the chair, and the almost verbatim note-taking produce an "unusually rich and complex rendering of patterns that invites rather than forecloses further interpretations" (p. 32). In conversation, "teachers engage in [the] joint construction of knowledge" (Cochran-Smith & Lytle, 1993, p. 94), as they make knowledge more explicit, challenge assumptions about common practices, produce many perspectives, and so encourage the consideration of many alternatives. Through oral inquiry, teachers build the "thick descriptions" (p. 95) that deepen their understanding of the local situation, while also opening up the larger implications of their work. Cochran-Smith and Lytle value the Prospect processes because they

> are particularly powerful ways for teachers to make explicit what is often implicit, to remember by drawing on past experiences, to formulate analogies between seemingly unrelated concepts and experiences, and to construct from disparate data patterns in students' learning. (p. 95)

The processes provide the time, structure, and values for paying close attention to the persons and things of/in the world and for bringing their many meanings into language—and so into a field of action.

DIALOGUE AS A WAY OF KNOWING

For me, given my long association with Prospect and phenomenology, this all takes me back to Merleau-Ponty (1962) and his definition of the act of dialogue as a knowledge-producing event that draws its power from the epistemological possibilities of intersubjectivity:

> In the experience of dialogue, there is constituted between the other person and myself a common ground; my thought and his are interwoven into a single fabric, my words and those of my interlocutor are called forth by the state of the discussion, and they are inserted into a shared operation of which neither of us is the creator. We have here a dual being, where the other is for me no longer a mere bit of behavior in my transcendental field, nor I in his: we are collaborators for each other in consummate reciprocity. Our perspectives merge into each other, and we co-exist through a common world. In the present dialogue, I am freed from myself, for the other person's thoughts are certainly his; they are not of my making, though I do grasp them the moment they come into being, or even anticipate them. And indeed, the objection which my interlocutor raises to what I say draws from me thoughts which I had no idea I possessed, so that at the same time that I lend him thoughts, he reciprocates by making me think too. (p. 354)

Dialogue is the lived experience of reciprocating voices that occurs through time, in history, and in a particular place, establishing a contingent "we," "a common world," and "a shared operation of which [no one] is the creator." In this way dialogue redefines and enlarges the self, as it takes place within the social dimensions of subjectivity. Merleau-Ponty highlights the duality of being in that space, as he points out that in dialogue the participants cannot be "mere bit(s) of behavior" for each other, but must be addressed and answered. In a similar way, Bakhtin (1986) claims, the stronger and more articulated the voices around us, the greater the chances for individuation. And, finally, dialogue produces knowledge as the temporal unfolding of meaning, as process, as *event*. As we answer and address each other and so are called forth from our more private worlds into a shared public space, we come to understand each other, albeit always partially, and to witness and to learn from each other's experiences.

According to Bakhtin (1986), this learning from a serious and sincere engagement with others, or otherness, happens, too, at the level of culture, where "a meaning only reveals its depths once it has encountered and come into contact with another, foreign meaning: they engage in a kind of dialogue" (p. 7). He notes that this dialogic encounter doesn't result in merging or mixing of the two separate cultures, because, while mutually enriched, the cultures maintain their own "unity and *open* totality" (p. 7, emphasis in original).

Merleau-Ponty (1962) asserts, too, that we do not become the other in the dialogic encounter:

> I perceive the grief or the anger of the other in his conduct, in his face or his hands, without recourse to any 'inner' experience of suffering or anger, and because grief and anger are variations of belonging to the world, undivided between the body and consciousness, and equally applicable to the other person's conduct, visible in his phenomenal body, as in my own conduct as it is presented to me. But then, the behavior of another person, and even his words, are not that other person. The grief and anger of another have never quite the same significance for him as they have for me. For him these situations are lived through, for me they are displayed. Or in so far as I can, by some friendly gesture, become part of the grief or anger, they still remain the grief and anger of my friend. . . . Although his consciousness and mine, working through our respective situations, may contrive to produce a common situation, in which they can communicate, it is nevertheless from the subjectivity of each of us that each one projects this 'one and only' world. (p. 356)

There is, finally, an irreducible difference that must be respected in collective work. The sense of commonality that is produced through dialogue must be vigilantly watched so that points of discord and difference can also be acknowledged. The witnessing of otherness enlarges our understanding of the world (and of our own self) but does not mean we become one in this dialogic encounter. Dialogue produces both a temporary and temporal dissolving of self/other—or perhaps, better, a juxtapositioning and overlapping of self/other—within a shared intersubjective situation and the deepening field of meaning.

Dialogue is also an *embodied* epistemological experience. As Alcoff (1998) reminds us, "Meaning and knowledge are not locked into language, but emerge at the intersection between gesture, bodily experience, and linguistic practice" (p. 19). It is at this intersection that oral inquiry takes place and why retrospective accounts fail to replicate fully the meaning and knowledge produced in dialogue. This is why it is so difficult to translate fully oral inquiry into written text.

POLITICAL MOMENTS IN THE CLASSROOM

Several years ago, a group of teachers in the Syracuse Writing Program met every other week for two years to learn about the political dimensions of our teaching—from considering what to do individually and institutionally about sexual harassment, to understanding how to respond to silence as an act of privilege, to coming to demarcate the limits as well as potentials of the classroom as a public deliberative site, and so forth. We called ourselves the Political Moments Study Group. As our method, we asked participants to tell a story from their current teaching that somehow fit under the large rubric of what we referred to (but refused to finally define) as "the political." Then we would ask questions of the storyteller until we had a full context in which to understand the story from many perspectives and many angles. We both stayed close to the lived life of the classroom and explored the larger implications and questions the story raised for us. We met biweekly, we talked for two hours, we described and discussed one or two stories each time, and we got a lot out of the meetings as teachers. I know, for one, how much my practice changed: Over the two years, I got braver and clearer in the classroom about how to work toward the democratic aims and social justice that motivate my desire to teach writing.

Something happened.

In organizing the group, I had wanted to know more about how to respond to various classroom episodes that disturbed or confused me or that disrupted the classroom in some way, but I also wanted to work with other teachers who shared the larger aim of defining the writing classroom as about more than skills or training, who envisioned the teaching of writing as one way of preparing people to deliberate in public forums about matters of consequence with those who do not always agree with them, and who valued the processes and outcome of collective labor.

In the Political Moments Study Group, I'd say that we shared an ethic or politics around the hope of setting up a writing classroom as a just and democratic space, even as we did not share more specific political beliefs. We were well aware that simple pedagogical mandates like "decentering authority" or "making everyone speak" were not only inadequate, but dangerously misleading. We could then all too easily assume that if we sat in a circle, if we allowed or even encouraged students to call us by our first names, if we learned things about their personal lives through class discussion or informal writing assignments, and if most of the students seemed relaxed and comfortable, *then* we had a democratic classroom. And *then*, if a student didn't like the class or didn't fit in or didn't like us or didn't participate, it was all too easy to write that student off as resistant or screwed up—and not take a hard look at the political realities of the writing class in a large private institution in the culture of the 1990s. That is, the classroom had to be politicized as a site, to be read through the many dimensions of power that circulate in any and all institutional settings, through the technologies of power that arguably would include our own "friendliness."

Sustained, structured conversation based in storytelling proved to be an excellent method for establishing a collective context for learning about the many dynamics of power involved in trying to have a democratic classroom. These micro-moments, when described and discussed over time, made readable and talk-able the many macro-dynamics of teaching composition at a private university. Quite simply, the stories—and the time to really discuss them—fueled the group and kept it moving. We listened from various perspectives (some more theoretically inflected than others), asked questions, told and retold the story, until its many possible meanings were more fully and precisely articulated beyond initial reactions. At the beginning of the project, for example, a teacher told a story about a very brief but disruptive moment in her class when a male student suddenly shouted something about it being dangerous to talk about race "on the hill" (i.e., on the Syracuse campus). Given time and careful attention, the story began to raise questions about women's safety in the classroom, about racial tensions in the university, about the anger and angst that characterize realities of difference in culture, about the role of talk in the classroom—and so on. The student became not some behavior-disordered guy, but a more complex person whose act resonated with larger cultural patterns. The teacher's response became not just the insecurity of a new teacher, but an instance that revealed the many dynamics a teacher has to take into account in any moment in the classroom, including her vulnerability as a woman and as a part-time teacher. The story, when talked about over time and in this deepening field of meaning, helped us to understand the episode and then to reimagine our role/s in it.

Furthermore, the Political Moments Study Group was an *event* where I not only learned things, but learned them in a context and across time. It was a time and place where we had ample opportunity to speak and to be listened to and where we all felt heard and respected as contributors. As I reread conversations in the book we published, I remember the gestures and inflections of the members of the group as they spoke, the felt sense of the discussion, the background of the stories we told. I hear, that is, respected and familiar voices.

As a group, we had decided to tape our conversations for further use. At times, I would transcribe a section of the discussion that had been muddled or unsettling in some way, so that we could return to it later as a group. After the first year, we decided to transcribe all the meetings to use as the basis for a collectively authored book. We read the transcripts, pruned them down, added contextual information or other references as needed, tried to keep the drama and meaning of real life conversation going in them, and identified themes or problems that later formed the basis of commentary and essay.

And we worried: Inevitably the transcripts, no matter how artfully edited, failed to reproduce the fullness, the embodiedness, the real experience of the exchange or to represent the new understandings we *knew* we had achieved. The shift from oral inquiry to written form proved frustrating, final, and flat. Yet we didn't want to mystify or render heroic what happens when teachers go about the ordinary act of discussing the daily life of the classroom, so we needed to have the edited transcripts there to show us at work in all that meant, including our very obvious (especially in retrospect!) confusions and limitations. The transcripts reveal teachers coming from different political perspectives and theoretical backgrounds trying to make sense out of stories about classroom events that deal with complex cultural and institutional dynamics of power. We sputter, we circle, we get blocked, we move too quickly from point to point, yet we persist in trying to unpack what we see going on in an event and to produce the precise and provocative languages that will help us to understand and reimagine the event.

We hoped that as other teachers would read the book, they would be able to imagine themselves into the conversations, finding themselves agreeing or disagreeing with us as well as gaining fuller knowledge about the politics of/in teaching, but mostly we hoped that they would be inspired to start their own group. We hoped, that is, that the value of a commitment to a sustained conversation about the political would become clear to others, because while such a conversation will not result in definitive answers or programmatic solutions, it keeps the many questions of the political open and readable and talk-able—and so act-able on.

As *Political Moments in the Classroom* (Himley, 1997) did, this book too has struggled with the questions of representing collective oral inquiry in written form. We are eager to add the Prospect processes into the national discussion about education. We want to participate in the reimagining of the possibilities of public education, since we are confident of the contribution Prospect has and can continue to make to that goal. To do that, we have had to demonstrate the processes at work so that other teachers might choose to practice them in their school settings and would have the knowledge to begin to do so. While edited transcripts are thus necessary, they are not sufficient for explaining the value/s of the Prospect processes and for explaining why very experienced teachers return again and again to Prospect weekends and summer institutes to describe a child's work or review a teacher's practice. The essays deepen the account by locating Prospect historically and disciplinarily and by developing themes more fully. But finally the book can only begin to represent all that happens and all that is learned during the *doing* of descriptive reviews.

THE POLITICS OF *BEMERKEN*

What is the political value of oral inquiry and the kind of understanding and wisdom it produces? As schooling is confronted at all levels with economic and social pressures, with more and more mandates, I am increasingly committed to the role of education in moving us all toward greater social justice and to resisting the corporate and bureaucratic forces that threaten public education.

But how does taking time to do a Descriptive Review of the Child or a review of a teacher's practice or a discussion of a story or two from a teacher's classroom experience serve that democratic larger aim?

Time is the key word here. I want to argue that it is in the *temporal unfolding* of this collective work that things happen: that the child announces him- or herself in richly complex and compelling ways, that new meanings emerge, that the full significance of the language we use is recognized, that ways to make changes become clear. It is in this temporal unfolding that possibilities open up. There are no shortcuts to really paying attention, to really taking notice, to really staying vigilant. Time is inevitably related to meaning. In talking about how writing teachers read student texts, for example, James Zebroski argues that temporality determines how and what a text means: He concludes that "the close reader reads an entirely different text in a completely different time warp from the holistic scorer" (cited in Himley, 1989, p. 15). He calls this "tempos of meaning."

The Prospect processes insist on *time* and *attention* and *vigilance* as the basis for new words, new meanings, new understanding, and reimaginings. For example, for the last two years the board of Prospect (about 20 of us) have met for an inquiry weekend as part of our long-range planning. After a very full day of informal panels on Saturday, we close on Sunday first by taking a half hour for each of us alone to look through our voluminous notes for strands of thought we deemed significant—and then by taking nearly three hours to listen to each other (again, while taking careful notes) bring these thoughts back to the group. This is clearly not efficient, but it is amazing what we learn from each other that would have been lost otherwise.

One of the big risks, then, is cutting down the time and shortchanging the process. A group may decide to cut out parts of the descriptive review process or members may come to understand each other's positions so well that they start anticipating them or saying too little or not listening well. Another risk that results from taking shortcuts is shallow consensus or forced homogeneity. The friendships (or even the hostilities) that form may work against confronting others, or the shared history of the group may unconsciously work against pursuing points fully enough.

The Prospect processes, like all oral inquiry, require and reward time: time set aside to do collective work, time taken to prepare carefully, time offered to listen and to be listened to, time truly devoted to children. In this way, the processes disrupt our efficiency, our daily pressures, our overdetermined responses, our autobiographical histories, our investment in conventional (and so oppressive) systems of thought. In so doing they open up in democratic ways new possibilities of thought, reflection, and action. They give us a chance to refuse our complicity with the world. I offer yet another quotation from Merleau-Ponty (1962):

> It is because we are through and through compounded of relationships with the world that for us the only way to become aware of the fact is to suspend the resultant activity, to refuse it our complicity (to look at it *ohne mitzumachen*, as Husserl often says), or yet again, to put it 'out of play.' (p. xiii)

All too often we are too tightly held by the ways of the world, too embedded in the discourses and technologies of thought and the regimes of truth, and too involved in moment and place and self really to take notice (or *Bemerken*) and give our full attention. Refusing to be complicitous with the conventional discourses of the social and the institutional is a good thing. It is a political act—not the only political act we might do, but a significant one. By holding off that discursive power, we open up space to reflect on word choice, identify assumptions, play out fuller meanings, look at connections and implications and effects, recognize and understand one another—see things differently. While it is possible to do this alone, of course, it is often more productive and surely more pleasurable to do it with others.

As participants in these processes, we develop other ways of seeing, alternative language, and powerful concepts for countering the dominant discourses of schools and culture that risk reducing us all to convenient categories. We acknowledge how much teachers always already know about the children in their classrooms and how powerful teacher–parent collaboration can be. We also remember and reassert the fundamental value we share of recognizing *all* children as capable learners and thinkers.

"INCHES MATTER"

The politics of oral inquiry might be characterized as *Bemerken,* or attention and vigilance. In developing the habit of mind of description and in insisting on the complexity and value of each and every person, Prospect teachers make a difference in the lives of their students.

To illustrate this, I'll end with two stories from the board inquiry weekend in March 1998. In the first story, Ann Caren, a teacher in the Ithaca school district in Ithaca, New York, tells stories about how "inches matter" and how small changes can affect a child's experiences in school and alter how a teacher sees and understands a child. This is a story about paying attention.

> A first-grade classroom teacher and the collaborating reading teacher who works half of each day in her classroom were talking about a 6-year-old boy who was having trouble learning how to read. They told me that the problem was that he didn't have a good memory. He couldn't remember symbols and words. He is taught them one day and doesn't remember them the next.
>
> I asked, "What kinds of things does he like to do in the classroom?"
>
> They said he is a smart child who likes to tell stories and has good ideas. He has ideas about everything, and he likes to talk about and describe these ideas. He does many things with his father, and he likes to talk about what they have done together. He remembers, in detail, the things he does with his father.
>
> So I responded by asking how they could get some of his story-telling and knowledge into the process of his learning to read. To me, it seemed so basic.
>
> As an aside, I'll mention that our school has adopted many of the new ideas about reading and writing such as Reading Recovery, "interactive writing" done with the whole class, and writing process where kids use invented spelling. What is often lost in the implementation of these new ideas is the opportunity for kids to tell stories, have them written down, and have the chance to reread their own personal stories to an adult.
>
> I suggested that they try that approach with this child. Let him tell a story, and the adult would write it down for him in a book. He could draw a picture to go with his story, and they could reread the

story together the next day, and he might be able to build up a sight vocabulary of words that have meaning for him from his stories.

A week later the reading teacher came to me and said, "It's incredible how interested this boy is in telling stories for his own book." That is a Prospect idea, building on strengths, seeing what the child can do.

This idea is analogous to something I learned at Prospect in the early days, the 1970s, about room arrangement. I learned that inches can make a difference. If kids are trying to come into a room and they are pushing around the doorway and you don't have enough space for them to get in and out easily, you can move things just a little bit, and it can make a big difference. You don't have to redo the whole room.

That's my image of trying to help teachers think about what they can do a little more of that's good for a child and what can we do a little bit less of that's bad for a child. Small changes may shift the child's experience and responses in school.

My second story is told by Jane Andrias, the director of Central Park East One, one of the public small schools in New York City. She talks about how difficult it is to struggle with the special education system in New York City. It is a story about vigilance.

The politics of special education is something we have come up against continually. I have to deal with it on a day-to-day basis more than anyone else because I have to be negotiating with the authorities. In its largest, most evil way it absolutely renders children invisible and it renders the parent powerless.

The child is described quantitatively and sketchily on several sheets of paper which are reviewed by absolute strangers who have never met her. It reminds me of a closing at a bank: The papers are passed around and every signs and mutters and you don't know exactly what has transpired. Children are placed in a particular category which dictates what kind of class they are assigned to, ranging from least to most restrictive environment. The system is convoluted and arbitrary. There is very little reason as to what happens and why it happens.

When I became director, I needed to find out as much as I could about this terrain and traverse it with tremendous persistence. I just do not bend. I simply do not bend. And now that's known.

Now when I go to a review at the Committee on Special Education, they see me and say, "Give her what she wants."

I bring the child with me in every form, except his or her physical presence. I do bring the parent. The child, as the child is described by the staff and the parent, is ever present. I bring letters about the child from anybody who knows the child and can offer any knowledge about the child. All of this is given to the review team. I am sure they are not particularly interested in what I bring, but they are somewhat annoyed and certainly worn down by it. In front of them I explain to the parent what her rights are and make sure she understands what is happening, particularly when it comes to signing any papers. I do not think we have made any impact in the sense of changing the system, but we have made an impact in the way they treat us and what they allow for us, just because they do not want to have to deal with us.

Yet we began in the school to have a creeping talk about the "special education children." So as a staff, we first did a reflection on the word *special*. We also started to do descriptive reviews of children who were placed in this "special" category, because the truth was that they were not visible to most of the people in the school. We spent a great deal of time looking not only at the children, but at our practice and our sense of success as teachers. As teachers, we had to become visible to each other again. I also did a lot of research about inclusion and brought it into the discussion. We had guest speakers, reflected on the word *inclusion*, visited established programs, and talked and talked and talked. This process took a lot of time and attention and hard work.

Now the idea of inclusion is not only not foreign, but it's absolutely at home in our school. We have become a school for all children. When children are spoken about now, no matter who they are, they are spoken about through their strengths, through what they bring to us, through what we can notice about them. The teachers are also spoken about through their strengths and what they have to offer. I am not saying that everything is wonderful, by any means, but there is a real shift in attitude.

Along with that has come a shift from the Committee on Special Education about who populates our classes. They have given us approval to leave spaces if we can't fill. That is not to say other children can't come here, but the concept of just "dumping" children or just putting them somewhere and forgetting about them and making believe they don't exist does not comply with our values, and it does not happen.

The issue here is balancing what is possible and warding off the evil by staying vigilant. It has taken time and will take more time.

Looking descriptively at children has been central to opening up new questions about our practice and new possibilities for our school.

SOMETIMES YOU *DO* HAVE TO BE THERE!

I return to Prospect and I continued to work with the Political Moments Study Group, because oral inquiry produces for me this complex site of resistance and affirmation. It offers a time and space for rethinking the given categories of thought that we are immersed in and for reasserting the values and aims that we need as a critical part of our work as teachers. We are all engaged in all kinds of activities: teaching, preparing for classes, reading books, giving presentations, keeping journals, designing curriculum, participating in meetings. Oral inquiry plays a role, too.

Sometimes we *do* just have to get together with others and do this kind of collective work. We need the richness and the surprise of sustained intellectual conversation. We need the pleasure of each other's company. We need the sense of solidarity that comes from respectful face-to-face interaction and that emerges not from homogeneity but from collective aims within a recognition of difference. We need new ideas and new words and new images and new visions to sustain us in our daily teaching lives. In the face of dehumanizing economic forces and depressing institutional realities, we need comrades.

APPENDIX

PROSPECT RESOURCES
AND RELATED PUBLICATIONS

For information on the following board members/consultants, institutes, or publications, please contact:

Prospect Archives & Center for Education & Research
Post Office Box 328
North Bennington, VT 05257–0326
802-442-8333
prospect@sover.net

THE PROSPECT BOARD

President: Cecelia Traugh, Director of Research and Evaluation, Institute for Literacy Studies, Lehman College, City University of New York, Bronx
Vice President: Rhoda Kanevsky, Elementary Teacher, Philadelphia
Secretary: Heidi Watts, Professor Emerita, Antioch New England Graduate School, Keene NH
Treasurer: Margaret Howes, Elementary Teacher, Stillwater NY

Beth Alberty, Director of Collections, Brooklyn Children's Museum, Brooklyn NY
Jane Andrias, Director, Central Park East 1, New York NY
Corrine Biggs, Consultant, Lifeworks Inventory Service, North Bennington VT
Paige Bray, Elementary Teacher, Graduate Student, Greenburgh NY
Ann Caren, Elementary Teacher, Ithaca NY
Patricia F. Carini, Independent Educator, White Creek NY
Kiran Chaudhuri, Secondary Teacher, New York NY
Carol Christine, Clinical Assistant Professor of Education, Arizona State University, Tempe AZ

Edward Chittenden, Research Psychologist, Educational Testing Services, Princeton NJ

Cecilia Espinosa, Elementary Teacher, Graduate Student, Phoenix AZ

Daryl Hartshorne, Educational Therapist, New York NY

Mary Hebron, Associate Director, Art of Teaching Graduate Program, Sarah Lawrence College, Bronxville NY

Margaret Himley, Associate Professor of English/Writing, Syracuse University, Syracuse NY

Linette Moorman, Director, New York City Writing Project, Institute for Literacy Studies, Lehman College, City University of New York, Bronx NY

Taeko Onishi, Elementary Teacher, Troy NY

Ellen Schwartz, Middle School Teacher, Northfield MA

Alice Seletsky, Elementary Teacher, New York NY

Lynne Strieb, Elementary Teacher, Philadelphia PA

INSTITUTES AND CONFERENCES

Prospect Summer Institute on Descriptive Process: a one-week introduction to Prospect's descriptive processes; Bennington VT

Prospect Summer Institute on Descriptive Inquiry: a two-week continuing study that welcomes those with prior experience of Prospect's processes; Bennington VT

Prospect Summer Insitute on Practice: a one-week institute on classrooms and curriculum using Prospect's descriptive processes; New York City

November Fall Conference: an annual weekend event on a theme such as "Creating Collaborative Working Groups in Schools"; location varies (near New York City)

Note: There is also an institute in Philadelphia each summer, and planning has begun for an institute in Phoenix, Arizona.

PUBLICATIONS

The Reference Edition of the Prospect Archives: This collection documents 36 children, each over at least five years, in slides, microfiche, and text. Sets of slides and written records on individual children may be rented. This edition is a part of the Prospect Archive, longitudinal collections of the art, writing, and other works by individual children, which totals over 250,000 pieces. This archive informs Prospect's view of children's growth over time.

The Prospect Review: This small journal, produced twice a year, features reviews of children, curriculum, and teaching and essays by teachers and others.

Prospect Papers: Occasionally, Prospect publishes selected talks and papers by Patricia F. Carini and other members of the larger Prospect community. Also available are documents explaining the descriptive processes in greater detail, including a procedural guide to the Descriptive Review of the Child.

PROSPECT-RELATED PUBLICATIONS

Compiled by Karen Woolf

Alberty, B. (1984). House and dwelling: Common themes in children's art. *School Arts, 83*(8), 23–81.

Allen, S. (1992). Student-sustained discussion: When students talk and the teacher listens. In N. A. Branscombe, D. Goswami & J. Schwartz (Eds.), *Students teaching, teachers learning* (pp. 81–92). Portsmouth, NH: Boynton/Cook Heinemann.

Bradbury, J. (1993). A reflection on the word "curriculum" at the 1992 Prospect Summer Institute. *Pathways: A Forum For Progressive Educators, 10*(1), 3–9.

Buchanan, J., Edelsky, C., Kanevsky, R., Klausner, E., Lieberman, G., Mintier, J., Montoya, B., Morris, E., Streib, L., & Wice, B. (1984). On becoming teacher experts: Buying time. *Language Arts, 61*(7), 731–736.

Bussis, A., Chittenden, T., Amarel, M., & Klausner, E. (1985). *Inquiry into meaning: An investigation of learning to read.* Hillsdale, NJ: Erlbaum.

Carini, P. F. (1987). *On value in education.* New York College Workshop Center Monograph.

Carini, P. F. (1988a). Another way of looking. In K. Jervis & A. Tobier (Eds.), *Education for democracy: Proceedings from the Cambridge School conference on progressive education* (pp. 10–28). Weston, MA: The Cambridge School.

Carini, P. F. (1989). Honoring diversity/striving for inclusion. In K. Jervis & C. Montag (Eds.), *Progressive education for the 1990s: Transforming practice* (pp. 17–31). New York: Teachers College Press.

Carini, P. F. (1993). *Images and immeasurables (II)*. Talk presented at Patterson Award for Excellence in Education to Teacher's Learning Cooperative. Philadelphia: Prospect Occasional Papers.

Carini, P. F. (1994). Dear sister Bess: An essay on standards, judgement and writing. *Assessing Writing, 1*(1), 29–65.

Carroll, D., & Carini, P. (1991). Tapping teacher's knowledge. In V. Perrone (Ed.), *Expanding student assessment* (pp. 40–46). Alexandria, VA: Association for Supervision and Curriculum Development.

Colgan-Davis, P. (1993). Learning about diversity. In M. Cochran-Smith & S. L. Lytle (Eds.), *Inside/outside: Teacher research and knowledge* (pp.163–169). New York: Teachers College Press.

Doan, A. (1996). *Prospect, reflection and voice.* Paper presented at the Conference on Reflection and Voice, Princeton Friends School.

Edelstein, L. (1995). Buddy and the zoobooks. *New York City Writing Project Newsletter, 15*, 4–7.

Engel, B. S. (1980). Prospect archives: Documenting children's growth. *Principal, 60*(2), 28–31.

Engel, B. S. (1981). Book review: *The art of seeing and the visibility of the person. Harvard Educational Review, 51*(14), 602–605.

Engel, B. S. (1986). Book review: *Inquiry into meaning: An investigation of learning to read. Harvard Educational Review, 56*(1), 85–89.

Engel, B. S. (1987). *Between feeling and fact.* Grand Forks, ND: North Dakota Study Group on Evaluation.

Engel, B. S. (1995). *Considering children's art: Why and how to value their works.* Washington, D.C.: National Association for the Education of Young Children.

Engel, B. S. (1996). Learning to look: Appreciating child art. *Young Child, 51*(3), 74–79.

Featherstone, H. (1998). Studying children: The Philadelphia teachers' learning cooperative. In D. Allen (Ed.), *Assessing student learning: From grading to understanding* (pp. 66–83). New York: Teachers College Press.

Futterman, A. (1996, February). Expanding the possible: A teacher's perspective on descriptive review. *Net News: The Lower East Side Network*, p. 7.

Gallas, K. (1998). *Teacher initiated professional development: The Lawrence school teacher study groups.* Research Report for the MacArthur/Spencer Professional Development Research and Documentation Program, Brookline, MA.

Hanhan, S. F. (1988). A qualitative and qualitatively different format for the evaluation of student teachers. *Action in Teacher Education, 10*(2), 51–55.

Hanhan, S. F. (1993). *Final report teaching evaluation development grant.* Grand Forks: Center for Teaching and Learning, University of North Dakota.

Harwood, L. (1987). A perspective on a child study group. *Reflections: The Brookline Education Journal, 4*(2).

Himley, M. (1991). *Shared territory: Understanding children's writing as works.* New York: Oxford University Press.

Himley, M. (1993). Deep talk. *Pathways: A Forum For Progressive Educators, 9*(2), 10–12.

Howard, J. (1988). On teaching, knowledge and "middle ground". In K. Jervis & A. Tobier (Eds.) *Education for democracy: Proceedings from the Cambridge School conference on Progressive Education* (pp. 118–125). Weston, MA: The Cambridge School.

Jervis, K. (1986). A teacher's quest for a child's questions. *Harvard Educational Review, 56*(2), 132–150.

Jervis, K. (1996). *Eyes on the child: Three portfolio stories.* New York: Teachers College Press.

Jervis, K. (1996). How come there are no brothers on that list?: Hearing the hard questions all children ask. *Harvard Educational Review, 66*(3), 546–576.

Jervis, K., with Carr, E., Lockhart, P., & Rogers, J. (1996). Multiple entries to teacher inquiry: Dissolving the boundaries between research and teaching. In L. Baker, P. Afflerbach, & D. Reinking (Eds.), *Engaging readers in school and home communities* (pp. 247–268). Mahwah, NJ: Erlbaum.

Jervis, K., & McDonald, J. (1997). Standards: The philosophical monster in the classroom. *Phi Delta Kappan, 563–569.*

Jervis, K., Mullins, D., & Stern, B. (1998). *In the face of my resistance . . . : Stephanie's parent and teacher gain a working trust.* Unpublished manuscript.

Jervis, K., & Wiener, A. (1991). Looking at children's work. In K. Jervis & C. Montag (Eds.), *Progressive education for the 1990s: Transforming practice* (pp. 114–124). New York: Teachers College Press.

Martin, A. (1983). Two writers. *Outlook, 44* 3–13.

Martin, A. (1984, June). Preschool screening. *Reflections: The Brookline Educational Journal,* pp. 20–21.

Martin, A. (1985). Back to kindergarten basics. *Harvard Educational Review, 55*(3), 318–320.

Martin, A. (1987, July/August). Encouraging youngsters to discuss their feelings. *Learning,* pp. 80–81.

Martin, A. (1988, November). Screening, early intervention and remediation: Obscuring children's potential. *Harvard Educational Review, 58*(4), 488–501.

Martin, A. (1989). Allowing the unconventional. *Teachers & Writers, 20*(5), 1–4.

Martin, A. (1990). Social studies in kindergarten: A case study. *The Elementary School Journal, 90*(3), 305–317.

Martin, A. (1992). Response to Chapter 2. In N. A. Branscombe, D. Goswami, & J. Schwartz (Eds.), *Students teaching, teachers learning* (pp. 42–45). Portsmouth, NH: Boynton/Cook Heinemann.

Martin, A. (1994). Deepening teacher competence through skills of observation. In S. Goffin & D. Day (Eds.), *New perspectives in early childhood education* (pp. 95–107). New York: Teachers College Press.

Martin, A. (1998). *Child study group: How has it shaped my assessment methods.* Research Report for MacArthur/Spencer Professional Research and Documentation Program, Brookline, MA.

Mishler, E. G. (1979). Meaning in context: Is there any other kind? *Harvard Educational Review, 49*(1), 1–19.

Mullins, D. (1988). What parents and teachers want for children. *Pathways: A Forum for Progressive Educators, 4*(3), 11–13.

Mullins, D. (1992). Narrative reports from parents and children. *Pathways: A Forum for Progressive Educators, 8*(3), 3–9.

Mullins, D. (1995). Journal excerpts. *Pathways: A Forum for Progressive Educators, 8*(2), 13–16.

Schwartz, E. (1992). The round table: Emergent curriculum in a primary class. In N. A. Branscombe, D. Goswami, & J. Schwartz (Eds.), *Students teaching, teachers learning* (pp. 22–41). Portsmouth, NH: Boynton/Cook Heinemann.

Schwartz, E. (1996). Clay boats. *Connect: K–8 Hands-On Science and Math, 9* (3), 1–5.

Schwartz, E. (1998, November). Teaching at the boundaries. *Process Papers, 3,* 6–19.

Stevenson, J. (1991). Expanding children's choice. *Writing Teacher, 4*(1), 17–20.

Strieb, L. Y. (1984). Trees: Excerpts from a teacher's journal. *Outlook, 50,* 3–33.

Strieb, L. Y. (1993). Visiting and revisiting the trees. In M. Cochran-Smith & S. L.

Lytle (Eds.), *Inside/outside: Teacher research and knowledge* (pp. 121–130). New York: Teachers College Press.

Strieb, L. Y. (1999). Communicating with parents: One teacher's story. In J. W. Lindfors & J. S. Townsend (Eds.), *Teaching language arts: Learning through dialogue* (pp. 251–274). Urbana, IL: National Council of Teachers of English.

Strieb, L. Y. & D. Jumpp. (1993). Journals for collaboration, curriculum, and assessment. In M. Cochran-Smith & S. L. Lytle (Eds.), *Inside/outside: Teacher research and knowledge* (pp. 121–130). New York: Teachers College Press.

Traugh, C. (1995, November). *Schools as workplaces for children and adults: Valuing work, collaboration, inquiry.* Paper presented at the November conference of Prospect Center, Litchfield, CT.

Traugh, C. (1996, November). *Keywords.* Paper presented at the Fall conference of Prospect Center, Litchfield, CT.

Traugh, C. (1997, November). *The authority of the question.* Paper presented at the Fall conference of Prospect Center, Litchfield, CT.

Traugh, C. (1996) *Tree: A curriculum about observation and description.* Unpublished manuscript.

Wice, B., Paul, P., Daniels, M., Lieberman, G., & Mitchel, K. (1992). Savoring children's work: Why do we collect children's work? *Pathways: A Forum for Progressive Educators, 8*(3), 10–15.

Woolf, K. (1986). Thoughts on continuity and community. *Pathways: A Forum for Progressive Educators, 2*(3), 1–7.

REFERENCES

Alcoff, L. M. (1998). Merleau-Ponty and feminist theory on experience. Unpublished manuscript.

Andrias, J., Kanevsky, R. D., Strieb, L. Y., & Traugh, C. (1992). *Exploring values and standards: Implications for assessment* (NCREST monograph). New York: Teachers College Press.

Bakhtin, M. M. (1986). *Speech genres & other late essays* (V. W. McGee, Trans.; C. Emerson & M. Holquist, Eds.). Austin: University of Texas Press.

Bissex, G. L. (1980). *GNYS AT WRK: A child learns to write and read.* Cambridge, MA: Harvard University Press.

Branscombe, N. A., Goswami, D., & Schwartz, J. (Eds.) (1992). *Students teaching, teachers learning.* Portsmouth, NH: Boynton/Cook Heinemann.

Buchanan, J. (1993). Listening to the voices. In M. Cochran-Smith & S. L. Lytle (Eds.), *Inside/outside: Teacher research and knowledge* (pp. 212–220). New York: Teachers College Press.

Carini, P. F. (1975). *Observation and description: An alternative methodology for the investigation of human phenomena.* Grand Forks, ND: North Dakota Study Group on Evaluation.

Carini, P. F. (1979). *The art of seeing and the visibility of the person.* Grand Forks, ND: North Dakota Study Group on Evaluation.

Carini, P. F. (1982). *The school lives of seven children.* Grand Forks, ND: North Dakota Study Group on Evaluation.

Carini, P. F. (1986). Building from children's strengths. *Journal of Education, 168*(3), 13–24.

Carini, P. F. (1995). *What would we create?* Paper presented at the November Fall Conference of the Prospect Center, Pawling, NY.

Carini, P. F. (1997). *. . . in the thick of the tangle what clear line persists . . .* Walker Gibson Lecture, University of Massachusetts, Amherst.

Carini, P. F. (in press). *Schools in the making, A collection of talks, 1988–1998.* New York: Teachers College Press.

Cochran-Smith, M., & S. L. Lytle. (Eds.). (1993). *Inside/outside: Teacher research and knowledge.* New York: Teachers College Press.

Dewey, J. (1938). *Experience and education.* New York: Macmillan.

Doty, M. (1995). Interview, Syracuse University, Syracuse, NY.

Drummond, M. J. (1994). *Learning to see: Assessment through observation.* York, ME: Stenhouse.

Duckworth, E. (1987). *The having of wonderful ideas.* New York: Teachers College Press.

Himley, M. (1989). A reflective conversation: "Tempos of meaning." In B. Lawson, S. S. Ryan, & W. R. Winterowd (Eds.), *Encountering student texts: Interpretive issues in reading student writing* (pp. 5–19). Urbana, IL: National Council of Teachers of English.

Himley, M., with K. Le Fave, A. Larson, S. Yadlon, and the Political Moments Study Group. (1997). *Political moments in the classroom.* Portsmouth, NH: Boynton/Cook.

Kanevsky, R. D. (1993). Descriptive review of a child: A way of knowing about teaching and learning. In M. Cochran-Smith & S. L. Lytle (Eds.), *Inside/outside: Teacher research and knowledge* (pp. 150–162). New York: Teachers College Press.

Keller, E. F. (1983). *A feeling for the organism: The life and work of Barbara McClintock.* New York: Freeman.

Kozol. J. (1991). *Savage inequalities.* New York: Crown.

Lopez, B. (1986). *Arctic dreams.* New York: Charles Scribner's Sons.

Lopez, B. (1992). *The rediscovery of North America.* New York: Vintage Books.

Martin, A. (1981). *The words in my pencil.* Grand Forks, ND: North Dakota Study Group on Evaluation.

Martin, A. (1983). *Reading your students: Their writing and their selves.* New York: Teachers & Writers.

Martin, A. (1986, March). Reporting on children by checklist: Sometimes/usually/always—or never? *Reflections: The Brookline Educational Journal,* pp. 6–7.

Martin, A. (1992). Narrative description: An alternative form of assessment. *Reflections: The Brookline Educational Journal,* 9(2), 5–7.

Martin, A. (1996, November). Checklists revisited. *The Prospect Review,* issue 8, pp. 12–16.

Martin, A. (1998, May). *Child study group: How it shaped my assessment methods.* Research Report for the MacArthur/Spencer Professional Research and Documentation Program, Brookline, MA.

Merleau-Ponty, M. (1962). *Phenomenology of perception* (C. Smith, Trans.). London: Routledge & Kegan Paul.

Morrison, T. (1997). *Lecture and speech of acceptance, upon the award of the Nobel Prize for literature delivered in Stockholm on the seventh of December, nineteen hundred and ninety-three.* New York: Knopf.

Nemerov, H. (1978). *Figures of thought.* Boston: Godine.

Park, C. (1972). *The siege: The first eight years of an autistic child.* Boston: Little, Brown.

Prospect Center. (1985). *Reference edition of the Prospect Archives.* The Prospect Center and Archive, North Bennington, VT.

Prospect Center. (1993–present). *The Prospect Review.* The Prospect Center and Archive, North Bennington, VT.

Rogers, V., Roberts, A. D., & Weinland, T. P. (Eds.). (1988). *Teaching social studies: Portraits from the classroom.* Bulletin #82. Washington, D.C.: National Council for the Social Studies.

Schwartz, E. (1987). An over-repeating story. *Teaching & Learning: The Journal of Natural Inquiry, 2*(1), 12–20.

Seletsky, A. (1985, May). Where the action is. *The Nation*, pp. 634–637.

Seletsky, A. (1988). My name is Alice: A fifth grade story of naming and family history. In V. Rogers, A. D. Roberts, & T. P. Weinland (Eds.). *Teaching social studies: Portraits from the classroom* (pp. 10–18). Bulletin #82. Washington, D.C.: National Council for the Social Studies.

Seletsky, A. (1989). How to build a Trojan horse. *New York Teacher*, p. 8.

Seletsky, A. (1990). The mark on the brick and other museum matters. *Journal of Museum Education, 15*(1), 15–17.

Strieb, L. (1985). *A (Philadelphia) teacher's journal*. Grand Forks, ND: North Dakota Study Group on Evaluation.

Strieb, L. Y. (1992). When a teacher's values clash with school values: Documenting children's progress. In J. Andrias, R. D. Kanevsky, L. Y. Strieb, & C. Traugh, *Exploring values and standards: Implications for assessment* (pp. 9–24). New York: Teachers College Press.

Traugh, C. (1989). *Creating knowledge in a school setting: A story.* Paper presented at the Progressive Education Conference, Chicago, IL.

Traugh, C., Seletsky, A., Kanevsky, R., Woolf, K., Martin, A., & Strieb, L. (1986). *Speaking out: Teachers on teaching.* Grand Forks, ND: North Dakota Study Group on Evaluation.

Weber, L. (1997). Inquiry, noticing, joining with, and following after. In B. Alberty (Ed.), *Looking back and thinking forward: Reexaminations of teaching and schooling* (pp. 48–67). New York: Teachers College Press.

Wice. B. (1994, November). Questions. *The Prospect Review, 4*, 1–7.

Whitehead, A. N. (1938). *Modes of thought.* New York: Macmillan.

Williams, R. (1961) *The long revolution.* New York: Columbia University Press.

Williams, R. (1976). *Keywords.* New York: Oxford University Press.

CHILDREN'S LITERATURE CITED

Berenstain, Stan, & Berenstain, Jan. (1978–present). *Berenstain bears*, First Time Book series. New York: Random House.

Cole, Joanna. (1983). *Bony legs*. Illustrated by Dirk Zimmer. New York: Simon & Schuster.

Cole, Joanna. (1987–present). *The magic school bus* series. New York: Scholastic.

Gannett, Ruth Stiles. (1988). *My father's dragon*. Illustrated by Ruth Chrisman Gannett. New York: Knopf. (Original work published 1948)

Hansen, Joyce. (1980). *Gift giver*. New York: Clarion.

Hansen, Joyce. (1986). *Yellow bird and Me*. New York: Clarion.

Laden, N. (1994). *The Night I Followed the Dog*. San Francisco: Chronicle Books.

Lamb, David. (1994). *Do platanos go wit' collard greens?* New York: I Write What I Like.

Morales, Iris. (1996). *Palante! Siempre palante*! Video documentary. New York: Latino Education Network Service/LENS.

Osborne, Mary Pope. (1992). *Magic tree house* series. Illustrated by Sal Murdocca. New York: Random House.

Paterson, K. (1977). *Bridge to Terabithia*. New York: Crowell.

Stine, R. L. (1992–present). *Goosebumps* series. New York: Scholastic.

ABOUT THE EDITORS
AND CONTRIBUTORS

Elaine Avidon is a co-director of Elementary Teachers Network (ETN) and a faculty member in the Department of Early Childhood and Elementary Education at Lehman College, Bronx, New York.

Patricia F. Carini is a co-founder of the Prospect School; a member of the Prospect board; and an author, speaker, and independent educator.

Kiran Chaudhuri is a teacher at East Side Community High School in New York City and a member of the Prospect board.

Mary Hebron is Associate Director of the Art of Teaching Graduate Program at Sarah Lawrence College and a member of the Prospect board.

Margaret Himley is Associate Professor of English and Writing at Syracuse University and a member of the Prospect board.

Rhoda Kanevsky has been a first-grade teacher in the Philadelphia public schools for 30 years, and is a founding member of the Philadelphia Teachers' Learning Cooperative (PTLC) and vice president of the Prospect board.

Karen Khan is a reading teacher at the Bronx New School in District 10 of the New York City public school system, who has taught pre-K–grade 1 and has participated in seminars and conferences at the Prospect Center, the Elementary Teachers Network, and the Center for Collaborative Education.

Anne Martin was a preschool through 4th-grade teacher for more than 30 years, mostly in Brookline, Massachusetts, and a longtime participant in summer institutes, who led a Prospect-inspired child study group in her own school for 10 years.

Ellen Schwartz has been a teacher for 16 years in the primary grades, currently teaching in Northfield, Massachusetts, and a member of the Prospect board.

Tara Shaw has been a teacher in Philadelphia urban schools for five years (first, third, and fourth grades), active in the Philadelphia Writing Project, and a member of Philadelphia Teachers' Learning Cooperative (PTLC). Recently she published an essay in the *Students at the Center* newsletter.

Lynne Strieb has been a first- and second-grade teacher in Philadelphia for 30 years and is a founding member of the Philadelphia Teachers' Learning Cooperative (PTLC) and a member of the Prospect board.

Cecelia Traugh is President of the Prospect board, director of Prospect Institutes, and director of research and evaluation at the Institute for Literacy Studies at Lehman College, Bronx, New York.

Betsy Wice has been a reading teacher for more than 30 years in Philadelphia and member of the Philadelphia Teachers' Learning Cooperative (PTLC).

Karen Woolf has been an elementary teacher for 25 years in the Hamilton-Wenham School District in Massachusetts, is a longtime participant in Prospect institutes and conferences and a doctoral student at the University of New Hampshire, completing a dissertation on collaborative inquiry at Prospect Summer Institute II.

INDEX

227